Cedar Mill & Bethany
Community Libraries

In Memory of
Leanna Angell

Shakespeare's Library

Shakespeare's Library

UNLOCKING THE GREATEST MYSTERY IN LITERATURE

Stuart Kells

COUNTERPOINT
Berkeley, California

Full source notes are available at stuartkells.com

Library of Congress Cataloging-in-Publication Data
Names: Kells, Stuart, author.
Title: Shakespeare's library : unlocking the greatest mystery in literature / Stuart Kells.
Description: First Counterpoint hardcover edition. | Berkeley, California : Counterpoint, 2019. | Includes bibliographical references and index.
Identifiers: LCCN 2018050854 | ISBN 9781640091832
Subjects: LCSH: Shakespeare, William, 1564–1616—Library. | Shakespeare, William, 1564–1616—Books and reading.
Classification: LCC PR3069.B6 K45 2019 | DDC 822.3/3—dc23
LC record available at https://lccn.loc.gov/2018050854

Jacket design by Donna Cheng

COUNTERPOINT
2560 Ninth Street, Suite 318
Berkeley, CA 94710
www.counterpointpress.com

Printed in the United States of America
Distributed by Publishers Group West

10 9 8 7 6 5 4 3 2 1

Contents

Shakespeare's
Library

Introduction

All literate people are shareholders in Shakespeare, the world's most famous author. We think of him and his creations as our common property and elemental heritage. We revere his plays and poems, and strive to know the man himself, to understand how he thought and lived, and how he wrote.

In 2018, original manuscripts are perhaps the best way for lovers of literature to get close to writers from the distant past. These handwritten texts tell a story beyond the words. The writing conveys personality and mood: calm and deliberative, or feverish and tumultuous? Sketches and doodles in the margins betray rumination and procrastination. The paper captures and holds something magical from the moment of literary creation.

Author manuscripts, letters, source books and, better still, diaries, are pathways for cerebral, tactile and even olfactory connection.

Who could resist connecting in such a way with Shakespeare? Imagine what it would be like to hold his original playscripts. For every species of book person, the idea of Shakespeare's library—his personal collection of manuscripts, books, letters and other papers—is enticing, totemic, a subject of wonder. How did he write? Who inspired him? Who appalled him? To know Shakespeare's books is to know Shakespeare the author.

Over the span of four hundred years, people sought his library out: in provincial towns and capital cities; in mansions, palaces, universities and public libraries; in riverbeds, cemeteries, sheep pens and partridge coops; and in the landscapes and corridors of the mind. The search became an international one, attracting academics, librarians, bibliographers, entrepreneurs, spirit guides, mystics, cryptographers, archaeologists, symbologists, graphologists, pharmacologists and every kind of opportunistic madman using every kind of technique. In all this time, the search came to nought. Not a trace of his library was found. No books, no manuscripts, no letters, no diaries. The desire to get close to Shakespeare was unrequited, the vacuum palpable.

The search for Shakespeare's library is much more than a treasure hunt, or a case of Shakespeare fetishism. The library's fate has profound implications for literature, for national and cultural identity, and for the global, twenty-first-century, multi-billion-dollar Shakespeare industry. It bears upon fundamental principles of art, history, meaning and truth.

Shakespeare's Library retraces the search. It does so by unfolding the search as the mystery story that it is, and by looking through the lens of the searchers themselves. Each searcher sheds light on the scale and scope of Shakespeare's library, the kinds of books and manuscripts it contained, and what happened to them and his other documents after he retired from writing and, a few years later, passed away at Stratford-upon-Avon in Warwickshire. Each searcher corresponds to a different conception of the library and a different conception of Shakespeare himself as an owner and gatherer of books. Workaday editor, gentleman bibliophile, shady frontman. Radical, fugitive, phantom or thief. Pornographer, forger or dupe. Francophile, classicist, lawyer or musician. Romantic or aesthete. Businessman or bumpkin. Librarian or anti-librarian. Author.

The questions about Shakespeare's library are closely bound up with the 'Shakespeare Authorship Question'—how he worked, what he wrote and, most controversially, *whether* he wrote at all. So much so that, to make any real progress, all these questions must be considered together. The writer's library cannot be separated from the extent of his authorial achievement and how it was accomplished. Depending on the answer to the Authorship Question, Shakespeare may have owned hundreds of books and manuscripts, or he may have owned none.

Two regrettable traditions foul the trail we must follow: the long tradition of Shakespeare forgery, and an even longer tradition of bad Shakespearean scholarship. To reach something like the truth, we must walk through noxious territory, consort with cranks and rogues, understand what they are capable of and expose their handiwork. Several searchers examined in this book are especially useful because they help define the mystery of Shakespeare's library. Others are valuable because their stories— and their crimes—equip us with the tools we need to solve it.

In my book *The Library: A Catalogue of Wonders*, I described how, in the 1990s, I found by chance an especially rare volume of

Elizabethan interest: an anonymously published, blue-paper copy of John Fry's *Pieces of Ancient Poetry from Unpublished Manuscripts and Scarce Books* (1814). Fry was a bookseller and an antiquarian. Always in poor health, he died young, having devoted his short life to the cause of bibliomania. In *The Library* I explained how that find led my wife, Fiona, and me into a bookish life, and how it prompted us to join the search for Shakespeare's library. Over the years, as authors, historians and affiliates of the International League of Antiquarian Booksellers, Fiona and I would make other remarkable finds, and we would assemble a unique collection of John Fry volumes, which would form the nucleus of our own library. Throughout those years, the life's work of a young bookseller from Bristol, long dead, would be our example and our guide in the quest to solve the greatest mystery in literature.

Part I

THE FIRST SEARCHERS

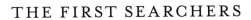

CHAPTER 1

William the Conqueror

More than four hundred years ago, William Shakespeare led an intriguing life. By all accounts he was a fun guy moving in a fun circle. One member of his London entourage, John Florio, is remembered as a consummate editor who gave the English language such indispensable phrases as 'higgledy-piggledy' and 'helter-skelter'. Shakespeare himself is blamed for 'blood-stained', 'eyeball', 'fancy free', 'seamy', 'zany' and hundreds of other poetic and prosaic innovations.

A street-brawling, heart-breaking actor and grungy man of letters, the Shakespeare who emerges drinking and smoking from contemporary documents is a kind of punk poet, a proto-rockstar, a sixteenth-century Russell Crowe, or Russell

Brand. Few documents about Shakespeare's life have survived, but a surprisingly high proportion of them concern his racy and bawdy exploits. When, for example, he got into trouble with a brothel keeper and two young women, his fearsome conduct was documented vividly in a writ. Another notorious incident followed a performance of the play we now call *Richard III*. Shakespeare's fellow actor Richard Burbage played the king and caught the attention of a beauty in the audience. The lady was so impressed by Burbage's performance that she invited him to her home that evening—so long as he promised to remain in costume and character. Shakespeare got wind of the assignation and went first to the lady's residence. Burbage arrived at the appointed time but Shakespeare was already inside, being 'entertained and at his game'. When the lovers were informed that Burbage was at the door, a triumphant Shakespeare sent his colleague a mischievous reply that contained a sharp lesson in English history. 'William the Conqueror,' he said, 'was before Richard the Third.'

The study of Shakespeare's life and authorship is every bit as exciting as the man himself. As they do in a Dan Brown thriller, the Rosicrucians and Freemasons enter the picture more than once. Some of the best known episodes of Shakespearean research read like outtakes from the Nicholas Cage film *National Treasure*. Searching for buried plunder in the bed of the River Wye at Chepstow Castle. Breaking into the Walsingham family tomb in St Nicholas Church, Chislehurst, to find evidence of a Marlowe–Shakespeare conspiracy. Molesting a commemorative bust of the man himself, in the hope of finding hidden manuscripts. Methodologically, in Shakespeare studies, anything goes.

The American codebreaker Elizabeth Wells Gallup found secret messages that directed her to Canonbury Tower, Islington. Full of expectation, she entered the tower room and went straight to the panelled wall where a hidden door was supposed to conceal 'rare papers'. Counting five panels along, she opened the cavity only to find it had been cleared of its contents. But, as always happens in this branch of the quest genre, there was another clue. Inscribed above the lintel was a list of monarchs that suggested—faintly, remarkably, implausibly—that Sir Francis Bacon was heir to Queen Elizabeth.

Cryptologists have gone to great lengths to discover clues about Shakespeare's life and authorship. In late-nineteenth-century Detroit, Dr Orville Ward Owen designed a remarkable machine for the specific purpose of reading messages hidden in the plays and in works by other authors published around the same time. Now a museum piece at Montana's Summit University, Owen's 'Wheel of Fortune' is a deranged contraption of gears and rollers and other moving parts that paint a false picture of busy industry. Owen believed his task as a cryptographer was to line up 'the connaturals, concurrences, correspondents, concatenations, collocations, analogies, similitudes, relatives, parallels, conjugates and sequences of everything relating to the combination, composition, renovation, arrangement and unity revolving in succession, part by part, throughout the whole'. No one has satisfactorily replicated his method.

Playing around with numbers is at the heart of Shakespeare studies. A whole branch of the discipline (which is not, it must be said, very disciplined) focuses on the mysterious references to 'shake' and 'speare' in the 1611 King James Bible. They are, respectively, the forty-sixth word from the beginning and the forty-sixth word from the end of Psalm 46—so long as certain words are excluded from the counting. Scholars in the same branch of Inexact Shakespearean Numerology count approximately 720 names of God and approximately 208 steps of the Great Pyramid, and detect pregnant meaning in the triangular number 153. It is both the number of Hail Marys when saying the Rosary, and the number of sonnets in Shakespeare's 1609 *Sonnets*—provided one sonnet is left out.

Across the Shakespeare literature as a whole, much is made of the myriad spellings of 'Shakespeare'. There are unsurprising variants, like Shakspeare, Sheakspeare, Shakspeyre and Shackspeer. And then there are variants that require a leap of faith: Shappere, Shakespea, Shaxkespere, Saxpere, Chacsper, Shakspurre, Shagsper, Schacosper, Schaftspere, Shaxberd. Over eighty variants have been recorded, not counting the international contenders like the Old German 'Sigispero', the French 'Jacques Pierre', the Arabic 'Sheikh Zubair' and the Italian 'Crollalanza'.

An everyday challenge in Elizabethan England, non-standard names are a challenge, too, for modern scholars trying to match poems and plays to people. The surname of playwright Christopher Marlowe is thought to have been spelt variously Marlo, Marloe, Marlow, Marlowe, Morley and Marley; we don't know for sure because these spellings may have belonged to more than one person. Many authors signed their work with initials; others adopted pseudonyms, pen-names or aliases. The actor Nicholas Tooley sometimes called himself Wilkinson. The translator and dramatist John Dancer also went by Dauncy; or maybe, as some believe, he didn't, and John Dauncy was a different person altogether.

Fans of Shakespeare's contemporary Sir Henry Neville have all sorts of fun with his surname—spelt variously Nevil, Neuill, Neuil, Neuyll, Neuel, Neveyll—and his punning family motto: *Ne Vile Velis*, meaning 'Form no vile wish or thought'. An epigram by Ben Jonson, 'To one that desired me not to name him', addresses both the general concept of anonymity and a specific anonymous recipient. Reading the epigram's second line, Neville scholar John Casson seized on two unremarkable words, 'any way', which, when voiced with a German accent, become 'any vay', supposedly a play on 'NEV' and a sign that Henry Neville was the epigram's anonymous addressee. References in other works to 'envy', and to Falstaff's original name 'Oldcastle' (a pun, it is claimed, on 'New ville'), have also been read as allusions to Neville.

In books published in Shakespeare's lifetime, his name was sometimes hyphenated as 'Shake-speare'. Ben Jonson's *The Poetaster* (1601) seems to have ridiculed the hyphen. The character Crispinus, a 'parcel-poet', sometimes spelled his name, pointedly, 'Cri-spinas'. Authors have since found all sorts of significance in Shakespeare's hyphen. Diana Price argued the hyphen signified a pseudonym, in the vein of 'Master Shoe-tie' or 'Sir Luckless Woo-all'. This is just one of the many phonological, ontological, editorial and typographical Theories of the Hyphen. Maybe the hyphen makes the name more striking, by highlighting its literal meaning—'shaking a spear'—which has been called political—a figurative threat to authority—as well as primal, armorial and phallic. Maybe the hyphen makes the name easier to remember, or serves another practical purpose.

When 'Shakspeare' was printed in italic font, as it was on several early quarto editions, the front foot of the 'k' was in danger of interfering with the tail of the 's'. Interposing a little spear prevents this, as does the insertion of an 'e'. This argument sounds convincing until we notice that the 'e' and the hyphen often appear together. Also, they are used even when 'Shake-speare' is printed in roman font, which poses no danger of foot-tail interference. According to other theories, the hyphen clarifies pronunciation of 'Shakespeare' by helping the 'e' lengthen the 'a', or by distinguishing 'Shake-speare' from, say, the mildly Francophonic

'Shak-espeare', or from 'Shakes-peare', a genuine possibility if we recall 'Shaxpere' was an alternative spelling of the playwright's name. All Theories of the Hyphen are as lame as these ones, and it is best to say as little about them as possible.

When exploring his world, we must always keep in mind that Shakespeare died long before lexicographers corralled English into the predicable beast we know today. In many other ways, too, we must leave our prejudices at the door. Shakespeare preceded much that we take for granted, like tube toothpaste, inexpensive glass, piped sewerage, the Enlightenment, American independence, newspapers, professional police, universal literacy, the 'literary life', compulsory education, the nuclear family and the rural picturesque. He flourished before tea and coffee reached the British Isles, and long before the animal rights movement; he and his entourage seem to have relished the cruel 'sport' of bear baiting.

Shakespeare lived at a time when witchcraft was taken seriously, and witchfulness was seen as valid grounds for setting a person on fire. 'Ringleader to all naughtiness', Satan was thought to walk the earth at the head of an army consisting of witches, possessed bodies and at least six divisions of secondary devils. Ben Jonson wrote numerous plays with occult themes, including *The Devil Is an Ass* (1616), a play partly set in Hell and in which Satan appears along with an inferior devil called Pug Deville (a name, incidentally, *not* claimed by the Nevillians as an allusion to Henry Neville). King James I wrote a treatise on the subject—*Daemonologie* (1597)—which denounces witches as devilish slaves. For ordinary people as well as the monarch, the boundary between science and magic was flimsy and unclear. People condemned evil witches while at the same time consulting 'good' or 'white' witches for medical advice.

In Elizabethan times, 'amateur' was not a word in English; nor was there a concept in the theatre of a 'director'. Shakespeare pre-dated modern ideas of literature, plagiarism and copyright. Different conceptions of authorial rights were symptomatic of different conceptions of authorship, ownership, piracy, forgery, truth and proof.

In the eighteenth and nineteenth centuries, Shakespeare scholarship flourished and interest in his work was intense. Editors and critics assembled a vivid and compelling portrait of the poet from Stratford-upon-Avon. He was gentle, mellifluous Shakespeare, a natural genius, the transcendent epitome of a literary man. This Shakespeare—whom author Henry Tyrrell called 'the acknowledged poet of the age, the friend of nobles and the pet of princes'—was often at the royal court, where he rubbed shoulders with Queen Elizabeth herself. One eighteenth-century image of Shakespeare has him on such intimate terms with the Virgin Queen, as her 'friend and admirer', that she gifted him 'a gold tissue toilet or table cover'. According to this image, Shakespeare was famous in his lifetime, feted by audiences and readers, venerated by his peers. This picture was so influential that, even today, we can't think of Shakespeare without it infiltrating our thoughts.

Just as the idealised image was taking root, however, scepticism was growing. As early as the sixteenth century, there were uncomfortable remarks about Shakespearean authorship and the extent to which he used the writings of others. In subsequent centuries those comments became a clamour; a colossal enterprise of scepticism emerged. The register of authors, thinkers, performers and dramatists who doubted Shakespeare's authorship includes Charlie Chaplin, Benjamin Disraeli, Ralph Waldo Emerson, Sigmund Freud, Henry James, William James, James

Joyce, Mark Twain, Orson Welles and Walt Whitman. Henry James wrote that he was 'haunted by the conviction that the divine William is the biggest and most successful fraud ever practised on a patient world'.

The scepticism has perhaps had the greatest influence on the Indiana Jones school of Shakespeare studies, whose adherents continue in their efforts to dig up clues, unravel ciphers and commune with the dead. These and more conventional researchers have a splendid goal: to prove William Shakespeare of Stratford—landlord, businessman, occasional moneylender—was or was not William Shakespeare of London—wild actor, serial miscreant and co-owner of theatres; and that one or both of these Shakespeares did or did not write the plays and poems many people regard as the highest achievement of English literature.

These primary controversies come in a multitude of variations, and branch into hundreds of secondary debates. Where did Shakespeare go to school? Was he educated at all? Did he poach deer? Was he a toper? Was he a Roman Catholic? Had he a Jewish girlfriend, the mysterious 'Dark Lady' of the sonnets? Who were W. H., T. T. and I. M.? And which real people were the targets of jests and jibes about Malvolio, Melicert, Phaeton, Aetion, Sogliardo and the Poet-Ape? The stakes are high: not just for English literature, but, if the Baconian heretics are to be believed, for the legitimacy of the British throne.

Who could resist the attractions of such a quest? And therein lies a problem. The price of admission into Shakespeare studies is trivially low: most of the documentary evidence and all the plays and poems are widely known and freely available in the public domain. Once inside the field, it is easy to become obsessed. Shakespeare scholars speak ruefully of addiction (another word coined by Shakespeare) and wasted years. Waylaid by the

Shakespeare Siren, they dare not go forward but cannot go back. The field is full of men and women with damaged reputations and impaired sanity. Many a leader in the field has met with a bad end. Among Shakespearean researchers (very, very broadly defined), more than one died from arsenic poisoning or narcotics; more than one perished in prison. There are serious whispers of a Shakespeare Curse.

CHAPTER 2

The Mystery

Though not quite a curse, and though most traditionalists vehemently deny it, there is certainly a problem at the heart of Shakespeare scholarship. The case against Shakespearean authorship is nowhere near as strong as the heretics would have us believe, but the case *for* is also weak. The historical record is incomplete and riddled with false leads. Much of the evidence is circumstantial and inconclusive, or was written at second or third hand, long after the fact.

Fabrications (like forged papers and plays) and falsities (like mis-dated books) impair the documentary record. John Payne Collier is one of several latter-day vandals who mischievously added to and subtracted from the documentary trail. John

Manningham captured the 'William the Conqueror' episode in his diary of 1601; Collier examined the diary in 1831, leading some scholars to treat it warily and a few to discount it altogether. But, on balance, for the time being, it is still regarded as genuine. Shakespeare's indirect entanglement in a palace intrigue (the Essex Rebellion) is a further source of mystery and skulduggery in the documentary record. Overall, Shakespearean biography is a conundrum.

As the basis for their work, biographical and literary researchers normally rely on registers (of births, deaths, marriages and baptisms), school enrolment records, academic transcripts, ledgers, account books, diaries, letters, drafts and inscribed books of various types, including 'presentation copies' and 'association copies'. (A presentation copy is a book inscribed by its author to a friend or fan. An association copy is a book demonstrably owned by someone famous. 'Association' here is used in the sense of 'guilt by association', not 'booksellers association'.) Scribbled notes can be incredibly important. Oscar Wilde's annotations in the margins of his books are a rich source of information, the closest he came to keeping a diary.

For historians of Shakespeare, though, such documentary pickings are slim. Aside from the poems and quarto plays published in his lifetime, few Shakespearean documents survive. Most of the seventy or so extant biographical records are arid administrative and legal papers like writs and wills. Much questionable work has been done to build around those records. Overbrimming with secondary detail, Shakespeare biographies are elaborate exercises in imagination and extrapolation. As Mark Twain remarked about the biographical Shakespeare, 'He is a Brontosaur: nine bones and six-hundred barrels of plaster of paris.'

Multiplicity deepens the conundrum. The little information

that we have looks as though it came from multiple Shakespeares living separate, parallel lives in London and Stratford. At the same time that Shakespeare was ostensibly a respectable citizen of Stratford, for example, he was charged in London with affray and disturbing the peace. At the time he was supposedly writing his most immortal and hilarious comedies, he was mourning the death, at the age of eleven, of his beloved son Hamnet. William Shakespeare purchased New Place, a grand house in Stratford, for sixty pounds or more when, in London, his theatre company was in financial difficulties and he was pursued for a five-shilling tax debt. The mainstream Shakespeare biographies valiantly attempt to knit together these disparate lives; to reconcile in one person and one narrative a ferret-race of incompatible facts. The results are universally unsatisfactory, and a spur to scepticism.

To distinguish between the Stratford Shakespeare and the London one, many sceptical authors name the former 'Shakspere' and the latter 'Shakespeare'. The Stratford man never referred to himself as 'Shakespeare' (as opposed to variants like 'Shakspere' and 'Shagspere'). More than once, he made a mess when writing his own name; ink blots mar several of the six surviving Shakespeare signatures. More than once, he signed in an abbreviated form.

His last will and testament is a precious document for Shakespearean biographers: three of the six signatures are there, and it is one of the most fertile records in a documentary desert. Tellingly, the will makes no reference to Shakespeare's former profession, his literary legacy or his stakes in two famous theatres. One part of the will does, however, link him to the London theatre world, and therefore connects the London and Stratford Shakespeares. The part in question bequeaths money to Richard Burbage (the man who lost out to William the Conqueror) and two other theatre-world celebrities: Henry Condell and John

Hemmings. The linking part was, however, added as an inter-lineation in a different hand, so the link is dubious.

In other ways, too, the will looks suspicious. The parchment, the handwriting, the contents, the annotations, the witnesses; all are causes for doubt and suggestive of conspiracy. One or more of the three Shakespearean signatures may well have been written by someone else, probably the lawyer Francis Collins. At five, the stated number of witnesses is atypically high. Most troubling of all: in the will, there is no trace of the great writer. After reading the will, Mortimer J. Adler pronounced a devastating judgement. The Stratford man's 'pathetic efforts to sign his name (illiterate scrawls) should forever eliminate Shakspere from further consideration in this question—he could not write'.

And then there is the simple problem of distance. Shakespeare scholars such as James Shapiro and Diana Price speak of Shakespeare 'commuting' between London and Stratford. After 1604, he had diverse commercial interests in the metropolis, but seems to have focused on his Warwickshire investments. Before then, he supposedly maintained residences in both localities and spent much time in each of them, especially in the 1590s and early 1600s. Commuting between London and Stratford is eminently practical in 2018. The trip takes about two hours by train or car. Not so, however, in 1600. For a middle-class Elizabethan like Shakespeare, the trip would have taken three days in each direction, provided there were no delays from incumbent hazards like highwaymen, rufflers, beggars, robbers, murderers, plunderers, cutthroats, vagabonds, horse-stealers, shady innkeepers and poor roads. To make the trip in safety and comfort was expensive and difficult. Shakespeare might have done it often, but he probably didn't. The life of Christopher Marlowe is informative here. Born in the same year as Shakespeare, and into the same provincial tradesman class, he hailed from Canterbury, a good deal closer to London. Once he became established in the capital, though, he seems seldom if ever to have made the trip back to his home town.

Much biographical scepticism has focused on the apparent clash between Shakespeare's modest provincial origins and the refined erudition of his writing. Charlie Chaplin's views typify one line of argument: 'In the work of the greatest geniuses, humble beginnings will reveal themselves somewhere, but one cannot trace the slightest sign of them in Shakespeare.' How, sceptics have asked, could a provincial entrepreneur become one of 'the universal geniuses of the world'? Biographers have looked in vain for signs of childhood prodigality or any other portent of adult excellence. Once Shakespeare arrived in London, he seems rapidly to have risen to the top of the theatre world, and rapidly to have gained an audience. How did he do it? Did he in fact do it? Was such a rapid rise even possible?

Contradictions are also apparent between the meagre facts of Shakespeare's life and the content of the works that bear his name. Like his father before him, Shakespeare lent money at interest. One of the most informative Shakespearean documents, and one with an early date, is a record of a loan of seven pounds that he advanced to John Clayton. Yet *The Merchant of Venice*, *Coriolanus* and *Hamlet* all condemn usurers. Most of Shakespeare's plays are concerned in one way or another with heterosexual love. In life, too, he seems to have delighted in the pursuit of women. Yet many of his sonnets were written from an altogether different perspective. This is such a striking feature of his verse that Bill Bryson characterised Shakespeare as 'English literary history's sublimest gay poet'.

Reading the plays creates a picture of a man closely familiar with law, science, falconry, statecraft, classical literature, Biblical studies, jurisprudence, navigation, Freemasonry, international affairs, the royal court and the aristocracy. How, the sceptics ask, could the son of a provincial tradesman display such knowledge of these high-flying fields and their specialised vocabularies?

Biographical contradictions are not the only reason why sceptics think there is a Shakespeare problem. Elizabethan and Jacobean London was a gossipy place. Literate people pumped out letters, books, pamphlets and plays on topical subjects, including each other. If Shakespeare was an important playwright and poet, he should have been captured and roasted extensively in the documentary chatter. Such contemporary references to Shakespeare, though, are rare. When they do occur, they are invariably cryptic, seemingly hinting at something mysterious or disreputable in the background. Even more striking are the documentary silences.

A year older than Shakespeare, Michael Drayton was born in the same county of Warwickshire. As a successful poet and dramatist, he moved in the same circles as Shakespeare. The two men could easily have met when Drayton lived in London, or when he stayed with the Rainsford family at the village of Clifford Chambers, less than three miles from Stratford. Drayton knew at least one member of the extended Shakespeare family. John Hall, husband of William's daughter Susanna, was the Rainsfords' family doctor. According to Hall's notebook, he treated Drayton for fever, with an 'emetick infusion mixed with syrup of violets', which 'wrought very well both upwards and downwards'. When not at the doctor's, Drayton immersed himself in English literary life. With his peers he exchanged scores of chatty and insightful letters and commendatory poems. His peers, that is, except for William Shakespeare.

John Chamberlain was another avid letter-writer who

pre-dated and post-deceased Shakespeare. Full of priceless details, his letters bear upon celebrity culture and reveal a sincere interest in the theatre world. Yet there is nothing in the letters about Shakespeare. In *An Account of the Life and Times of Francis Bacon* (1878), James Spedding observed that Chamberlain's letters were 'full of news of the month, news of the Court, the city, the pulpit and the bookseller's shop…court masques are described in minute detail, authors, actors, plot, performances, receptions and all, [yet] we look in vain for the name of Shakespeare'.

The author, poet and diplomat Sir Henry Wotton was another serial letter-writer. He became provost of Eton in 1624. The list of recipients of his letters includes King James I and Henry, Prince of Wales, along with an alphabet of other worthies: Sir Edmund Bacon, Sir Francis Bacon, Sir Edward Barrett, Dr Hugo Blotius (librarian of the Hofbibliothek), Isaac Casaubon, Robert Cecil, John Donne, Sir Thomas Edmondes, Lord Zouche. Wotton's *Reliquiae Wottonianae* (1651) captured the personalities of his literary world. Notably, he also described the fire that destroyed the Globe theatre during a 1613 performance of 'All is True' (*Henry VIII*).

> King Henry making a Masque at the Cardinal Wolsey's house, and certain cannons being shot off at his entry, some of the paper or other stuff, wherewith one of them was stopped, did light on the thatch, where being thought at first but idle smoak, and their eyes more attentive to the show, it kindled inwardly, and ran round like a train, consuming within less than an hour the whole house to the very ground. [One] man had his breeches set on fire, that would perhaps have broyled him, if he had not by the benefit of a provident wit, put it out with a bottle of ale.

Again, Shakespeare is not mentioned.

Other books from the period are strangely silent about Shakespeare, as are some important contemporary diaries. Philip Henslowe owned and managed the Rose and other playhouses. Shakespeare supposedly wrote and acted for him. Henslowe's working diary, discovered by the monumental Shakespeare scholar Edmond Malone, covers the pinnacle of Shakespeare's career (1592 to 1603). Henslowe was thorough. His inventory of costumes and props reads in part:

> Green hats for Robin Hood and 1 Hobbyhorse. Trumpets and drum and treble viol. 1 rock, 1 cave and 1 Hellmouthe. 1 tomb of Guido, 1 tomb of Dido, 1 bedstead. 8 lances and a pair of stairs for Phaeton. 1 golden fleece and 1 bay tree. Tamburlaine's bridle and wooden mattock. Mercury's wings and dragons. Imperial crowns and ghosts crowns. Cauldron for the Jew.

The folio diary describes Henslowe's theatrical business: takings from performances, and remittances to playwrights such as George Chapman, Henry Chettle, Thomas Dekker, Drayton, Thomas Heywood, Ben Jonson, John Marston, Thomas Middleton and John Webster. (Also there are mentions of Marlowe's plays, such as *Doctor Faustus* (1592), *Tamburlaine the Great* (1587) and *The Jew of Malta* (1589), but the one mention of 'Marloe' by name is thought to be a later forgery.) One way or another, the leading dramatists are present. Except for one. Shakespeare is never mentioned.

Shakespeare's son-in-law—'upwards and downwards' Dr Hall—wrote a diary, too, but the part covering Shakespeare's lifetime is missing. Philip Henslowe's stepson-in-law and business partner Edward Alleyn was another diligent diarist. Apart from acting in plays (some of them Shakespearean in title and in plot) and co-owning theatres, he was also, by royal patent, Master of the Bears, Bulls and Mastiff Dogs. Like Henslowe, Alleyn recorded in a diary his transactions with notable actors and playwrights. Shakespeare's name is conspicuously absent.

Appearing in several editions in the early decades of the seventeenth century, Peacham's *Compleat Gentleman* (1627) lists the 'English Poets of our owne nation'. After bowing to the especially esteemed 'Sir Ieoffrey Chaurcer the father', Peacham notes John Gower, John Lydgate, John Harding, John Skelton, Sir Thomas Wyatt, Thomas Sternhold, Heywood, Sir Thomas More, Dr Thomas Phaer, Arthur Golding and Henry, Earl of Surrey. Elizabethan poets receive a special mention:

> In the time of our late Queene Elizabeth, which was truly a golden Age (for such a world of refined wits, and excellent spirits it produced, whose like are hardly to be hoped for, in any succeeding Age) above others, who honoured Poesie with their pennes and practice...were Edward, Earl of Oxford (Edward de Vere); Lord Buckhurst (Thomas Sackville); Henry Lord Paget; Sir Philip Sidney; Edward Dyer; Edmund Spencer; Samuel Daniel.

Peacham, though, left Shakespeare out.

There are other gaps, too, in the documentary record. Shakespeare's Stratford school records are missing (we do not know for sure if he went there at all, or to any other school), as are the deeds of his Stratford properties. There is no record of his theatrical tours. No one in Stratford ever referred to him as a writer. In the 'lost years' between 1585 and 1592 and between 1603 and 1607 there is nary a trace of him. About Shakespeare the man, his literary contemporaries seem to have known little and to have written even less. He never wrote a word about himself, or, if he did, no such word has reached us.

After Queen Elizabeth died in 1603, much of the great outpouring of grief and reflection was expressed in print. William Shakespeare, though, wrote not a single elegy or tribute or recollection. Ben Jonson was Shakespeare's colleague and rival in the theatre world. When Jonson died in 1637, there was a great display of public lamentation, and he was interred in Westminster Abbey. Edmund Spenser, John Fletcher, Francis Beaumont, Chapman and Drayton (Dr Hall's violets could not save him) were all honoured in a commensurate way after their death. Shakespeare's passing, though, was greeted in London with silence.

The biggest gap, however, and the most enduring mystery, is Shakespeare's missing library.

CHAPTER 3

The Quarry

None of Shakespeare's friends and associates left behind a description of his library. Nor is there a record of it being dispersed at the time of his death. His will refers neither to books nor manuscripts. In fact, as we've already heard, it gives no sign of a literary career at all, or even a literate one. Contemporary dramatists such as Francis Beaumont, Thomas Dekker, John Fletcher, Robert Greene, Thomas Heywood and Ben Jonson all left behind plays in manuscript. No Shakespeare playscript, though, has ever been found. (Part of the manuscript of a play about Sir Thomas More has been attributed to Shakespeare, but the part is small and the attribution contentious.)

We do, however, know a few things about Shakespeare's

relationship with books. He wrote plays according to a method that has been labelled plagiaristic; 'appropriative' is a more polite term, and historically more accurate. Quantities of prior plays, poems, novels, histories and almanacs fed into his writing. The breadth of his sources is exceptional; they number in the hundreds and span diverse eras, countries and genres. By some means, Shakespeare had contact with most or all of these source texts.

During his career, a network of libraries linked bookmen to one another. Jonson, for example, used Francis Bacon's library, and John Florio used the Earl of Southampton's. Shakespeare probably knew John Bretchgirdle's clergyman's library in Stratford and printer Richard Field's working library in London. Shakespeare referred to libraries as 'nurser[ies] of arts' (in *The Taming of the Shrew*) and characterised them as treasure troves and cure-alls. Titus Andronicus invites Marcus Andronicus and Lavinia to 'Come, and take choice of all my Library, / And so beguile thy sorrow'. *The Tempest* seems to have been written late in Shakespeare's life. Many scholars have read it as his theatrical farewell, and the sorcerer Prospero as his alter ego. Prospero tells Miranda, 'Me, poor man, my Library was dukedom large enough', and later confesses: 'Knowing I loved my books, he furnished me, from my own Library, / With volumes that I prize above my dukedom.'

Shakespeare's plays and poems reveal a close familiarity with the physicality of books and the mechanics of their production. The sonnets abound with such references:

'Thou shoulds't print more, nor let that copy die' (Sonnet 11)
'So should my papers, yellowed with their age / Be scorned' (Sonnet 17)
'Show me your image in some antique book' (Sonnet 59)

'That in black ink my love may still shine bright' (Sonnet 66)
'The vacant leaves thy mind's imprint will bear' (Sonnet 77)

Book terminology also permeates the plays. In *Romeo and Juliet*, Lady Capulet tells Juliet about the handsome suitor, Count Paris: 'This precious book of love, this unbound lover, / To beautify him, only lacks a cover.' In *As You Like It*, Orlando exclaims: 'O Rosalind! these trees shall be my books / And in their barks my thoughts I'll character.'

Love's Labour's Lost contains book-making terms such as printing, ink, lead, letters, text, formes, numbering, pencils, superscripts, bookmen, sheets (of paper) and the coloured letters of illuminated manuscripts. In *Antony and Cleopatra* there are references to abstract, almanac, period and 'nonpareil' (a size of printer's type). In *The Merry Wives of Windsor* we find second edition and madrigals; in *Hamlet*, index, parchment, preface, volume and writing; in *As You Like It*, contents, indents and the printer's devil (a printer's errand boy); and in *Pericles*, books, points, calendars and quoins (wedges for locking up type). *All's Well that Ends Well* adds publisher and 'finisher', a tradesman in a bindery. In *The Taming of the Shrew* (act 4, scene 4), Shakespeare makes a racy joke about copyright:

> *Lucentio*: And what of all this?
> *Biondello*: I cannot tell, except they are busied about a counter-feit assurance. Take you assurance of her, 'Cum privilegio ad imprimendum solum' [i.e. 'With exclusive rights to print']. To the church, take the Priest, Clerk, and some sufficient honest witnesses.

In addition to such material from the poems and plays, doubtful oral traditions have come down to us. One anecdote concerns

Ben Jonson, with whom Shakespeare seems to have maintained a complex relationship of mutual affection and perpetual jousting. The anecdote sees Jonson 'in a necessary-house' (in other words, on the lavatory) 'with a book in his hand reading it very attentively'. Shakespeare notices Jonson thus engaged and says he is sorry Jonson's memory is so bad he cannot 'sh-te without a book'.

If Shakespeare had a library, we can readily visualise its contents. Apart from working drafts, along with manuscripts and copies of his principal literary and historical sources, he probably owned reference works: writing guides, dictionaries and foreign-language instruction manuals. Examples of the latter include Claude de Sainliens' *A Treatise for Declining of Verbes* (1590); Sainliens' *The French Littleton: A Most Easie, Perfect and Absolute Way to Learne the Frenche Tongue* (1591); William Stepney's *The Spanish Schoole-master* (1591); John Eliot's *Ortho-epia Gallica* (1593); and G. Delamonthe's *The French Alphabet, Teaching In a Very Short Tyme, by a Most Easie Way, to Pronounce French Naturally, to Reade it Perfectly, to Write it Truely, and to Speake it Accordingly* (1592). All these titles were printed or published by the Stratford-born bookman Richard Field.

Shakespeare is thought to have written at least thirty-eight plays, two epic poems and 154 sonnets. As many as seventy Shakespeare quarto editions were produced during his lifetime, by a variety of publishers and printers (this includes plays that went into multiple editions), and Shakespeare probably retained copies of these. Some quarto plays identified Shakespeare as the author, some did not, and none did so before 1598. In that year, quarto editions of *Richard II* and *Richard III* named him as author; and the quarto of *Love's Labour's Lost* was issued as 'Newly corrected and augmented by W. Shakespere'. The latter quarto was published at the 'Shoppe in the Pultrie', a street historically associated with poulterers. The 1609 quarto editions of *Pericles* and *Troilus and Cressida* stated they were written by William Shakespeare. Some of his plays, though, continued to appear anonymously after 1598. The 1599 *Romeo and Juliet* quarto is an example.

The same plays appeared under different titles. *Much Ado About Nothing*, for example, was registered and performed as *Benedick and Beatrice*. *Twelfth Night* was also known as *Malvolio*. (The comical part of *A Midsummer Night's Dream* was separately printed in quarto, and was acted under the title *Bottom the Weaver*.) With the exception of *Othello*, from 1622, all the pre-Folio quartos were first published before Shakespeare retired to Stratford, in about 1611.

Of the many hundreds of book owners I've studied, the overwhelming majority left behind evidence of their ownership—bookplates, book-labels, signatures, marginal notes, manicules, inscriptions, imprecations. That is the case today and it was true, too, of book collectors in Shakespeare's day. Sixteenth- and seventeenth-century collectors often wrote their names on title pages or other leaves of their books. John Bretchgirdle was vicar of Holy Trinity Church in Stratford. He probably baptised the infant William Shakespeare, and certainly had one of the best libraries in town. On each of his title pages, Bretchgirdle wrote 'Jo. Bretchgyrdles Book', along with details of where he bought the book. Edward Alleyn wrote his name twice in his books, once on the title page and once on the verso of the last leaf. Among other Shakespeare contemporaries who were also book-markers, Ann Raynor used a tidy and legible script to sign her books on the inside of the front cover, while Humphrey Dyson ink-stamped the date on his books in a manner as idiosyncratic as a signature.

Apart from writing 'Will: Boothby' on his title pages, Sir William Boothby had his books bound in armorial calf, goatskin and vellum. A folio volume from his library, now in a private collection, is bound in calf with raised bands that divide the spine into even compartments, each one featuring Boothby's lion's-paw crest stamped in gold. The sixteenth-century book collector Robert Dudley, Earl of Leicester, also had his books bound in personalised leather covers. Those bindings were decorated with his initials and his coat of arms—a muzzled bear chained to a ragged staff—stamped in gilt on the upper cover. Dudley's home was Kenilworth Castle, near Stratford-upon-Avon.

Mystery and controversy surround the Shakespeare family arms and motto. In 1596 the College of Heralds granted a coat of arms to John Shakespeare. Most scholars believe the College was responding to an application from William Shakespeare in his father's name. Unlike John, his son could afford the steep cost and possessed the steep ambition to apply for a crest. The Shakespeare application was not smooth sailing; it had to be submitted more than once. A supplementary request to combine the crest with that of the Arden family was rejected.

The application was so controversial that the Shakespeare arms were cited as a factor in the 1602 complaint by a heraldry official that coats of arms were being granted to undeserving commoners. The Shakespeares' application does appear to have exaggerated their wealth and over-egged their connection to the better sorts of Ardens, who had lived in the district since at least 1438. The Shakespeares may also have paid a bribe in lieu of proof of their noble lineage. They could not prove, for example, that a warrior ancestor had defended Henry VII—because he almost certainly had not. Nevertheless, William Shakespeare was soon referring to himself as a 'gentleman'.

The final 'letters patent' version of the Shakespeare family arms has been lost, but we do have drafts and a detailed description: 'Gold, on a Bend, Sables, a Speare of the first Steeled Argent. And for his creast or cognizaunce a falcon, his winges displayed Argent standing on a wreath of his colours.' Variant versions add a helmet and tassels. The spear was an unavoidable inclusion (and, in gold and silver, an aspirational one). Complementing the arms was the motto, *Non sanz droict*, 'Not without right'. The claim, sometimes made, that Shakespeare used this motto on many of his documents is patently false. On nearly all the surviving documents the motto is absent. It seems to have been composed specifically for the arms application. (An alternative theory, not widely accepted, is that the motto is not a motto at all but a record of the application's initial rejection—*Non, sanz droict*, 'No, without right', the comma making all the difference.)

Both the arms and the motto quickly drew ridicule. Pretentious characters populate Ben Jonson's *The Poetaster*. Pompous Pantalabus is a writer and social climber who 'takes up all' and claims to be a 'gent'man'. Crispinus, the 'parcel-poet' who made fun of Shakespeare's hyphen, boasts about his own coat of arms:

Chloe: Are you a gentleman born?
Crispinus: That I am, lady; you shall see mine arms if't please you.
Chloe: No, your legs do sufficiently show you are a gentleman born, sir: for a man born upon little legs is always a gentleman born.
Crispinus: Yet, I pray you, vouchsafe the sight of my arms, Mistress; for I bear them about me, to have 'em seen. [*Showing Chloe a paper*] My name is Crispinus, or Cri-spinas indeed; which is well expressed in my arms, a face crying *in chief*, and beneath it a bloody toe, between three thorns *pungent*.

(This suggests another Theory of the Hyphen: a symbol of the Elizabethan nouveau riche.)

Jonson was even more explicit in *Every Man out of his Humour* (1600). Sogliardo (a rustic clown) tells Sir Puntarvolo (a foolish knight) and Carlo (a jester) how proud he is of his new coat of arms (act 3, scene 1):

> *Sogliardo*: I' faith, I thank God. *I can write myself a gentleman now*; here's my patent, it cost me thirty pounds, by this breath.
>
> *Puntarvolo*: A very fair coat, well charged and full of armory.
>
> *Sogliardo*: Nay, it has as much variety of colours in it, as you have seen a coat have; how like you the crest, sir?
>
> *Puntarvolo*: I understand it not well, what is't?
>
> *Sogliardo*: Marry, sir, it is your boar without a head, rampant. A boar without a head, that's very rare!
>
> *Carlo*: Ay, and rampant too! troth, I commend the herald's wit, he has deciphered him well: a swine without a head, without brain, wit, anything indeed, ramping to gentility...
>
> *Sogliardo*: On a chief argent, a boar's head proper, between two ann'lets sables.
>
> *Carlo (to Puntarvolo)*: 'Slud, it's a hog's cheek and puddings, in a pewter field, this.
>
> *Sogliardo*: How like you 'hem, signior?
>
> *Puntarvolo*: Let the word be, 'Not without mustard': Your crest is very rare, sir.

The comical conversion of 'Not without right' into 'Not without mustard' may be a reference not only to Shakespeare in general but to Shakespeare in particular, via an allusion to *II Henry IV* (act 2, scene 4): 'He a good wit? Hang him, baboon! His wit's as thick as Tewkesbury mustard; there's no more conceit in him than is in a mallet.'

The search for Shakespeare's library provides an intriguing perspective on his purchase of arms. Was he assembling a collection of books that he would clothe in beautiful calfskin and morocco? Was he planning to display his heraldic crest on the books' front covers and spines? Did 'gentle Shakespeare', in other words, yearn for a proper gentleman's library? Notwithstanding Jonson's lampoon, every connoisseur of leather-bound tomes would swap a limb for an original volume displaying Shakespeare's crest. With my wife, Fiona, I've searched far and wide for just such a volume.

A few of our finds are exciting and suggestive. Perhaps the most intriguing one was previously owned by the Lane family. A theological work by Agostino Tornielli, it was published in Milan in 1610, then shipped to England where, in 1615, it was bound in brown calfskin in a distinctive style. The book's spine is divided by raised bands into eight compartments decorated with golden sprays of laurel. The cover panels feature a rectangular decoration with, in the centre, an image blocked in gilt showing the tragic story, from Ovid and used by Shakespeare in *A Midsummer Night's Dream*, of Pyramus and Thisbe. (The story also influenced *Romeo and Juliet*.) In the image, Pyramus lies on the ground, expired, and Thisbe ends her own life by spearing herself on an upright sword. A lion flees but Cupid stays to watch the spectacle.

Apart from the handsome leather cover, the edges of the text-block are beautifully decorated with elaborate patterning: snail and lion motifs within laurel wreaths on a field of gilt 'fleurons', or printers' flowers. Three other bindings in the exact same style, with the exact same gilt block, have also been documented. All four volumes date from before the year of Shakespeare's death, except for one which was bound in that year. The latter volume, bound in black turkey, is especially notable because it is a copy of Ben Jonson's *Workes* (1616), a book closely connected to Shakespeare.

The owner of the four bindings is not known, but there are a few hints. Do the fleurons signify a literary career? That would fit the depiction of Pyramus and Thisbe, which suggests a deep interest in literature (the owner chose a literary motif over a royal, ecclesiastical, political or military one) and possibly a deep interest in Shakespearean literature. In tiny letters, the cover image is signed 'I. S.' No one knows whether the initials are those of the block-maker, the bookbinder, the bookseller, the book's owner, a patron or a dedicatee. No one has stepped forward to claim them. One person with those initials is 'Iohannes Shakespeare', William Shakespeare's father, a man who made part of his living by dealing in leather hides, no doubt some of them for bookbinding.

Sotheby's sold the book in 1926. Maggs Brothers of London bought it then sold it to Henry Clay Folger. It is now in the Folger Shakespeare Library, not attributed to any early owner.

Apart from this intriguing foursome, Fiona and I found many other armorial bindings from the right period. Not one of them, though, displays Shakespeare's crest. Not one of them is conclusively traceable to his library.

Nor have we found a Shakespeare bookplate. A German innovation, the idea of using printed pictorial labels to link books to their owners dates from the mid-fifteenth century. The earliest English armorial bookplate—a woodcut plate commemorating a gift from Sir Nicholas Bacon—dates from 1574. Though slow to take off (the next two English examples date from 1585) they gradually became more popular, and by the end of the seventeenth century were *de rigueur* for English ladies and gentlemen. Shakespeare may well have had one made, featuring his crest and motto.

Bookplate or no bookplate, tracing the provenance of bindings is difficult. A longstanding principle of bibliography is that bindings are, strictly speaking, not part of the books they protect and adorn. Books, according to this view, begin and end with their preliminary and terminal leaves. Binding scholarship, and detailed descriptions of bindings in catalogues, are recent phenomena. Researchers looking today at early catalogues are lucky if the type of leather is briefly identified. Such identifications are usually just a single word, indicating the type of animal that provided the hide—'calf', 'goatskin', 'vellum' (a beautiful and hardy form of calfskin)—or the approximate geography of where the leather came from—'morocco', 'turkey', 'russia'.

The risk of *remboîtage* poses another problem for the study of bindings and their provenance. *Remboîtage* is a type of fakery in which a desirable binding is removed from an unremarkable book and then added to one that is more valuable or exciting. Crude examples of this crime are easy to spot: the binding is too large or too tight; the wear and tear do not match up; the binding style pre-dates the book's publication date; or there is another hint of mischief. But skilful pairings can fool even the most accomplished specialists.

The sad case of John Blacker demonstrates that, in the collection and connoisseurship of bookbindings, there are far worse crimes than *remboîtage*. In the 1870s and '80s, Blacker bought a spectacular collection of beautiful Renaissance bindings from the English bookseller Bernard Quaritch. Quaritch in turn sourced the bindings from a Frenchman, Monsieur J. Caulin. Crafted by masters of the bookbinding art, the bindings had been commissioned by 'every important French sixteenth-century collector: Grolier, Mahieu, Anne de Montmorency; French kings and their wives and mistresses, François I, Henri II and III, Catherine de Medici, Diane de Poitiers; popes and cardinals'. The texts inside were mundane and not very valuable, but the bindings lifted them into the rare-book stratosphere. They became Blacker's most precious treasures. To guard them from light and dust, he stored them in custom-made, velvet-lined boxes and 'coffrets', all of which were perfumed and some of which could only be opened with golden keys.

Utterly obsessed, Blacker began to treat his collection as though it were a reliquary, or a harem. At every opportunity he sat alone in his dining room with one of the books, gloating: 'If anyone came into the room he would throw a square of silk over the book to prevent it being seen.' The library was thought to be worth seventy thousand pounds. That is, until Caulin was exposed as the notorious forger Louis Hagué. Disastrously, not a single one of the Caulin–Hagué bindings was genuine. Though Blacker discovered the fraud himself on a visit to Blois, his first reaction was blind denial; the bindings just had to be real. Even after Hagué came to London and confessed, Blacker refused to let go of the illusion. He died in April 1896, trapped in an obstinate, optimistic madness. In 1897 the books were bundled up and sold at Sotheby's as 'A Remarkable Collection of Books in Magnificent Modern Bindings, formed by an Amateur (Recently Deceased)'. The proceeds totalled a mere £1907. The silver coffrets were more valuable than the books they housed.

Partly because of the dispersal of the Blacker collection and Hagué's own library, fake bindings now turn up surprisingly often. Though rare-book librarians are permanently on the lookout, fakes have infiltrated major collections. The Folger Shakespeare Library contains several forgeries including, on a 1555 volume by Conrad Gesner, a fake 'Catherine de Medici' binding by none other than Louis Hagué. Let us take care, then, when searching for Shakespeare's bindings.

If he was indeed assembling a fine library, we know a little about what his books might have looked like. In the middle and later decades of the seventeenth century, the rise of Puritanism shifted bookbinding fashions towards simplicity and austerity; rich decoration was a radical and dangerous act. But in Shakespeare's day the most delightful bindings were sumptuously decorated with gilt ornamentation: stars, dots, blocks, chevrons, cartouches, centrepieces, arabesques, ellipses, flowers, diamonds, rolls and scrolls. Rooms of books bound in this way look like collections of jewels.

Thinking about Shakespearean bookbindings sparks off other exciting thoughts. Robert Southey's 'Cottonian Library' consisted for the most part of books bound by his daughters and their friends in floral cotton remnants. The delightful homecraft bindings make the books look soft, fresh, warm and eminently embraceable. Like Edward Alleyn, Shakespeare probably was entitled to keep his own acting wardrobe. Imagine Shakespeare's children covering his books in fragments of the knotted and embroidered costumes he wore when playing the Ghost in *Hamlet*, and that his children and grandchildren wore when playing games of Scaramouches. What would such an artefact be worth? What would it tell us about Shakespeare's life and character?

Following in Bretchgirdle's footsteps, Reverend John Ward was Stratford's vicar from 1662 to 1681. An anecdotal tradition, dating back at least to Ward's day and possibly to Ward himself, speaks of a Stratford reunion between Shakespeare and Jonson late in the Bard's life. At that time, Shakespeare was enjoying a respectable retirement. Jonson was getting older, too. As a young man, his skin had been remarkably clear and fair; by late middle age, though, a life of hard drinking had taken its toll. Jonson described himself in geographical terms as having a 'mountain belly' and a 'rocky face'. John Aubrey claimed the geography was wonky; Jonson 'had one eye lower than tother and bigger'. Thomas Dekker found other similes for Jonson's face: it was like 'a bruised, rotten russet apple, or a badly pock-marked brass warming pan'.

According to the reunion tradition, the two playwrights went drinking together and reprised the 'wit-combats' they had so energetically engaged in at London's Mermaid Tavern during their glory days. Shakespeare was living out his retirement at New Place, the grand home he bought a decade earlier. In the century after his death, the building would be substantially rebuilt, and then entirely demolished. Surviving drawings, though, show a sizable three-storey edifice with five gables and multiple outbuildings. Plenty of room for a large private library. (Legal documents from 1635 and 1637 refer to the home having 'a study of books'.) During Jonson's Stratford sojourn, did he visit the library at New Place, perhaps before the old rivals went out drinking? Did they spend a few moments swapping stories, surrounded by the artefacts of Shakespeare's literary life? Did Jonson see bindings decorated with Shakespeare's crest? Could he hold his tongue, or did he just have to say something about wanting to be a gent'man?

CHAPTER 4

The Search Begins

If there is a Shakespeare library waiting to be found, the next step is to go looking for it. But where to look? What happened to Shakespeare's books after his death?

Many possibilities present themselves. The books could have passed to Shakespeare's surviving family and direct descendants. Rumours have long circulated that his Bible and other relics passed to John Hart, a chairmaker and descendant of Shakespeare's sister Joan, who died in 1646. Or the books may have passed via his daughter Susanna and her husband Dr Hall to their daughter, Elizabeth, Shakespeare's last surviving descendant. Elizabeth's marriage to Sir John Bernard conferred on her a title, Lady Bernard, but no children. Her possessions may have passed to her executor, Edward Bagley, or to Sir John's daughters from an earlier marriage. (One of Lady Bernard's belongings has been identified: a copy of the 1599 'Breeches' Bible, tenderly inscribed to her husband.)

Alternatively, Shakespeare's books might have passed to the Arden branch of the family, or to the Sheldons of Beoley. (Ralph Sheldon's wife, Anne Throckmorton, was sister-in-law to Edward Arden, one of the 'better' Ardens.) Sheldon's sister Anne Sheldon Daston was the mother-in-law of Ralph Huband, from whom William Shakespeare purchased a lease of tithes in 1605. As author and bookseller Alan Keen has pointed out, Ralph Sheldon's grandson, William Sheldon, owned the Burdett-Coutts copy of the 1623 First Folio; perhaps he had other Shakespeare items as well.

The books may instead have passed to John Hemmings, Shakespeare's fellow actor and ostensibly a co-editor of the First Folio. Hemmings died in 1630. Seven of his children survived into adulthood. One, a son named William, lived until 1653. The Hemmings daughters married into the Atkins, Smith, Sheppard, Merefield and Ostler families. These marriages produced descendants who may have inherited Hemmings' 'accompt-books and theatrical contracts', and perhaps part or all of Shakespeare's library.

Or the books could have fallen into the hands of Thomas Russell, Esq., whom Shakespeare appointed, along with Francis Collins, to oversee his will. The son of a member of parliament, Russell was educated at Queen's College, Oxford. In or around 1596, he moved to Alderminster Manor, about four miles south of Stratford-upon-Avon. (In 1596 he sued William Parry, a Stratford butcher, for an unpaid debt.) Shakespeare bequeathed him five pounds. Russell almost certainly had both a library and an appreciation of Shakespeare's literary status, whatever it was. He knew people connected with Shakespeare's theatrical career, including Anne Digges. (Leonard Digges wrote a memorial poem for the preliminary pages of the First Folio. His widowed mother Anne knew John Hemmings as well as Henry Condell, purportedly Hemmings' First Folio co-editor.)

The Russells were well connected, including to Sir John Harington (godson of Queen Elizabeth and author of *The Metamorphosis of Ajax* (1596)), to Tobie Matthew senior (Dean of Christ Church at Oxford and Archbishop of York) and to Tobie Matthew junior (close friend of Sir Francis Bacon and John Donne, and retainer of the Earl of Essex). Any one of these Russell connections is a possible transmission route for part or all of the library. These and other promising chains of provenance would be followed when, in the eighteenth century, the searchers first set out.

Nicholas Rowe, the first author to attempt a biography of Shakespeare, was among the earliest searchers. His brief biography is full of errors, and as a searcher, too, he did not get far. He advertised for people to come forward with Shakespearean documents. It seems few people did; in writing his book, Rowe relied heavily on anecdotal evidence, much of it apocryphal, some of it collected in Stratford-upon-Avon on Rowe's behalf by the aged Shakespearean actor Thomas Betterton. Apart from speaking to locals, Betterton consulted the parish register at Holy Trinity Church, using methods that account for large and small inaccuracies in Rowe's *Some Account of the Life &c of Mr William Shakespear* (1709).

The next we hear of a search on the ground is the story of Reverend James Wilmot. Though Wilmot's search is said to have been extraordinarily thorough, and though it revealed a great deal, both it and a subsequent search by members of the Ireland family were not entirely satisfactory.

Born in Warwick in 1726, Reverend James Wilmot became a Fellow of Trinity College, Oxford, before leading an eminent life in London. He befriended parliamentarians and came to know the literary men of the day such as Samuel Johnson, Laurence Sterne and Thomas Warton, the poet laureate. Retiring in about 1781, he became rector at the village of Barton-on-the-Heath, sixteen miles south of Stratford-upon-Avon. In his retirement he continued to pursue his literary interests. With the help of a London bookseller he augmented his library and strengthened its Elizabethan and Jacobean nucleus, especially the writings of Shakespeare and Bacon. When the bookseller asked him to emulate Rowe and write a Shakespeare biography, Wilmot went to Stratford in search of the traces he expected to see left behind by a writer of Shakespeare's stature. He interviewed townsfolk and conducted other research in and around the town. The people of Stratford regaled him with colourful local folklore, like the story about the cakes that hailed down one Shrovetide and injured hapless pedestrians. And the one about the church tower wickedly removed by the devil. And the one about the unusually tall and ugly man who threatened to bewitch the cattle of local farmers. Why, Wilmot wondered, had Shakespeare not used these fascinating characters and stories in his plays? Most importantly for Wilmot's search, the local people told him Shakespeare, the son not of a glover or leather-trader but an illiterate butcher, was:

> at best a Country clown at the time he went to seek his fortune in London, that he could never have had any school learning, and that that fact would render it impossible that he could be received as a friend and equal by those of culture

and breeding who alone could by their intercourse make up for the deficiencies of his youth.

Thoroughly, painstakingly, meticulously, the reverend searched for Shakespeare's books and manuscripts. Interrogating bookcases, book chests, drawers, closets and cabinets, Wilmot inspected every private library and every holding of letters and documents within fifty miles of Stratford. In Warwickshire his search radius encompassed Charlecote Park, home of the Lucy family; Coughton Court, home of the Throckmortons; Ragley Hall, home of the Conways and ancestral seat of the Marquess of Hertford; Baddesley Clinton, home of the Ferrers; Packwood House, the Fetherstons; Upton House, the Childs; Farnborough Hall, the Holbechs; and Arbury Hall, the Newdegates. Not too far away in Gloucestershire and Oxfordshire and Worcestershire were other august seats such as Snowshill Manor, Chastleton House, Broughton Castle and Hanbury Hall; these, too, fell within the compass of Wilmot's search.

Most of the local gentry had roots dating back to Shakespeare's day; their libraries were at least two centuries old. Surely they would have purchased a selection of his books upon his death, or would otherwise have come upon his manuscripts and other papers. Yet none of them seemed to have done so. None of them, in fact, seemed to know anything useful at all. Wilmot unearthed not a single volume that betrayed any evidence of having been owned by Shakespeare. He calculated that the poet must have produced over a quarter of a million manuscript pages. Yet he found not a single one.

The failure of his search led Wilmot to a tectonic conclusion. Shakespeare was not an author at all. He was an illiterate frontman for the true creator of the plays and poems, Sir Francis Bacon. Bacon was the only man with the necessary depth of intellect and breadth of learning, encompassing an intimate knowledge of France, Italy, the law, government and philosophy. Having made this earth-tilting deduction, Wilmot wrote extensive notes about it, and shared his conclusions with friends and visitors. The Baconian theory, though, was far too hot for publication. Even Wilmot's unpublished notes were dangerous. Near the end of his life, he arranged for all the 'bags and boxes of writing' in his bedroom to be burned 'on the platform before the house'. His heretical hypothesis did, however, survive the fire.

James Corton Cowell, one of the visitors to Wilmot's home, had taken accurate notes of their conversations. 'Wilmot does not venture so far as to say definitively that Sir Francis Bacon was the Author,' Cowell reported, 'but through his great knowledge of the works of that writer he is able to prepare a cap that fits him amazingly.' Cowell had travelled to Warwickshire from Ipswich looking for details of Shakespeare's life to include in a presentation for his local philosophic society. When finally given, the address to the society was a lightning bolt. Cowell outed himself as a Shakespeare heretic: 'A Pervert,' he confessed, 'nay a renegade to the Faith I have proclaimed and avowed before you all.' Shakespeare, he said, had destroyed his manuscripts to conceal the fact of Bacon's authorship. The names of characters and the details of plots in Shakespeare's plays provided ample confirmatory evidence, as did the fact that they indicated a sound knowledge of legal principles and method. Stylistic similarities in the works of Bacon and Shakespeare clinched the case. Bacon must have been Shakespeare. Having heard these revelations, the Ipswich audience was, by all accounts, scandalised.

The next major search after Wilmot's was a curious kind of family excursion. In the late eighteenth century, Samuel Ireland lived at

8 Norfolk Street, the Strand, with one Mrs Freeman. Formerly a favourite of the Earl of Sandwich, she was now Samuel's house-keeper, amanuensis, mistress and the mother of his children: Anna, Jane and William-Henry. A dogged collector, Samuel assembled a creditable library and a small gallery of artworks. A minor artist in his own right, he dealt in prints and paintings from time to time, and was an authority on Hogarth. He also dabbled in writing and publishing, producing illustrated books of pictur-esque views and topographical tours such as the intermittently racy *A Picturesque Tour Through Holland, Brabant, and Part of France* (1790). (The tour's highlights include a brothel and a town whose young women trade favours for gingerbread.)

Samuel and Mrs Freeman revered Shakespeare, rearing their children on readings of his plays. In William-Henry's teens he became an assiduous browser of bookstalls, making many Elizabethan and other finds that pleased his father. In the summer of 1793, Samuel and William-Henry visited Stratford-upon-Avon. William-Henry, though he later claimed to have been sixteen at the time, was eighteen years old. The Irelands had as their escort a tall, muscular, beetle-browed rustic named John Jordan. Formerly a wheelwright, Jordan had remodelled himself as a local antiquary and tourist guide.

At Shottery, just outside Stratford, Jordan led the Irelands to Hewlands Farm and the oak-beamed farmhouse that came to be known as Anne Hathaway's Cottage. The moment was one of irresistible historicity, and Samuel just had to have a Shakespearean memento. Anne's relatives owned an ancient bed; Samuel tried to buy it but seems to have failed despite multiple ardent offers. He did succeed, however, in buying another piece of furniture, which was sold to him as Shakespeare's courting chair, and another intimate relic: a four-inch-square tasselled purse, made from supple leather and decorated with bugle beads, 'a present from Shakespeare to his love', Anne Hathaway.

From another Stratford family the Irelands bought a goblet fashioned from a mulberry tree that Shakespeare was said to have planted. There were limits, however, to their desire for relics; they seem to have resisted the temptation to recover bones from the charnel-house at Holy Trinity Church.

Physical relics were all well and good, but Samuel's true prey was literary. Where were the manuscripts that would provide him with a portal to Shakespeare's creative life and work? Interrogating all, he learned that a quantity of manuscripts had been moved from New Place to nearby Clopton House at the time of the Stratford fire of 1742. Intoxicated by the scent of rare paper, Jordan and the Irelands went to Clopton House full of expectation. There, they experienced one of the most brutal let-downs in the history of humankind.

Clopton House's occupant, a gentleman farmer named Williams, got straight to the point. 'By God I wish you had arrived a little sooner! Why, it isn't a fortnight since I destroyed several baskets-full of letters and papers, in order to clear a small chamber for some young partridges which I wish to bring up alive: and as to Shakespeare, why there were many bundles with his name wrote upon them. Why it was in this very fireplace I made a roaring bonfire of them.' A stunned and appalled Ireland cried, 'My God! Sir, you are not aware of the loss which the world has sustained. Would to heaven I had arrived sooner!' Farmer Williams' elderly wife verified the baleful story and chided her husband. 'I do remember it perfectly well! And, if you will call to mind my words, I told you not to burn the papers, as they might be of consequence.' Shell-shocked, Ireland inspected the little chamber and found nothing but partridges.

The ornithological trauma sent Samuel's appetite for Shakespearean documents to fever pitch. He would, he asserted, happily give half his fine library to become possessed of even a single Shakespeare signature.

Back in London, the Irelands found their son a job in the office of a conveyancer. Thus employed, and aware of his father's appetites, William-Henry ramped up his scrutiny of bookstalls and anywhere else he could acquire old books, manuscripts, pamphlets, letters, leases, deeds, wills, contracts, rent rolls, prints, sketches; indeed, any miscellaneous old paper or parchment or vellum. He caught spectacular fish. One of his first finds after the Stratford visit was a quarto volume bound in vellum featuring the crest of Queen Elizabeth and containing a dedicatory letter. Then came an old deed—signed by Shakespeare and Michael Fraser, dated 1610—which William-Henry said he found in a chest of old papers at the home of a prosperous banker.

A delighted Samuel took the deed to several authorities, all of whom confirmed its authenticity. Father pressed son to redouble his search for documentary treasures. William-Henry came up with the goods. A promissory note from John Hemmings, followed by even bigger bounty: a letter from Shakespeare to the Earl of Southampton, Henry Wriothesley, the dedicatee of two volumes of Shakespeare's poems. In the letter, Shakespeare expressed his gratitude—a 'Budde which Bllossommes Bllooms butte never dyes'—and apologised for not replying sooner. Remarkably, William-Henry's sources also furnished Southampton's reply, in which he admonished his friend for only accepting half of a proffered cash sum. Another recovered document was a firecracker: a fervent disavowal by Shakespeare of Catholicism.

Experts called at Norfolk Street to interrogate the documents and their discoverer. The documents were confirmed as genuine, their discoverer a peculiar genius. Samuel beamed: his life's ambitions had been fulfilled, his meagre paternal investment gloriously rewarded. William-Henry, though, was just getting started. More letters followed, as did Shakespearean contracts, receipts, a pen-and-ink sketch of the playwright and a colour drawing of him as Bassanio.

Then came an incomparable prize: a manuscript catalogue of Shakespeare's library. Extending to over thirty pages, the catalogue is a simple inventory of titles and publication dates. The last date is 1613, indicating that, if Shakespeare made the catalogue, he did so in the latter part of his Stratford retirement. The compiler wrote in an idiosyncratic, almost indecipherable script—a daunting blend of italic and secretary hands—but many titles can be made out. There are classical literary works, like Sir John Harington's 1591 translation of *Orlando Furioso* ('Orlandoo Furiosoo'), as well as contemporary ones, like Edmund Spenser's *Shepherds Calendar* ('Shepheardes Calenderre'), probably the 1579 edition (an impudent hole now obscures the date). There are plentiful Italian editions, several of them evidently by Matteo Bandello, as well as titles in Latin and Greek.

In all, the catalogue features a thousand tantalising volumes. Its discovery reverberated throughout the literary world. Leading bibliophiles were dazzled and compelled. The catalogue is intriguing because it aligns very well with how we know Shakespeare worked. He certainly used *Orlando Furioso* as a principal source for *Much Ado About Nothing*, and Spenser's *Faerie Queene* (1590) for several plays. Indeed, most of his work drew heavily on the writings of others. Even his greatest plays, *Hamlet* and *King Lear*, took major plot elements and characters from prior plays, which were called *Hamlet* and *King Leir*, the latter registered in 1594. *Romeo and Juliet* was based substantively on an Italian novel from

1530. Raphael Holinshed's 1587 *Chronicles of England, Scotland and Ireland* were a principal source for the history plays.

Whole slabs of *Antony and Cleopatra* were lifted from Thomas North's 1579 translation of Plutarch's *Lives*. Plutarch's 'the poop whereof was of gold' becomes in Shakespeare 'the poop was beaten gold'; 'the sails of purple' becomes 'purple the sails'; 'the oars of silver', 'the oars were silver'. This is Shakespeare laundering prose into drama. In his defence, let us note again that there was no equivalent in his day of the modern concept of plagiarism. Borrowing was commonplace; part of a venerable tradition, which dated back at least as far as early mediaeval times, of incrementally improving hallowed texts. (Nevertheless, as we will see later, authors did complain.)

William-Henry, now confirmed as a magician of documentary research, went one better, producing actual books and manuscripts from Shakespeare's library. First came books with Shakespeare's signature and initialled annotations: Johan Carion's *Chronicles* (1550); Thomas Churchyard's *The Worthiness of Wales* (1587); Spenser's *Faerie Queene*; and a copy of James I's *Daemonologie*, containing the curtly dismissive note, 'Impossyble, WS'. Then, even better, Shakespeare manuscripts: a less ribald version of *Lear*, called the *Tragedye of Kynge Leare*; leaves from a less raunchy version of *Hamlet*, called *Hamblette*—yes, *Hamblette*; and a hitherto entirely unknown play, *Vortigern, An Historical Tragedy*.

The Ireland documents caused a sensation. In his final year of life, diarist James Boswell visited the treasure trove at Norfolk Street and announced, 'Well, I shall now die contented, since I have lived to witness the present day.' He kissed the papers and thanked God for revealing them. A few pilgrims were more sceptical, but most were firmly in Boswell's camp. The documents and the attention were a boon for the Irelands, who began to worry that a Shakespeare descendant might come forward to claim the cache that William-Henry had so miraculously assembled. Once again, providence came to the rescue. William-Henry gave forth an astonishing document that showed the Ireland and Shakespeare families were irrevocably intertwined.

In 1604, another William Henry Ireland, a hyphen-less haberdasher from London, had leased the Blackfriars gatehouse that William Shakespeare would later purchase. In 1794, the new William-Henry discovered a 'Deed of Gift' that his ancestor and namesake had received from Shakespeare himself. In heavily Elizabethan prose, the deed told of how the playwright, along with his 'Masterre William Henry Ireland ande otherres', had taken a boat up the Thames. The voyagers were 'much toe merrye throughe Lyquorre', to such an extent that the boat tipped over midstream. All the men could swim, all except Shakespeare. When the swimmers reached the bank, Ireland noticed Shakespeare's absence. Informed that the Bard was 'drownynge', Ireland 'pulled off hys Jerrekynne and jumpedd inn'. Finding Shakespeare 'withe muche paynes', Ireland dragged him nearly dead to the riverbank.

Accompanying the deed was a document bearing the Shakespeare and Ireland coats of arms. In the document, Shakespeare expressed his gratitude to Ireland for 'hys havynge savedde mye life'. On the strength of this discovery, Garter Principal King of Arms Sir Isaac Heard suggested that the Irelands should combine their arms with Shakespeare's. Samuel was elated, and even more so when first an invitation and then an escort arrived at Norfolk Street; he was to enjoy an audience with the Prince of Wales.

Though the meeting progressed awkwardly, the Prince made

approving noises about the papers' authenticity. A proud Samuel arranged for his son's discoveries to be published; they appeared on Christmas Eve, 1795, in a sumptuous folio, richly adorned with facsimiles and colour illustrations. Despite its exhausting title and rich price of four guineas, subscribers snapped up *Miscellaneous Papers and Legal Instruments under the Hand and Seal of William Shakespeare, Including the Tragedy of King Lear, and a Small Fragment of Hamlet, from the Original Manuscripts in the Possession of Samuel Ireland*. Preparations were set in train for a gala performance of *Vortigern*. John Philip Kemble, the greatest actor of the era, signed up (with, it is true, reservations) to play the lead role: the courtier Vortigern. The world premiere at the Theatre Royal, Drury Lane, was initially slotted for April Fool's Day, 1796, but was pushed back a day, 'for fear', in the words of Shakespeare scholar Jonathan Bate, 'of the enterprise seeming Foolish'.

CHAPTER 5

The Master
Investigator

Lawyer, scholar and editorial genius Edmond Malone is remembered as the man who guided and improved drafts of James
Boswell's *Life of Johnson* (1791), helping to make it the greatest
of all English biographies. Born into a Dublin legal family in
1741, Malone attended the Molesworth Street school, where he
fell in love with Shakespeare's works. After completing a BA
at Trinity College he commenced studies at the Inner Temple
and was called to the bar in Dublin. While practising law he also
completed literary projects, including editing an unfinished and
unpublished poem by Alexander Pope.

Short of stature and mild of manner, Malone 'created a favour-
able impression by his urbanity of temper, kindliness, and social

ease'. His father's death left him with an inheritance and a modest income that allowed him to leave Ireland and the law, and to set up in London as a man of letters. There, he befriended Samuel Johnson and James Boswell, as well as Sir Joshua Reynolds and Horace Walpole. The first true historian of early English drama, he became the greatest of all Elizabethan scholars. His literary life's work would be to establish an authentic text and chronology of Shakespeare's works.

After editing a version of Rowe's life of Shakespeare, he embarked on a new, accurate version. In Malone's biographical research, he followed every possible lead, however tenuous, that might find for him Shakespearean relics and documents, and Shakespeare's library.

A self-appointed prosecutor of crimes against Shakespeare, Malone did not share Boswell's enthusiasm for the Ireland documents. When they appeared in their lavish book form, he scrutinised them with a sceptical eye and the formal rules of legal evidence. He studied the facsimiles' handwriting, orthography, vocabulary, phraseology and history. Immediately he noticed problems. The letters contained words not used in Shakespeare's time—words like 'whimsical', 'accede' and 'witty'. The Queen's signature was an obvious fake, the handwriting a dead giveaway. When compared with genuine specimens of Elizabeth's writing, 'no magnifying glasses or other aids are requisite: it is only necessary for any person, however unconversant with ancient manuscripts, to cast his eye on the facsimiles...to be convinced that the pretended Letter of Queen Elizabeth to Shakespeare is a manifest and bungling forgery.' And there were other problems, too.

On 31 March 1796, the results of Malone's investigation appeared under the title *An Inquiry into the Authenticity of Certain*

Miscellaneous Papers and Legal Instruments. Five hundred copies of the four-hundred-page book sold within the first forty-eight hours. Readers devoured every sensational page. Literary London had of course been duped. Many 'experts' were left looking foolish. Speaking of which, the *Inquiry* appeared just before the *Vortigern* premiere—too late to cancel the performance, which degenerated into a farce when, all as one, cast and audience ridiculed the incompetent dialogue and plotting and characterisation. When Kemble reached the line, 'and when this solemn mockery is o'er', he voiced it with comedically poignant emphasis.

Malone's *Inquiry* exposed this and other Ireland documents as crude fakes full of elementary errors and stark anachronisms. He remarked, with restraint, on 'the absurd manner in which almost every word is over-laden with both consonants and vowels'. An excruciating example is the purported letter to 'Anna Hatherrewaye', which reads in part, 'I praye you perfume thys mye poore Locke with thye balmye Kysses forre thenne indeede shalle Kynges themmeselves bowe ande paye homage toe itte'.

To produce the forged letters and deeds, William-Henry had started with genuinely old papers, no doubt first furnished through his work in the conveyancer's office. When he ran out of paper there he turned to other sources; at Verey's bookshop in St Martin's Lane he cut blank flyleaves from old folios and quartos. To make old-looking ink, he employed a cocktail of dyes normally used for paper marbling. To add another antiquarian touch, he tied documents into bundles using string he filched from an old tapestry in the House of Lords.

Constructing the 'Shakespeare library catalogue' was child-ishly simple. William-Henry plucked the books' titles and dates from eighteenth-century sources such as Edward Capell's *Notes and Various Readings of Shakespeare* (1779–83) and David Erskine

Baker's *Biographia Dramatica* (1782). He may also have used seventeenth-century bibliographies like Francis Kirkman's and Gerard Langbaine's. Langbaine was one of the first to comment in print on the extent to which Shakespeare relied on prior sources. For William-Henry's purposes, Langbaine's section on Shakespeare was especially helpful, as it identified the principal sources for each play.

Samuel Ireland maintained that his son was not smart enough to pull off a deception of such ambition and complexity. Malone, though, mocked the ease with which the fraud was perpetrated. To compile the catalogue, all the forger need do was to transcribe 'Mr Capell's List' and then add 'from any old Catalogues whatever might be wanting...By turning over the pages of the late editions of Shakspeare, I make no doubt, the names of a thousand books or tracts of his age, might be collected in a few days: and names alone are wanting to make a catalogue.'

After selecting suitable titles from such published sources, William-Henry then used his unique linguistic formula to transform them into pseudo-Elizabethan gibberish. He also seems to have made up some of the titles; it is hard to tell, as much of the catalogue has since been destroyed and much of the remainder is indecipherable. When selecting genuine titles for the inventory, William-Henry was astute enough to choose only titles that had been printed before Shakespeare's death. He used the same approach when gathering actual books that he claimed had Shakespearean provenance.

Point by point, Malone dismantled William-Henry's library evidence: the catalogue, the books, the inscriptions. To the rhetorical rejoinder, 'But some of the books themselves have been produced,' Malone responded, 'I make no doubt of it':

But are old books so very difficult to be procured? And could not two or three hundred have been picked up on stalls, and elsewhere, in five or six years, during which this scheme may have been in contemplation? Within these few years past the price of Holinshed's *Chronicle* has doubled, in consequence of his having been pointed out as the author whom Shakspeare followed in his Historical Plays, and of our poet's daily-increasing reputation: yet still it is without much difficulty to be procured...The same observation may be made on many other valuable books of that age...But valuable or costly books were not always necessary; worthless books, when duly appropriated by writing our poet's name forty or fifty times in them, would do just as well.

Picking apart the spurious library, Malone showed how the whole enterprise could be accomplished by even the clumsiest of fraudsters.

With respect to smaller tracts, a different process was to be pursued, for they could not be safely exhibited as Shakspeare's, while they remained in miscellaneous volumes. It is well known to the collectors of these rarities, that very often pieces extremely discordant, both in their subjects and dates, are strangely blended together under the same covering. Thus 'The Golden Legend,' printed by Wynken de Worde, or the 'Gorgeous Gallery of Gallant Inventions,' or Greene's 'Art of Connycatching,' or 'A Fig for Momus,' or 'The Nest of Ninnies,' or 'The Art of Swimming' (not by the renowned William Henry Ireland of Blackfriars, but by Christopher Middleton)...may happen to be bound up [with] 'The Unloveliness of love-locks,' or 'Papers Complaint against the paper-spoylers of these times,' which belong to a period subsequent to Shakspeare's death. No such volume therefore could be safely exhibited as his. What then is to be done? The process is extremely simple. The *unknown gentleman* from whose store-house all these rarities have issued, has nothing to do but to cut out such tracts as are dated prior to 1616; and after each of them has been separately cloathed with morocco or vellum, or any other covering that fancy may direct, and the name of William Shakspeare has been written in the upper, lower, and side margin of twenty or thirty pages, it becomes a most valuable relick, miraculously preserved for near two hundred years, and now first displayed to the gazing world…In two months two hundred such volumes might be procured. Let us then hear no more of Shakspeare's Library.

Though the Ireland forgeries included a document showing the Shakespeare family coat of arms, William-Henry seems to have lacked the skill and wherewithal to forge Shakespearean bindings. The Irelands did, however, have their own fake Shakespeare volumes uniformly bound in green goatskin. Thus bound, they remain today as sad curiosities in collections such as the British Library's and the Folger's.

Adding insult to injury, farmer Williams' partridge coop story was almost certainly another hoax, a practical joke made by a Stratford-upon-Avon local at the expense of nosy and naive antiquarians. The Stratford historian Robert Bell Wheler reported that Williams confessed to the prank. A note in the British Library describes the farmer as 'a country wit who amused himself with telling the story in order to ridicule Mr Ireland'. At least he didn't burn Shakespeare's papers.

Let us return to Reverend James Wilmot's failed Warwickshire search. Many scholars have emphasised that failure as a turning point in Shakespeare studies, one that led to the first overt questioning of Shakespearean authorship. Allardyce Nichol (1932), F. E. Halliday (1957), Reginald Churchill (1958), H. N. Gibson (1962), Graham Phillips and Martin Keatman (1988 and 1994), Peter Sammartino (1990), Samuel Schoenbaum (1991 and 2006), Ian Wilson (1993), Jonathan Bate (1997), John Michell (1999 and 2004), Virginia M. Fellows (2006), Bill Bryson (2007) and William Rubinstein (2008)—these and other authors took the Wilmot–Cowell papers seriously, seeing them as crucial for the birth of scepticism in general and the Baconian heresy in particular.

That the first doubts about Shakespeare's authorship were raised when people could not find his library is an appealing idea. But the appeal, unfortunately, is illusory. The whole Wilmot story—the exhaustive search, the revelatory Cowell papers, the shocked Philosophic Society—is a bigger hoax than farmer Williams' paper bonfire or William-Henry's catalogue.

To their great and lasting credit, a group of leading orthodox and unorthodox Shakespeare scholars revealed the Wilmot–Cowell papers as forgeries. The first revelation was made in 2003 by a physicist and amateur Shakespeare scholar, Dr John Rollett, who lived at Ipswich, about 150 miles east of Stratford. After 'many hours spent in the Suffolk Record Office', Rollett found no evidence of an Ipswich Philosophic Society, and no references to the supposed lecturer or president. When he examined the Wilmot–Cowell papers at London University, he thought the paper stock and the handwriting seemed much more recent than 1805.

Rollett shared his misgivings with two leading academics: Dr Daniel Wright, Director of the Shakespeare Authorship Research Centre at Concordia University; and, Professor Alan

Nelson, a documents expert from U. C. Berkeley. Looking closely at the papers, Wright noticed that several of the Wilmot–Cowell arguments in favour of Baconian authorship had not been put forward until well after 1805. Nelson, too, thought the manuscript was a forgery; this was later confirmed by a palaeographer. The papers were 'a Baconian spoof'.

Announcing the findings in his 2010 book *Contested Will*, James Shapiro added further evidence that the language was anachronistic, probably dating from the twentieth century. All these scholars did well to spot the fake, but in hindsight the papers were obviously bogus, just too good to be true—something they had in common with the Ireland forgeries. Let us all be wary of future 'discoveries'.

The field of Shakespeare studies is still coming to terms with the implications of the Wilmot–Cowell forgery. For our present purposes, one point is key: the most thorough of the first searches *never happened*. Well into the eighteenth and nineteenth centuries, in one or more of those private libraries already mentioned, Shakespeare's books could have been sitting there all along, waiting to be found.

The Ireland episode shows how easy it is to fake association copies. Though recklessly executed, the forgeries convinced many people. William-Henry's creative efforts sparked off an appalling tradition of copycats. In nearly every decade since, a new 'discovery' has been announced: Shakespeare's copy of Florio's *Montaigne* (1580), Halle's *Chronicles* (1548), Bacon's *Essays* (1597), Lambarde's *Archaionomia* (1568). Shakespeare's prayer book. Shakespeare's journal. Shakespeare's dictionary. Shakespeare's almanac. Shakespeare's Greater London phone book.

Halle's *Chronicles* were a source for the history plays. In 1940,

Alan Keen, an antiquarian bookseller, purchased a copy that contained what appeared to be early marginal annotations. Keen, along with Roger Lubbock, later argued that the annotations were in Shakespeare's hand, and that the book was Shakespeare's own copy, the very one he used when writing his plays. Keen and Lubbock presented a weight of evidence, including a chain of provenance back to the aristocratic Worsley family, with whom Shakespeare may have spent time in Lancashire in his youth. The case, which Samuel Schoenbaum called 'unilluminating' and 'suppositious', has yet to be proven.

Thomas North's translation of Plutarch's *Lives* has already been cited as a Shakespeare source. The Shakespeare Birthplace Trust has a copy of that work, published in 1579 and printed by Thomas Vautrollier and possibly his Stratford-born apprentice, Richard Field. The Trust's *Lives* has interesting provenance; it was owned for a time by the Fifth Earl of Derby, Lord Strange, whose company performed early Shakespeare plays. An annotation by the Earl's widow, Alice, can only be read under ultra-violet light. Tantalisingly but inconclusively, the annotation inscribes the book to 'William'.

Apart from obvious Ireland forgeries, the British Library holds a 1603 copy of Florio's translation of Montaigne's *Essays*. The copy is signed on the flyleaf, 'William Shakespeare'. In the eighteenth century the book belonged to a clergyman who lived near Stratford-upon-Avon and 'who is known to have shown the volume to his friends before the year 1780'. The Library bought the book in 1837 or 1838. Though initially regarded as genuine, the signature was subjected to rigorous analysis by principal librarian and first director of the British Museum Edward Maunde Thompson, who denounced it as a forgery produced in 'a more practiced hand and one more expert than is usually to be found in such Shakespearean curiosities'. Thompson reached the same conclusion about a similar signature on a volume of Ovid in the Bodleian.

In 1573 the lexicographer John Baret published *An Alvearie, or Triple Dictionarie in English, Latin, and French*. A second edition appeared in 1580. Shakespeare almost certainly used one of these editions as a source of words and sayings—and inspiration. For Gertrude's line in *Hamlet*, 'Your bedded haire, like life in excrements, / Start up, and stand an end', Shakespeare may have noticed the *Alvearie* entry for 'stare', 'His haire Stareth or standeth on end'. In writing the words, 'Oh that this too too solid Flesh, would melt, / Thaw, and resolve it selfe into a Dew', he seems to have been inspired by the definition of 'thawe': 'resolve that which is frozen'. 'Forsworne' ('perjured, false, that hath broken his oth') echoes Sonnet 152:

> In loving thee thou know'st I am forsworne,
> But thou art twice forsworne, to me love swearing;
> In act thy bed-vow broake, and new faith torne,
> In vowing new hate after new love bearing.

In 2008, the search for Shakespeare's library collided with the internet era. New York booksellers George Koppelman and Daniel Wechsler purchased a 1580 *Alvearie* on eBay, where it had been listed as 'an early Elizabethan dictionary with contemporary annotations'. The book features many marginal notes and symbols, and much underlining. Appearing on a terminal blank page is what Koppelman and Wechsler call a 'word salad', a rich selection of French words and their corresponding English ones. After matching many of the notes and highlighted words to lines from Shakespeare, the two booksellers co-authored a monograph in which they argued the eBay *Alvearie* was Shakespeare's own copy.

The Shakespearean connections are indeed fascinating. One example: next to the *Alvearie* entry for 'scabbard' ('vide sheath') someone has written 'vagina'. This brings to mind for Koppelman and Wechsler Juliet's suggestive, 'Yea noise? then ile be briefe. O happy dagger, / This is thy sheath, there rust and let me dye'. Like several of the most promising association copies, the *Alvearie* was printed by Richard Field. The book includes phrases that Shakespeare used, some of which are underlined or circled or asterisked. Koppelman and Weschler have been admirably transparent about the book's content and their method. Nevertheless, they are probably wrong. The handwriting doesn't match, the chain of provenance is broken, the attribution argument too improbable, too circumstantial.

(Another recent 'discovery' is far less credible. In what the editor of *Country Life* called 'the literary discovery of the century', botanist Mark Griffiths claimed to have found, in a 1598 edition of John Gerard's *The Herball or Generall Historie of Plantes*, the only portrait of Shakespeare that was executed in his lifetime. The argument rests on an arcane code of rebuses, ciphers, heraldry and floristry—an argument so patently ridiculous that the whole thing must be a publicity stunt.)

When the alleged association copies are examined as a group, it is easy to see that the handwriting and inscriptions are worryingly variable. More than one person has been at work, more than one person with mischievous intent. Some annotations are very brief, others wax lyrical with suspiciously helpful additions like addresses and occupational information. Most of the discoveries are obvious try-ons, and not a single one has been authenticated. To do so is difficult. Malone's critique continues to apply: it is easy to obtain an old book and add old-looking writing that is difficult to expose, whether chemically or orthographically. In an annotated sixteenth- or seventeenth-century book, it is hard to tell which of the annotations are contemporary and which are eighteenth-, nineteenth- or even twentieth-century additions. William-Henry Ireland was not the only forger to use genuinely early documents along with specialised inks that confound detection. Some documents feature a thwarting combination of old and new ink.

Even genuinely old annotations must be treated with care. Suppose the writing in a marked-up book is shown, through chemical or spectral analysis, to date from Shakespeare's day. Suppose also that the words appear to align with the contents of Shakespeare's plays. It does not necessarily follow that the Bard made the marks or owned the book. The inscriptions could have been added by a fan, an editor, a collaborator, a relative, a bookseller, a critic. Or the similarity could simply be coincidental.

A 1570 Bible in the Folger Shakespeare Library contains more than a thousand underlinings and notes, possibly in the hand of Edward de Vere, Earl of Oxford. Many of the marked passages can be linked to Shakespeare's plays. These linkages have been cited as evidence that de Vere authored those plays. What are we to make of this? The annotations, even if they were added at an early date, do not prove the Folger Bible was a Shakespearean source, or that the annotator was a Shakespearean author. The notes could have been made *after* a reading of the plays, by de Vere or someone else, perhaps intrigued by the Shakespearean echoes. They could be evidence of a predecessor text, perhaps used by Shakespeare. Or, as always, the echoes could be the result of chance. Without strong provenance and corroboration, it is difficult to prove that any particular 'ancient' book belonged to any particular person, or that any one book was used in the writing of another.

Trying to match the language of an inscription with the language that Shakespeare used is problematic for other reasons as well. Select any two Elizabethan authors and you will see commonalities in their vocabulary, grammar and turns of phrase. Looked at in isolation, the harmonies intensify, readily suggesting an important connection between the two authors, even one as close as tautology. But such a connection is nearly always an illusion, a symptom of blinkering. Educated Elizabethans used the same language, employed overlapping vocabularies, read the same or similar books, knew the same or similar people, frequented the same places and were interested in similar matters. Focusing on resemblances tends to magnify them. Looked at in isolation, any literate Elizabethan can be made to fit Shakespeare's jerkin.

Let us take stock. Two of the earliest searches for Shakespeare's library were, to say the least, unsatisfactory. The first, Wilmot's, did not take place at all. The second, equally colourful, was at least partly a fabrication, and was relayed to us by forgers and fantasists. In the search for Shakespeare's library, we are back to square one.

CHAPTER 6

The Bibliomaniac

Born in Calcutta in 1776 and orphaned on a voyage to England, Thomas Frognall Dibdin came into the care of his wider family. His first tutor, John Man, lived in a divey part of Reading called Hosier's Lane. In Man's private bookroom, young Tom caught 'the electric spark of bibliomania'. Man purchased books 'by the sack-full'. When he brought them home he tumbled them out on the floor; his pupil, standing by, pulled from the pile illustrated editions of Horace, Ovid, Aesop and other authors who piqued his boyish interest.

At the age of twelve, Dibdin moved to Stockwell, where he learned French and drawing, and acquired, without paying for it, his first book: an odd volume of Shakespeare, containing *Macbeth*,

A Midsummer Night's Dream and *The Merry Wives of Windsor*. As a recently printed volume in a broken set, the book had no commercial value. But Dibdin was excited 'almost to delirium' by the find, and decided to try his hand at drama. Shunning spy-high, soldiers, scrumping and other 'ordinary games of youth', he rose early to pursue 'drawing and dramatic composition; and, ere my fourteenth year, was the author of three exceedingly bloody tragedies'. This mania, though, was cured by a 'simple but severe incident':

> I had brought these plays (of which I now recollect only the names of two—viz. *Jasmin* and *The Distressed Brothers*) home to my aunt, Mrs William Compton; a lively and sensible woman, and much disposed to humour my vagaries in many ways. I begged she would read them, and challenged her approbation. She *did* read them, or as much as she *liked* of them; but studiously pronounced no opinion. One evening, on retiring to rest, and receiving the bedchamber candlestick from the servant, I found a piece of paper at the bottom of the candle, to keep it steady in the stick, upon which my hand-writing was but too visible. I stopped—and read 'Act III, scene V', and found it to be a fragment of my beloved *Jasmin*! Retracing my steps with a precipitancy which may well be conceived, I enquired of the servant '*where* she had got this?' 'Sir,' said she, 'my mistress gave it me as WASTE PAPER TO LIGHT THE FIRE.'

Bookstalls and bookshops held irresistible charms. One of Dibdin's first purchases, and a milestone in his nascent bookmanship, came from the window of Mr Collins' shop in Walbrook: Theobald's edition of Shakespeare's *Works*, along with three other books. 'I disdained to let the shopman carry them home for me, but took them triumphantly under my arm'.

At Oxford, Dibdin founded a literary debating club called The Lunatics. A mysterious incident with a girl led to a hasty marriage and an even hastier exit from the university. He left without taking his degree, but set up anyway as a practitioner of the law. This he practised, without success, before taking Holy Orders and devoting his life to the church, and to literature.

The Bishop of Winchester appointed him a deacon; three months later, after a three-minute exam, he became a priest. Dibdin's ecclesiastical duties made only small demands on his time and ardour, leaving plenty of room for his true calling, books. He found himself enraptured by their contents, but also, perhaps even more so, by their outward properties: their bindings, formats, illustrations, typography, title pages. In 1802 Dibdin published his first bibliographical work, *An Introduction to the Knowledge of Rare and Valuable Editions of the Greek and Latin Classics*. Several of the classics were source texts for Shakespeare's plays. The slight volume sold rapidly and gave Dibdin what little encouragement he needed to become the biggest bibliomaniac in history.

In 1809 Dibdin published *Bibliomania or Book-Madness*. Dedicated to the great collector Richard Heber, the book helped fuel a fashionable hunger for rare and precious volumes. A second edition, much revised and expanded, followed two years later. In *Shakespeare and His Times* (1817), Nathan Drake called Dibdin's book 'the most fascinating which has ever been written on Bibliography...It is composed in the highest tone of enthusiasm for the art, and its dialogue and descriptions are given with a mellowness, a warmth and a raciness, which absolutely fix and enchant the reader'. Netting its author two hundred pounds, the second *Bibliomania* emboldened Dibdin to attempt a much more significant enterprise: a deluxe, career-defining, seven-volume catalogue of the remarkable Renaissance library of Dibdin's new friend and patron, George John, Second Earl Spencer of Spencer House, St James's Place and Althorp in Northamptonshire.

In the opinion of their author, these and subsequent works 'set wealthy and well educated men a-stirring to collect materials, which, but for such occasional excitement, might, in the end, moulder in oblivion'. In a forty-year literary career, Dibdin applied and popularised terms and a perspective that booklovers now take for granted. According to this perspective, first editions ('editiones princepes') are best and rarity is a virtue. Vellum beats morocco, which in turn beats ordinary calf. (The critic and poet Leigh Hunt described Dibdin 'leaping up to kiss and embrace every enticing edition in vellum and every sweetly toned, mellow-toned, yellow morocco binding'.) Copies printed with wide margins ('large paper copies') are to be preferred. Fatter margins are more amenable, more luxurious; some bibliophile editions have margins so generous that only 'a rivulet of text trickles down the middle of the page'. Adhering to the fashions Dibdin helped create, prospectuses and colophons announced breathlessly that 'only a hundred copies', or, better still, 'only fifty copies' had been taken off the press. Special copies ('specials') were another dimension of the vogue; the most desirable of these were printed on coloured or otherwise exotic paper: 'yellow paper, blue paper, writing paper, on *papier de Hollande, de Chine*, or *d'Inde*'.

Worshipping primacy of publication was something new. In the seventeenth century, collectors replaced old editions with new ones, and regarded this as an improvement. On 6 November 1683, Sir William Boothby wrote to the bookseller Michael Johnson: 'I have sent you my old Josephus, and desire you to send me one of the last and best edition.' He wrote similarly about Livy's

Theatrum Historicum, John Cowell's *The Interpreter* (1607) and Robert Burton's *The Anatomy of Melancholy* (1621). The Bodleian library had a copy of the 1623 First Folio of Shakespeare's plays— until the library disposed of it when the 1663 'enhanced' third edition became available.

In the production of his editions, Dibdin collaborated with William Bulmer, the finest English printer of the era, and Charles Lewis, London's foremost bookbinder. Lewis was so successful that he earned opprobrium for dressing above his tradesman station by 'wearing tassels to his half boots'. When Dibdin produced an enlarged edition of Joseph Ames and William Herbert's *Typographical Antiquities* (1810–19) the subscribers included all the leading bookmen of the day—Richard Heber, Francis Douce, Edmond Malone, Earl Spencer, Mark Masterman-Sykes—as well as King George III. The orphan from Calcutta had come a long way.

According to the bookman Colin Franklin, 'books are tedious things—unless you own them'. Becoming the owner of an especially rare and desirable book can have a magical effect. The most famous example of a life transformed by a single book purchase is the tale of John Ker, Third Duke of Roxburghe.

Under George III, Ker had shouldered weighty responsibilities: Lord of the Bedchamber, Knight of the Thistle, Groom of the Stole and Knight of the Garter. In Italy on the Grand Tour he came across a 1471 Christopher Valdarfer edition of Giovanni Boccaccio's *Decameron*. Shakespeare used the *Decameron* as the principal source for *All's Well that Ends Well*. The Valdarfer edition, the first known printing, was so rare that many authorities denied it could be found at all. Ker bought it for a hundred guineas. Back in London it was celebrated as a magnificent prize, and Ker was a changed man. He had caught the most virulent strain of the bibliomania virus.

Like Earl Spencer, Ker became one of the few noblemen of the time who preferred books over bloodstock and gambling. For the next four decades, he hunted rare volumes, and especially the rarest editions of Shakespeare's works, or books relating to Shakespeare, or to his sources or his peers. Ker acquired all four seventeenth-century folio editions of Shakespeare's plays. He also bought a large number of Shakespeare quartos, and much else besides. If Shakespeare ever owned a quantity of books, the chances are that some of them made it into Ker's collection.

The Roxburghe Library became the greatest of the age, and exemplified the mounting interest in Shakespeare and his world. According to the Pall Mall bookseller Robert Harding Evans, Ker 'idolized the talents of Shakespeare and Cervantes, and collected everything that could illustrate their works'. (Members of one branch of Shakespearean heresy claim that Francis Bacon wrote not only the works of Shakespeare but *Don Quixote* as well, of which Cervantes' version is a Spanish translation.) At its core, the library was a Shakespeare library, and the most illustrious book sale ever held was a Shakespeare library sale. After Ker's death, Evans sold the Roxburghe Library at auction. George Nicol prepared the catalogue and William Bulmer printed it. The 1812 sale became a defining moment in Shakespeare bibliography and indeed bibliography of every kind. Ten thousand items were dispersed, in sessions that extended over forty-six days. Napoleon Bonaparte was rumoured to have bid through a go-between while at the same time invading Russia. The auction raised £23,341 for Ker's estate—an enormous sum in 1812.

Three bibliophiles in particular—the Duke of Devonshire, Earl Spencer and his cousin the Marquess of Blandford—drove the Roxburghe Sale prices into the stratosphere. Ker's fifteen Caxtons (volumes printed by England's first printer) brought record prices: the Duke of Devonshire paid £1060 for the *Recuyell of the Histories of Troy* (1464). Before the Roxburghe Sale, no one had ever paid more than a thousand pounds for a book.

George Spencer-Churchill, Marquess of Blandford and later the Fifth Duke of Marlborough, was a notorious spendthrift. He splurged so much on books and manuscripts that he would soon be bankrupt. The Roxburghe Sale, though, coincided with the high point of his resources and his acquisitiveness. He bought the Valdarfer *Decameron* for £2260, a record price for a single book, and one that stood for many decades afterwards. When the crunch came for the Marquess, creditors seized his estates and sold his books. He was reduced to renting out Blenheim Palace's fishing and hunting grounds at an hourly rate.

At the Roxburghe Sale, Earl Spencer had bid against the Marquess and helped run up the *Decameron* to the record value; Dibdin likened the contest to a mediaeval joust. At the distressed sale of the Marquess's library, the fight became a fizzle: Earl Spencer bought the *Decameron* for £918 15s, less than half the bubbly Roxburghe price. Many other titles also failed to realise their Roxburghe price for many years after the sale. John Morgan Rice, for example, bought a rare volume at the sale, Richard Edwards' *The Paradyse of Daintie Devises* (1580), for fifty-five pounds and thirteen shillings. The very same copy was sold, at the dispersal of Rice's library in 1834, for twelve pounds.

On the day the *Decameron* was sold, Dibdin dined with jubilant bibliophiles at St Alban's Tavern. There and then, the diners resolved to found a club that would become the world's most prestigious and exclusive book fraternity. Earl Spencer was the inaugural president, Dibdin vice-president. The members adopted rules that would preserve the club's exclusivity: one black ball would be enough to disqualify a candidate from membership. Despite these efforts, the Roxburghe Club's members were soon ridiculed by publications such as the *Museum* and the *Edinburgh Literary Courant* as being 'very considerable' in wealth but 'so-so' in intellect.

Undeterred, the Roxburghers established a schedule of regular meetings to drink, gourmandise and talk about books. They began publishing Members' Books for presentation to each other; the books sought to revive the rarest sixteenth- and seventeenth-century pamphlets and other small works.

In preparing his Member Book, Earl Spencer had many sources to choose from. His library at Althorp, Northamptonshire, contained tens of thousands of volumes; some estimates put the number above a hundred thousand. The library occupied five large rooms. The height of bookish discernment, it was rich in desirable books, many of them handsomely bound in leather featuring Spencer's coat of arms. The library was off limits to most visitors, but Spencer gave Dibdin free access to what was probably the best private library in the western world.

In Shakespeare's day, drama was regarded as low literature, far inferior to poetry. Indeed, drama rated so poorly that many library cataloguers did not even bother to identify individual plays. Sir Edward Dering assembled a substantial library that included over 225 plays, but he seldom recorded their titles, listing them instead merely as gatherings of 'playbooks'. Author Robert Burton did the same. He bequeathed his substantial library, which included many plays as well as poetry and novels, to two Oxford institutions: the Bodleian and Christ Church. (Burton's copies of *Venus and Adonis* (1593) and *The Rape of Lucrece* (1594) are still in the Bodleian.) Burton's play quartos were the first to be admitted into the Bodleian Library. The 'founder' of the library (actually the reviver), Sir Thomas Bodley, famously disliked the idea of including plays in the library. He made his views very clear:

> I can see no good reason to alter my opinion, for excluding suche bookes, as almanackes, plaies, and an infinit number, that are daily printed, of very un-worthy matters…Happely some plaies may be worthy the keeping : But hardly one in fortie. For it is not alike in Englishe plaies, and others of other nations : because they are most esteemed, for learning the languages and many of them compiled, by men of great fame, for wisedom and Learning : which is seldom or never scene among us. Were it so againe, that some litle profit might be reaped (which God knowes is very litle) out of some of our play-bookes, the benefit thereof will nothing neere counter-vaile, the harme that the Scandal will bring unto the Librarie, when it shall be given out, that we stuff it full of baggage bookes…This is my opinion…and the more I thinke upon it, the more it doth distast me, that suche kinde of bookes, should be vouchsafed a rowme, in so noble a Librarie.

Like Bodley, many scholars and readers ranked the best English publications well below the best classical and Continental works. Dibdin would later strive to elevate the status of drama and English books, but his Spencer catalogue reflected the old prejudices. He placed Shakespeare's works well down, as 'miscellaneous English books'; after 'Miscellaneous Latin books'; after editions of Ariosto; and after more than a hundred pages of Greek and Latin classics and editions of the Bible.

In the catalogue of his library, Earl Spencer wished to show off more than just his books. Dibdin's *Bibliotheca Spencereana* is notorious in book-collecting circles for its 'posh totty': racy engraved portraits of the handsomest Spencer women. The Duchess of Portsmouth, Lady Denham and Mrs Middleton, appearing in the roles of Juliet, Ophelia and Desdemona. Breasty etchings, though, are not the only highlight of Spencer's library. He also had a First Folio Shakespeare.

Published in 1623, *Mr William Shakespeares Comedies, Histories, & Tragedies* contained thirty-six plays, eighteen of them appearing in print for the first time. Dibdin regarded the book as a prize, though far from the apex of Spencer's collection; the Aldines and Ariostos were more alluring. Nor was the Spencer copy of Shakespeare's works in perfect condition. But Dibdin's 1822 catalogue entry ignored the flaws, gushing instead about the book's completeness and the Henry Walther binding, which Dibdin called Walther's *chef d'œuvre*.

Shakespeare's Works. 1623. Folio

First folio edition. The knowing need not be informed of the price and importance of this impression: yet a tougher question is rarely agitated among bibliographers than 'as to what constitutes a fine and genuine copy of it?' After having seen the copy lately obtained by Mr Grenville, and that, yet more recently, by Mr James Boswell, and carefully examined the present—I am abundantly convinced that this is, after all, but a disagreeable book—as to typographical execution. Every leaf of the present copy was carefully examined by the late George Steevens, for his Lordship...The leaves are, throughout, exceedingly clean...The binding of this copy, by Walther, is worthy of its intrinsic worth. It is in blue morocco, lined on the sides in the Grolier style, and the back is thickly studded with gold in the manner of Roger Payne.

Only two years later, in *The Library-Companion* (1824), Dibdin painted a rather different picture of the 'exceedingly clean' leaves.

The verses opposite are genuine, but inlaid, and there are many tender leaves throughout. There are also, in the centre of some of the pages, a few greasy-looking spots, which might have originally received the 'flakes of pie-crust' in the servant's hall.

Spencer and Dibdin put the greatest store in pristine copies. It seems unbelievable to modern booklovers, but Spencer often had his books *washed*, to remove antique soiling and inscriptions. (How many Shakespearean inscriptions did he wash away?) He also routinely sent his acquisitions to be rebound in gold-tooled goatskin. This had a similar effect of obliterating information left by former owners.

The 'flakes of pie-crust' quotation in the Spencer catalogue is from George Steevens' *The Plays of William Shakespeare* (1803). The former owner of the Spencer First Folio, Steevens was one of the leading eighteenth-century Shakespeare editors. Having seen many folios suffer with the passing of time, Steevens laid claim to 'the merit of being the first commentator on Shakespeare who strove, with becoming seriousness, to account for the frequent stains that disgrace the earliest folio edition of his plays, which is now become the most expensive single book in our language'.

Though Shakespeare was not, like Fox the Martyrologist, deposited in churches, to be thumbed by the congregation, he generally took post on our hall tables; and that a multitude of his pages have 'their effect of gravy,' may be imputed to the various eatables set out every morning on the same boards. It would seem that most of his readers were so chary of their time, that (like Pistol, who gnaws his leek and swears all the while) they fed and studied at the same instant. I have repeatedly met with thin flakes of pie-crust between the leaves of our author. These unctuous fragments, remaining long in close confinement, communicated their grease to several pages deep on each side of them. It is easy enough to conceive how such accidents might happen...still it is no small elogium on Shakespeare, that his claims were more forcible than those of hunger.

Throughout his adult life, Steevens made a daily round of London's bookshops. At his home on Hampstead Heath he assembled an excellent Elizabethan library that included many quarto editions of Shakespeare's plays. Steevens studied Shakespeare's sources and undertook other Shakespearean research. In 1766 he reprinted twenty of the quartos. Impressed, Samuel Johnson encouraged him to prepare a complete edition of Shakespeare's plays. The resulting ten-volume *Works of Shakespeare with the Corrections and Illustrations of Various Commentators* appeared in 1773.

A decade and a half later, Steevens had become an incorrigible eccentric, irascibly engaged in pointless battles on all fronts. Anonymously he promoted Boswell's claims as Johnson's biographer, mainly to annoy Sir John Hawkins, the official candidate. He perpetrated public hoaxes, such as a spurious account of the fictitious 'Java upas tree'; and the tombstone of the mediaeval king 'Hardyknute', supposedly excavated in Kennington but actually engraved with Steevens' own Anglo-Saxon-style composition, on a chimney slab. Steevens published, in the *Theatrical Review*, a fake Shakespearean letter. Purportedly written in 1600 by George Peele to Christopher Marlowe, it concerned Shakespeare's annoyance at being accused of stealing Edward Alleyn's words to compose the speech in *Hamlet* on 'excellencie of acting'. As his madness coalesced, Steevens denounced Shakespeare's poems and was accused of pilfering and forging documents. In the latter years of his life, Steevens was more than a little crazy.

This was the same George Steevens who learned, in the 1780s, that Edmond Malone was working on a definitive edition of Shakespeare's writings (the edition appeared in 1790). Gripped by the kind of competitive jealousy normally seen only in ice-skating, Steevens issued, in 1793, fifteen volumes that he hoped would be received as a virtuoso edition of Shakespeare's works—a display of his wide knowledge of Elizabethan literature; confirmation of his editorial mastery; and a demonstration of his superiority over Malone. Steevens was a dogged researcher and competent editor. His unhinged eccentricity, though, made him unreliable. One of his quirks was to pepper footnotes with obscene and spurious interpretations, then foist them on enemies. History remembers Malone's as the better edition.

Today, the 1623 edition of Shakespeare's plays is the world's most famous book of literature. It is universally referred to as the 'First Folio', but things were not always so. If a time-traveller met Shakespeare on his deathbed and referred to the 'First Folio', the Bard would be baffled. When the book eventually appeared, Shakespeare had been dead for seven years. He had no direct involvement in its production and was probably not even involved in conceiving the idea of a collected edition of his plays. If the same time-traveller went to 1623 and met an early purchaser of Shakespeare's works, and again mentioned the 'First Folio', she would receive the same look of bafflement. That term does not appear in the book at all. The great Shakespeare editors of the eighteenth century, such as Johnson, Malone and Steevens, were the first to use the term, but they used it not as we do today (not, that is, as a proper noun) but as a neutral, factual description, distinguishing the 1623 folio from the other three that followed it in the seventeenth century. Dibdin's Spencer catalogue is a turning point, after which the term 'First Folio' starts to be used in the sense we use it today—as a sexy label bursting with bibliographical glamour.

Though both Dibdin and Steevens emphasised the book's price, copies were changing hands at modest values in comparison to the Roxburghe First Folio price, and very much below the benchmark set by Ker's *Decameron*, which sold for more than twenty times the price of his First Folio.

In a footnote to the First Folio entry, Dibdin expressed his sadness at the passing, in the weeks in which he was finalising *Aedes Althorpianæ*, of James Boswell the younger. Only six months before, Boswell had finished editing Malone's twenty-one-volume edition of Shakespeare's works. (Like a force of nature, the length of Shakespeare editions—and the number of volumes—increased steadily from the seventeenth century into the nineteenth.) According to Dibdin, Boswell had paid £120 for John Philip Kemble's copy of the First Folio—an inferior copy partially made up of leaves from later editions.

In keeping with the attitudes set in the seventeenth century, Spencer's Shakespeare quartos were unworthy of individual descriptions in *Bibliotheca Spencereana*; they were catalogued as an undifferentiated group.

Despite the low ranking of the First Folio in Spencer's catalogue, and despite Dibdin's description of its typography as 'disagreeable', he would help make it the most collectable book of all time. In furtherance of that cause, he conducted in 1824 a census of First Folio owners. The census, focusing on the London area, would be the first of many. Over the years, the censuses would grow in scope and cachet. The world's wealthiest men and women would compete to be included among the list of First Folio owners. (The latest census runs to 960 somewhat inaccurate pages.)

At the peak of his career, Dibdin was the most famous and influential bibliophile of his day. He taught a generation of bookmen what to appreciate and how to appreciate it. The latter years of his life, though, were unhappy. Dibdin's expertise as a bibliographer did not match his enthusiasm. Many of Spencer's books were written in languages and printed in characters that Dibdin could not read. He catalogued them anyway; errors were inevitable and plentiful.

Dibdin was forever proposing new books, but he managed money and work poorly. Many proposed projects failed to launch. Padded with rambling anecdotes, in-jokes, cringeworthy obsequiousness and over-long footnotes (taking up successive pages, even earning their own extensive infra-footnotes) his ebullient books fell out of fashion. Henry Crabb Robinson sketched a portrait in 1826. Dibdin was a 'vain man', 'very pleasant', 'exceedingly gay', and 'too boyish in his laughter (especially for a Doctor of Divinity)'. Worst of all, he was a 'Jerry Diddler' who 'published very costly books by subscription and borrowed everywhere'.

Critics tore apart Dibdin's *The Library-Companion* variously for its sloppy inclusions and incompetent exclusions. He searched libraries throughout the British Isles and on the Continent, leaving a trail of errors. A book of a bibliographical tour of Scotland and northern England fell flat. In the same way that farmer Williams had had fun with the Irelands, a Scotsman tricked Dibdin into thinking the 'Codex Club' was a Roxburghe-style

Scottish bibliophile society. A critic by the name of Turnbull found so many errors in the *Northern Tour* that he invited people to whip Dibdin's bottom.

An apparently random episode of arsenic poisoning brought Dibdin close to death. His daughter complained of the burden of caring simultaneously for her father and her mother.

> I assure you it is only with the utmost difficulties I can go on. The Chemist and our medical man must be paid to say nothing of washing and wine which are indispensable with the nature of his complaint. I should almost feel happy when it pleases the Almighty to remove him out of his trials and difficulties.

The Roxburghe Club refused to ease her burden or to support her or her mother after Dibdin's death. One Roxburgher—Earl Spencer—had insured the bibliographer's life for a thousand pounds, but does not seem to have paid any of the proceeds to Dibdin's widow.

Shakespeare may have owned many books. He may even have commissioned armorial bindings, but he could never have been a full-blown, Dibdin-esque bibliophile. Shakespeare could not have cared less about whether his books were first printings or not. The very concept of a bibliophile was defined almost two centuries after his death. Veneration of primacy, the cult of scarcity, making love to vellum bindings; much that entertains collectors and bibliographers today would have mystified Shakespeare. By the turn of the nineteenth into the twentieth century, firstness would be, for the field of book collecting, both a pillar and a drug. Dibdin was 'patient zero' for several book pathologies, including 'point mania'—searching for and arguing about small and usually spurious indicators of primacy of issue—and the twentieth-century rage for 'modern firsts'.

Like Pope and Theobald and Steevens, Dibdin was an unreliable scholar. Like Wilmot and Rowe and the Irelands, he was an unreliable searcher. He did, however, make interesting discoveries. *Bibliotheca Spencereana* includes an exceptionally rare copy of Shakespeare's 1609 *Sonnets* (only thirteen copies are known today). The Spencer copy was inscribed with 'Commendations to my very kind Ffriend 23: M'. Why 23? Who was M? Was he or she the author or the subject of the inscription? Dibdin's Spencer catalogue is also useful as a record of Shakespearean sources. It notes, for example, pre-Shakespeare editions of *Romeo and Juliet*.

Bibliotheca Spencereana should also be remembered as the place where the First Folio received its modern title. But the man who christened the First Folio was not the man to find Shakespeare or his library. It is not difficult to catalogue his faults. Dibdin was starstruck by England's aristocrats, intoxicated by the rarefied air of their libraries. Frivolous, giddy, inconsistent, he was too much of an enthusiast, too taken by surfaces, too much the Jerry Diddler. Dibdin represents another wrong turn in the search for Shakespeare and his library. It is not quite a tragedy that history remembers him as the 'world's worst bibliographer'.

Looked at in those terms, the fact that Dibdin found nothing is neither a surprise nor a disappointment. He might have missed something. During his lifetime, other searchers would take a closer look.

CHAPTER 7

The League of
Radical Gentlemen

Yorkshireman, clergyman and minor poet, Francis Wrangham
nurtured the search for Shakespeare's library during the reign
of King George III. As a student first at Magdalene College and
then at Trinity Hall and Trinity College, Cambridge, Wrangham
had excelled at university. He was Third Wrangler in the
Mathematical Tripos, and in 1787 won a medal for the best Greek
and Latin epigrams; later that year his winning entry was printed
handsomely as a single octavo sheet. He developed republican
views (the new breed of rulers could never live up to his idealised
picture of the Virgin Queen) and was thereafter denied prefer-
ment at Cambridge. Injurious gossip branded him 'a friend to the
French revolution, one who exulted in the murder of the king'.

Despite these setbacks, he embarked on a fruitful literary and ecclesiastical life, amassing a wide circle of friends, who described him as an 'attractive personality', an 'affectionate father', a 'tall slight man of exceedingly gentle and attractive manners', possessing a countenance 'of classical elegance'. Wrangham was on friendly terms with Lord Spencer, Thomas Frognall Dibdin and other Roxburghers. He also knew celebrities such as Sir Walter Scott, Leigh Hunt and William Wordsworth, with whom he collaborated on minor literary and republican projects. From Wrangham House at Hunmanby, North Yorkshire, he maintained an effusive correspondence with a wide circle of these and other bookmen, among them Thomas Arnold, James Montgomery, William Hone, Dawson Turner and John Gibson Lockhart, author of a *Life* of Scott.

In 1808 Leigh Hunt and his brother John founded the radical and much-prosecuted newspaper the *Examiner*, which Wrangham—an opponent of slavery and supporter of Israel—distributed enthusiastically. The paper's most sensational trial resulted from Hunt's disenchantment with the Prince Regent. Hunt called him a 'corpulent libertine and violator of his word'—a blatant libel—and in February 1813 he began two years of imprisonment in Horsemonger Lane Gaol: what Ann Blainey called 'a triumphant two years of martyrdom'.

In December 1808, Wrangham penned a prescient letter to Hunt, with whom he shared a love of Elizabethan literature. (When challenged to choose a 'library of one', Hunt 'was torn between Shakespeare and Spenser'.)

> I am at a loss whether to sympathise with you in the way of congratulation or of condolence, on the subject of your impending prosecution [for the Prince Regent libel]. As a proof of what to your readers needed no proving—your

energy—it will undoubtedly bring you earlier to that pre-eminent celebrity which I have sanguinely anticipated for you, and by all my little efforts laboured to promote. This, by giving a wider diffusion to your opinions, out of evil may educe good…May I beg to be favoured henceforth with your Monday edition, which will leave out nothing material, I trust, of its elder brother's contents. I shall be obliged to you likewise for the title-page, preface, &c., as *I* shall assuredly bind you up, whatever the law may do.

Wrangham continued to support Hunt and to make common cause in progressive politics. In his literary efforts, Wrangham rendered Petrarch into sonnets, which he submitted to the Lee Priory Press. Wordsworth asked Wrangham to destroy the manuscript of one of their collaborations: an intemperate satire imitating Juvenal. In all likelihood Wrangham kept it. The most enduring picture of him is of a 'conscientious clerical dignitary with a consuming passion for rare books and eccentric bibliographic detail'. The archdeacon's friend and neighbour Sydney Smith was fully alert to the intensity of Wrangham's bibliomania. He counselled Mrs Wrangham: 'If there be a single room which you wish to preserve from being completely surrounded by books, let me advise you not to suffer a single shelf to be placed in it; for they will creep round you like an erysipelas till they have covered the whole.'

Leigh Hunt's biographers portrayed him as an 'immortal boy', a gentle soul who retained child-like traits well into adulthood. For many years Wrangham, too, kept up 'the elegant tastes of youth and college'. Dibdin portrayed him in his library 'stretching himself at length in the Elizabethan chair, in the midst of his Plantins and Elzevirs', watching the last glimmer of the day tipping the Cheviot hilltops. He maintained strong connections with other private collectors, and in 1822 would himself be elected to Roxburghe membership.

For his Roxburghe Member Book he chose a little volume called *The Garden Plot, An Allegorical Poem, Inscribed to Queen Elizabeth*. It was written by the sixteenth-century poet and dramatist Henry Goldingham. Though unpublished in Shakespeare's lifetime (or indeed before the Roxburghe edition), it had circulated in manuscript in the 1580s and Shakespeare probably knew of it. Wrangham had it printed in nostalgic 'black letter' type. The reception was not universally positive. In Dibdin's *Reminiscences of a Literary Life* (1836), the critical reverend called the archdeacon's choice 'unworthy'; the content was suitable neither for a clergyman nor a Queen. Wrangham replied with infinite patience, pointing out errors in Dibdin's recollections.

> In returning my most heartfelt thanks for the very kind manner in which you have characterized me in many parts of your *highly interesting* volumes, for the suggestion of literary employments so highly flattering to me, and for the friendly honesty of your censure of my poor Garden-Plot, I ought I know to attach a formal disclaimer of all fitness, &c., but it would at once be too formal and too hypocritical for the habits of our intercourse. I will therefore only *meo more* note two or three slight errata in your extracts relative to me which I hope you will soon be called to set right in a second edition.

Wrangham's regard for books—especially ones that were privately printed or had uncommon features like coloured paper, private imprints and special bindings—was equally infinite. He used his network of friends and bookmen to assemble a library that he hoped would be 'extensive rather than expensive'. In the library's extent, his success was absolute. He owned tens of thousands of books, booklets and manuscripts, neatly organised into folio, quarto, octavo and duodecimo sections. Books from around the world, encompassing an astonishing range of subjects: angling, gardening, magic, history, travel, classics, science, mythology, art, archaeology, poetry, drama.

Dibdin ribbed Wrangham for his eclecticism: 'The Archdeacon yet continues to woo his muse in his miscellaneous and wide-spreading library. He is yet as rapturous as ever over the charms of Bibliomania.' Many of the books were merely 'reading copies' in tired condition. Wrangham confessed to preferring 'tattered and dusty' old books over new titles. His library did, however, contain a good deal of treasure. Wynkyn de Worde's edition of *Synonima* by Johannes de Garlandia, 1518 (an edition unknown to Dibdin). A 1603 printing of James I's *Daemonologie* (the edition Dibdin dubbed 'the author's opus maximum') and a 1619 printing of his *A Meditation upon the Lord's Prayer*. A Second Folio Shakespeare. And many other rare volumes from the period.

Ever the fisherman, Wrangham dropped hints in his correspondence with publishers about them sending him complimentary copies and offprints, even better if on apricot or stone-coloured paper. In his letters to booksellers he offered to swap his duplicates for books in their stock. For titles he could not obtain this way, he politely sought discounts—a mutually beneficial way to move slow-selling items, he argued—and he informed the merchants of the cheapest means of dispatch. Mrs Wrangham showed admirable tolerance for the books, some of them improper, that took over her house. She accommodated them as best she could and, from time to time, tried to limit her husband's expenditure. As a clerical father of six children, perhaps he should not indulge in 'the luxury of large paper copies' when ordinary editions would do. He mostly followed her advice, but sometimes the special copies were irresistible and had to be paid for somehow. 'I must make up this prodigality by economy in some other quarter,' he remarked after an especially juicy purchase.

In one of the many curious twists in the story of Shakespeare's library, the creators of the Cowell–Wilmot forgeries seem to have selected Wilmot, and to have built his imaginary identity, in part with an eye to Wrangham's real one. The transformation of Wrangham into Wilmot is simple. Turn Yorkshire into Warwickshire, conveniently congruent with the Bard's home town. Swap Trinity College, Cambridge, for Trinity College, Oxford. Replace Wordsworth, Scott and Hunt with their predecessors Warton, Sterne and Johnson. Sprinkle in a hint of Dibdin. Otherwise leave everything else unchanged, and the archdeacon becomes the reverend. This sleight of hand could have been perpetrated by the nineteenth-century fantasist Olivia Serres, or by a more recent Baconian activist.

(A serial fraudster, Serres wrote a bogus 1813 biography of Wilmot, which she dedicated to the Marquess of Blandford and in which she falsely gave Wilmot authorship of the 'Junius' letters. Serres claimed at different times to be Wilmot's granddaughter, Wilmot's niece, George III's niece and George III's daughter.)

In 1812, soon after the Roxburghe Sale and at the height of the *Examiner* trouble, a youth of twenty called at Wrangham House. John Fry arrived carrying an introduction from his fellow Bristolian Sir Francis Freeling, First Baronet, fellow of the Society of Antiquaries and founding member of the Roxburghe Club.

Freeling had worked his way up through the postal service to become England's postal supremo: Secretary of His Majesty's

General Post Office. Along the way he collected a large library that was even stronger than Wrangham's in Shakespeareana and Elizabetheana, and even more eclectic. Apart from a witchcraft collection and a complete set of the Roxburghe Club issues, it contained very naughty books like *The Scourge of Venus, or the Wanton Lady* (1613, the only known copy); possibly the only surviving copy of *Loyal Garland* (1686); and several Caxtons, including *The Morale Prouerbs Cristyne of Pyse* (1478), which Dibdin classified 'among the Scarcest Pieces of Caxton's Press'. Bibliomania was a strong theme. Apart from Dibdin's *Reminiscences*, the library contained nineteen other Dibdin titles, as well as books Freeling had bought with enthusiasm at the Roxburghe Sale.

At Fry's first meeting with Wrangham, the young bookseller spoke of his strong appreciation for 'ancient' books, especially those from the reign of Elizabeth. He deplored editors like Pope who claimed to have 'improved' and 'modernised' Shakespeare but had in fact, in the words of the *British Critic*, 'purged and castrated him, and tattooed and beplaistered him, and cauterised and phlebotomised him'. Displaying an impressive knowledge of Elizabethan drama and early printed books, Fry outlined his plans to study and promote the foundation texts of English literature, and to help preserve their integrity. And he announced that he was on a quest. He was looking for Shakespeare's library.

In an advertisement at the end of the *Inquiry*, Malone's publishers had appealed for information about Shakespeare's papers, of whose existence Malone was certain.

> Though Mr Malone has already obtained several very curious and original Materials for the Life of Shakspeare, he will be extremely obliged by any further Communications on that Subject. He has always thought that much Information might be procured, illustrative of the History of this extraordinary

Man, if Persons possessed of ancient Papers would take the trouble to examine them, or permit others to peruse them.

In particular, Malone was sure that Shakespeare's granddaughter, Lady Bernard, had left behind 'Coffers and Cabinets, in which undoubtedly were several of her Grandfather's Papers'. John Fry was one of several aspiring young bibliographers to take up Malone's challenge.

Fry shared Wrangham's politics and was a fellow supporter of the *Examiner*. Both men were radicals in another sense, too. In the nineteenth century, to admire the original Shakespeare, with all his wildness and bawdiness, was a daring act. Influenced in part by Ker's collection and the Roxburghe Sale, Fry's taste had taken an early and ardent turn towards Elizabethanism. 'Surely,' he wrote, 'it can require but little examination to decide that the latter half of the sixteenth century was the period of England's greatness. The heart swells with rapture at the idea that one female reign contained the greatest Poets, Heroes, Statesmen, Philosophers and Warriors that any nation ever produced in the same portion of time.' Among the great poets, three stood tallest. Shakespeare, Spenser and the slightly later Milton were 'Fancy's sweetest children', a triumvirate of literary genii, and Shakespeare ranked uppermost among them. (Virginia Woolf rated Milton highest.) In Wrangham's drawing room, Fry praised 'the magic muse of the divine Shakspere', and confided his goal of rescuing—from obscurity, neglect and 'shelves of dust'—important documents that would extend understanding of the Elizabethan drama.

William-Henry Ireland had uncovered, in fraudulent form, exactly the kind of Shakespearean association copies that Fry now yearned to find in genuine form. Ireland and Wilmot had used fantasy to search for phantoms; Fry would conduct a real search. Almost a generation younger than the forger, Fry had been an impressionable teenager in the golden era of British bibliomania. By the age of sixteen or so he was already dealing in books and busily cultivating an antiquarian sensibility. At the age of eighteen Fry subscribed to Dibdin's exhilarating *Typographical Antiquities*, and began publishing fragments and extracts from exceptionally rare books and manuscripts housed in the greatest libraries of Elizabetheana.

Fry's first three books appeared in 1810. One of the debut volumes was *A Selection from the Poetical Works of Thomas Carew, with a Life of the Author, and Notes, by John Fry* (price four shillings, boards, in crown octavo). Another was *The Legend of Mary, Queen of Scots: And Other Ancient Poems, Now First Published from MSS of the XVIth Century* (the poem in question was possibly an inspiration for *Hamlet*). Longmans received these two Fry titles with enthusiasm and published them to feed the Elizabethan poetry craze. Carew's verse was mostly amatory in nature; Fry called it 'mellifluous', the same word Heywood and Meres had used to describe Shakespeare.

Fry was interested in tracing Carew's use of ideas and vocabulary from Milton, Spenser and especially from Shakespeare. The Nymph's lines in Carew's 'A Pastorall Dialogue', 'The yellow planets and the grey / Dawn shall attend thee on thy way', reminded Fry of *Romeo and Juliet* (act 3, scene 5): 'Yon light is not day-light, I know it well; It is some meteor / To light thee on thy way to Mantua.'

Carew's 'Boldness in Love':

Mark hoe the bashfull morne in vaine
    Courts the amorous Marigold
With sighing blasts and weeping raine;
    Yet she refuses to unfold:
But when the planet of the day

Approacheth with his powerfull ray,
Then she spreads, then she receives
His warmer beames into her virgin leaves.

echoed *Winter's Tale* (act 4, scene 3): 'The marigold that goes to bed wi' the Sun, / And with him rises weeping.' Fry noted other parallels, too, including the use of the Saxon word *hind* or *hinde*, meaning servant, both in Carew and in *The Merry Wives of Windsor*. These observations reveal Fry cultivating an especially sharp eye for the detection of poetical recycling.

Fry's Carew collection was well received by the *British Critic*: 'This is a chaste, elegant, and classical Publication. We have always encouraged Works of this description, and should be glad if the Editor would extend his critical labours to the Works of many of Carew's contemporaries.' But a man by the name of Griffiths, writing in the *Monthly Review* (1810), thought he had overdone the identification of sources and parallels. Griffiths' review abounded with patronising criticisms of the teenager's editorial method.

In the first place, we would suggest to him that the use of the same epithet by two authors is no certain mark of imitation; and that, were it so, the multiplication of parallel passages might be carried on *ad infinitum*: nay, there would indeed, in that case, be nothing new after Homer...Because Carew calls the wind 'whispering,' we need not be told that Milton in various passages does the same; nor need we be referred to *Mister* Todd's notes on that author, as our editor quaintly refers us. The 'dimpled stream' is an expression, like the foregoing, to be found throughout the whole range of English poetry...The image is natural, and would obviously strike any beholder.

The reviewer concluded by pointing out minor date errors and encouraging the editor to make further extracts from the works of Carew's contemporaries, while making sure that he 'excluded all intimations of parallel passages that do not contain manifest indications of plagiarism. The present editor would do well to read Bishop Hurd's Treatise on this subject, before he published again.' Other reviewers were even harsher, and one was especially damning of another Fry publication that appeared in 1810, *Metrical Trifles in Youth*. Four years later, Fry wrote with disarming openness about how he had been subjected to 'malevolent aspersion' and 'spiteful malignity' after producing his debut books, 'in a fit of youthful enthusiasm, when scarcely eighteen years old, independent of controul and without a friendly adviser to check an aspiring mind...That he now regrets this premature appearance it is unnecessary to add'.

Fry's feelings about *The Legend of Mary, Queen of Scots* (and its critical reception) were more uniformly positive, though the story is a harrowing one. Mary acceded to the Scottish throne as an infant. Once she attained her majority, her life became a series of disasters: a brief marriage to the Dauphin of France; marriage to her cousin, Henry Stuart, who was murdered just two years later; marriage to the man suspected of the murder; and long periods of confinement, mostly at the behest of her cousin, Queen Elizabeth, ending with Mary's execution on the flimsiest of pretexts. These and later books show Fry's desire to preserve and revive early texts. They also show him developing a practical brand of scientific bibliography for which Malone's demolition of the Ireland forgeries provided the methodological benchmark.

Francis Wrangham shared Fry's ambition to revive Elizabethan authors. He also shared Fry's view that Malone's rival eighteenth-century editors had diminished Shakespeare.

In the catalogue of his library, Wrangham cited the *Gentleman's Magazine* on the amounts received by Pope (£217 12s), Theobald (£652 10s) and Johnson (£475) for editions of Shakespeare. 'Thus,' Wrangham quoted, 'has the Poet *enriched* those, who have *impoverished* him.'

Unoffended by Fry's reference to 'shelves of dust', the archdeacon gave his erudite visitor immediate and unfettered access to the sprawling library at Wrangham House. A long friendship began, in which there was much swapping of books and anecdotes and clues. Impressed by Wrangham's 'enlarged and cultured mind', Fry used his connections with Thomas Fry & Co., a bookshop in Bristol's High Street, to help the archdeacon expand his library, and even to improve it by restoring missing pages to the most time-worn volumes. Freeling had introduced Fry to the leading literary lights of Bristol. Wrangham now did the same in London, introducing Fry to the lords, scholars and collectors such as Francis Douce and John Morgan Rice who would consume his stock like hotcakes, admit him into their marvellous libraries, subscribe with gusto to his publications, and make common cause with him in his quest.

Wrangham wrote to Lord Spencer describing his refreshing new acquaintance as 'a very enlightened and intelligent young bookseller' and buzzing over his bibliographical faculties. In an era that lacked bibliographical professionals, men such as Freeling, Wrangham and Fry stepped forward to join a noble enterprise. Reckless editors were attacking the textual integrity of Shakespeare. Thieves and forgers were pillaging libraries. In response, the noble amateurs created a network that operated as a league of bibliographical superheroes. In answer to Malone's call to arms, and using weapons he had wrought, the bookmen pledged to preserve the reputations and genuine texts of Elizabethan and

Jacobean authors. Fry described the enterprise as an endeavour to protect and promote 'the poetical treasures of the Elizabethan era...all the sublimity, the magnificence, the heroism, the imagery, and the vivid charms of the age'. He would finish what Malone had started.

In pursuit of Shakespeare, Fry searched institutional collections like the Bodleian, but he also scoured the libraries of clergymen and scholars, and the patrician collections of the minor and major aristocracy. These private libraries were ideal places in which to look: a direct chain of provenance connected them to Shakespeare's world. Some early institutional libraries spurned 'low' drama and had replaced early editions with 'better' new ones, just as the Bodleian had done with its First Folio. Compared to university libraries, private libraries were more likely to hold literature that people actually liked and read, including politically unpopular and morally naughty books. (Wrangham owned works that were banned in Shakespeare's day, such as 'Leicester's Commonwealth' (1584).)

Private libraries were the natural environment for the rarest private editions, either printed or in manuscript, that circulated in and since Elizabethan times. Small editions and unpublished manuscripts could pass under the radars of censors and other authorities. Often not registered with the Stationers' Company (an early form of copyright protection and print regulation), these editions were the preserve of antiquarians and connoisseurs; their mode of distribution was ideal for the works of those poets and dramatists who were seen as too radical, too heterodox or too sexy. Those rare texts are the source of much that is known about the literature and book culture of Shakespeare's world.

Many of the manuscripts were written in the notoriously difficult 'secretary hand', a scribbly gothic script that is striking for its inconsistency and incongruity—features appreciated by Elizabethans who, as the palaeographer Leon Kellner observed, liked to shake things up. 'Uniformity was shunned, variety commended as a grace of style. In spelling, in declension and conjugation, in the structure of sentences, in word-formation we notice a deliberate preference for variation.' To aid his search, Fry mastered the secretary hand.

He also adopted a bibliographical method that today seems very modern. He was interested in the completeness of the books he examined; he noted any defects such as missing leaves and plates. Scrupulous in acknowledging his own sources, he called conjecture conjecture, and was meticulous in noticing and correcting his own errors. Following a lead that Dibdin had half started, Fry and his Malonite network advanced the study of provenance. They traced books back through chains of multiple prior owners, as revealed by bookplates, inscriptions and signatures, and they published their findings in books and catalogues.

Freeling's copy of Anthony Munday's *True Historie of the Three Years Fasting of a Maiden of Confolens* (1604) was, for example, 'Bindley's Copy' (James Bindley was an eighteenth-century English official, book collector and antiquarian). Freeling's copy of Munday's *Palmerin of England* (1596) was 'Col. Stanley's Copy, in russia'. Many of the books in Wrangham's, Freeling's and Rice's libraries had come, via the hands of Ker and Masterman-Sykes, from eighteenth-century collections such as those of Johnson, Steevens and Ames, and could be traced even further back to seventeenth-century owners such as Sir William Boothby and Frances Wolfreston.

To zero in on Shakespeare, Fry studied annotated eighteenth-century editions of the plays, as well as bibliographies and reference works from that century, like Thomas Warton's *History of English Poetry* (1774–81). He also studied, from earlier centuries, the silences, sources and contemporary references. He noticed, for example, how the section on English poets in Peacham's *Compleat Gentleman* (1627), as mentioned in chapter 2, referred to Heywood, Sidney, Dyer, Spenser, Daniel and de Vere, but not to Shakespeare. And he noticed how thoroughly the early English poets had made use of Latin and French sources.

Equipped with his bibliographical and palaeographical toolkit, Fry followed a trail from shelf to shelf, book to book and page to page in his friends' libraries. As Malone and Rowe had done, he appealed to owners of 'ancient papers' to make them available for scholarly examination. What he found would turn the search for Shakespeare's library upside down.

CHAPTER 8

The Mystery Deepens

Two hundred years ago, and two hundred years after Shakespeare's death, John Fry and his associates conducted a thorough search for traces of Shakespeare's library. Fry documented his findings in letters, catalogues, unpublished manuscripts and three new publications: *Pieces of Ancient Poetry from Unpublished Manuscripts and Scarce Books* (1814); an edition of George Whetstone's *Metrical Life of George Gascoigne* (1815); and the wide-ranging *Bibliographical Memoranda* (1816). In their style of publication, all three targeted the Georgian appetite for special rarities, and all harked back to the private editions that had circulated in Shakespeare's day. Of *Pieces*, a total of 102 copies were printed, including six 'specials' on blue paper; of the *Metrical*

Life, a hundred copies; and of *Bibliographical Memoranda*, again a hundred copies, one of which was 'accidentally destroyed'. The *Metrical Life* was produced from Edmond Malone's own copy of the notoriously rare 1577 original.

The leading collectors of the era—men such as Francis Douce, Mark Masterman-Sykes and the two Francises, Wrangham and Freeling—snapped up Fry's publications. When he came to acknowledge the men whose libraries he had used, Fry gave special thanks to Wrangham for 'friendly favours', and to Freeling for 'unreserved liberality'.

One of Fry's subscribers was infamous trickster William-Henry Ireland, who bought one of the special 'large paper' copies of *The Legend of Mary, Queen of Scots* (1810) using proceeds from the sale of his bogus curiosities, or money he had borrowed from one of his few remaining friends. (In an 1811 letter to Richard Garnett, Joseph Ritchie wrote of Ireland: 'He is a man of very engaging manners and extremely communicative, but talks rather too much of what books he has published and what he intends to publish.') In the year in which *Pieces* appeared, Ireland moved to France where he worked in the Bibliothèque Nationale, no doubt perpetrating further mischief.

Freeling's library contained a remarkable curiosity: for Spenser's *Faerie Queene* (first edition, 1590–96) the catalogue citation reads, 'From Ireland's Shakspeare Library, with numerous Manuscript Notes pretended to be Shakspeare's, forged by Ireland, in green morocco'. According to Freeling, at the height of public belief in the Ireland hoax, the two Spenser volumes 'attracted more notice, curiosity and veneration from the believers in the Shakspeare Forgery, than any of the Printed Books in the pretended Shakspeare Library. Spenser illustrated with Notes by Shakspeare was hailed as an inestimable Treasure. Ireland, in his

Confessions, says that a Gentleman offered Sixty Pounds for the copy.'

In his search for Shakespeare's library, John Fry made many contributions to our understanding of the sources Shakespeare used for his plays and poems. He pointed out two early sources for *Troilus and Cressida*: 'Troylus and Cresseyde' in John Skelton's *Philip Sparowe* (1568); and a manuscript, on vellum, of Geoffrey Chaucer's *Troilus and Creseide*. Fry also pinpointed two *Merchant of Venice* sources: Alexander Silvayn's *Orator* (1596), which includes the 'Story of a Jew, who would have a pound of a Christian's flesh for his debt'; and John Gower's epic *Confessio Amantis* (1483), which Caxton printed and which includes the casket-choosing plot device.

Among the other source books he studied were Anthony Munday's rare play, *Two Italian Gentlemen* (1584, a source for *Two Gentlemen of Verona*); Barnaby Riche's 1581 *Fruites of Long Experience* and 1594 *Farewell to Military Profession* (the latter a source for *Twelfth Night*); John Eliot's *Ortho-epia Gallica* (1593), which influenced *The Rape of Lucrece*; William Painter's *Palace of Pleasure* (1566), 'the earliest collection of Romances in the era of Elizabeth' and the book that 'supplied Shakspeare with the fables of many of his Dramas'; and Thomas Bedingfield's translation of *Cardanus Comforte* (1573), the inspiration for the 'To be or not to be' soliloquy.

Another important source in Freeling's library was Saviolo's *Practice of the Use of the Rapier and Dagger; and the Honor of Honorable Quarrels*, 'very rare, in russia, gilt leaves', 1595. Stabbing was the principal cause of death in Shakespeare's plays. Freeling's library catalogue identifies Saviolo as a source both for Shakespeare and for Jonson: 'This work throws considerable light on the affected manners of "our gallants" in the days of Elizabeth, and elucidates several passages in Shakspeare and Ben Jonson. It is strikingly alluded to in *As You Like It*, the *Alchemist*, and *Every Man in His Humour*.'

Freeling also owned one of the most important Shakespeare source books of all: Holinshed's *Chronicles* in two folio editions: the 1577 first edition, and the expurgated 1587 'best edition'. The latter was a primary reference source for *Macbeth* as well as *Cymbeline*, the history plays and parts of *King Lear*.

Freeling introduced Fry to another essential resource for Shakespeare research: a 'matchless' collection of Robert Greene's works. Greene has been labelled England's first professional author. A less sympathetic appellation would be the sixteenth century's greatest hack. Versifier, farceur, romantic novelist, social historian, crime reporter and adapter of foreign works, Greene wrote prolifically—poetry, plays and prose; fiction and non-fiction; and blends of fact and fiction—on a great variety of subjects. Many of his books found wide audiences. His popular *Defence of Cony-catching* sold for three pence and kicked off a series of irresistibly colourful underworld accounts: *A Notable Discovery of Coosnage, Now Daily Practised by Sundry Lewd Persons called Cony-catchers and Cross-biters* (1591); *The Second Part of Cony-catching* (1591); *Thirde and Last Parte of Cony-catching* (1592); *A Disputation Between a Hee Cony-Catcher and a Shee Cony-Catcher* (1592); and the pseudonymous *Defence of Cony-catching* 'by Cuthbert Cony-catcher' (1592). ('Coosnage' or cozenage is trickery, such as in cards and dice; 'cony-catchers' are con-artists; 'cross-biters' are swindlers.)

Greene's personal appearance and habits were notorious. 'Who in London hath not heard', asked writer Gabriel Harvey, of Greene's 'dissolute and licentious living; his fonde disguisinge of a Master of Arte with ruffianly haire, unseemely apparrell, and more unseemely Company?' According to Freeling's catalogue:

[Greene's] dissipated habits made him fairly acquainted... with the Profligates of every grade. He has accordingly depicted in glowing terms, and with poignant raillery the Humours of the Times; and laid open the Practices of Cheats, Sharpers, Courtezans, &c. with a raciness and animation scarcely to be found in any other writer of the Period. His Descriptions are living Pictures, Painted with the hand of a Master; he possessed great fertility of imagination, vividness of fancy, a strong perception of the ludicrous and real pathos. The Poetical Pieces scattered through his Prose Works, as well as his Dramas, evince the high station he might have attained as a Poet, had he sacrificed more at the shrine of Apollo, than at those of Bacchus and Venus.

Freeling's Greenes included a dubious pamphlet of dubious origin that is also one of the most important Shakespearean documents. Greene's *Groats-worth of Witte* (1592) is exceedingly rare: Freeling's was one of only two known copies. The pamphlet contains what is probably the first citation of Shakespeare as a playwright: a cryptic, hyphenated reference to 'Shake-scene', the 'upstart Crow'.

Edmond Malone was the first to properly identify the reference as an attack on Shakespeare (aged twenty-eight at the time), whom Greene accused of stealing other authors' works and passing them off as his own. Fry, too, saw *Groats-worth* as an attack, and focused on the text that Greene most probably thought Shakespeare had filched: Greene's 1588 pastoral romance, *Pandosto*, the basis for *The Winter's Tale*. (Greene may also have been put out by Shakespeare and Marlowe revising Greene and

George Peele's original versions of the three parts of *Henry VI*.)
Freeling's catalogue calls *Groats-worth* 'a very interesting tract,
as Greene gives in it an exposition of his own follies and dissipa-
tion…and makes an attack upon Shakespeare, who he says, "is in
his owne conceyt the onely Shake-scene in a countrey"'.

Fry studied Greene volumes that Shakespeare probably used
as sources, and may have owned. Other exceptional sixteenth-cen-
tury rarities in that category include Chaucer's *Workes* (1561);
Thomas Cutwode's *Caltha Poetarum, or The Bumble-Bee* (1599);
William Percy's *Sonnets to the Fairest Coelia* (1594); Edward
Hake's *Newes out of Powles Churchyarde* (1579); Stephen Gosson's
Schoole of Abuse (1587); Bartholomew Chappell's *Garden of
Prudence* (1595), thought to be the only extant copy; and Richard
Crompton's very rare *Mansion of Magnanimitie* (1599), dedicated
to the 'Earle of Essex, Earle Marshall of England'.

In the spectacular Shakespearean library of Reverend John
Morgan Rice, Fry found other extreme rarities, including
Thomas Watson's *Hekatompathia or Passionate Centurie of Love*
(1581), dedicated to Edward de Vere. In the eighteenth century,
George Steevens had pronounced Watson a 'much more elegant
Sonnetteer than Shakespeare'. According to Rice's catalogue,
Watson's Sonnets 'should form part of a Shakespeare Library'.

> Shakespeare appears to have been among the number of his
> readers, having in the following passage of Venus and Adonis,
> 'Leading him Prisoner in a red-rose chain,' borrowed an idea
> from his 83rd Sonnet, 'The Muses not long since intrapping
> Love In chains of Roses'.

Rice also owned John Florio's *Second Frutes, with 6000 Italian
Proverbs* (1591); George Puttenham's *Art of English Poesie* (1589,
annotated by Steevens); and the 1603 compilation of work by

poets expressing their 'Sorrowes, Joy, or Lamentation for Queen Elizabeth and Triumph for the prosperous succession of King James'. Another of Rice's prizes was a very rare book that had passed through the libraries of Steevens and the Duke of Roxburghe: Arthur Hall's *Ten Books of Homers Iliades* (1581), thought to be 'the first appearance of a part of the *Iliad* in English Dress'. Robert Harding Evans called the translation 'frequently very singular and whimsical'. An example is the anachronistic line: 'Sound friend (quoth Nestor) what you say, as true is as the Byble'. Rice also possessed what was thought to be the only remaining copy of Munday's *Banquet of Daintie Conceits* (1588), 'unknown to Warton, Ritson, Ames, and Herbert'.

Fry studied dispersed libraries such as Ker's, Steevens' and Malone's. He retraced the searches made by Rowe, the Irelands, and celebrated eighteenth-century antiquary and bookman William Oldys. Oldys wrote a variety of books, among them a life of Sir Walter Raleigh and (with John Taylor) a book on curing blindness. Dibdin opined in *Bibliomania* that Oldys' *The British Librarian* was 'a work of no common occurrence, or mean value. It is rigidly correct, if not very learned.' With Samuel Johnson, Oldys had worked for the bookseller-publisher Thomas Osborne, famous for producing *The Harleian Miscellany* (1744–46) and for being knocked down by Johnson with a folio. 'Sir,' Johnson told Boswell, 'he was impertinent to me, and I beat him.' Oldys built an important collection of early books and manuscripts. His famous copy of Gerard Langbaine's *Dramatick Poets* contained extensive annotations of much Shakespearean interest.

One of several antiquarians who 'helped' Shakespeare's descendants with their relics, Oldys seems to have been better than most. The Folger includes a copy of *Poems on Several Occasions* inscribed by a sixth-generation descendant of Joan Shakespeare.

A gift from My Dear
Father
Thomas Hart
With manye items of my
Noble Ancestors Joan Shakespeare
Had it not been for the great
Spirit of Kindness of Mr William
Oldys I should not of had the
joy of having in my safe keeping
our great Poets Bible, in the little
Chest with the keys

Throughout Oldys' life he was frequently in financial trouble; in 1761 he died deep in debt. His friend and creditor John Taylor paid for the funeral 'and obtained possession of [Oldys'] books and valuable manuscripts'. The bookseller Thomas Davies sold the books and a portion of the manuscripts.

Bibliographical Memoranda is the principal source for details of the dispersal of Oldys' library. Taylor's son told Fry that the dispersal led to trouble:

> Mr Oldys had engaged to furnish a bookseller in the Strand, whose name was Walker, with ten years of the life of Shakespeare unknown to the biographers and commentators, but he died, and 'made no sign' of the projected work. The bookseller made a demand of twenty guineas on my father, alleging that he had advanced that sum to Mr Oldys, who had promised to provide the matter in question.

The sale of Oldys' books would disappoint Taylor as well as Walker. Fry was shocked by the 'trifling prices' achieved by important sixteenth- and seventeenth-century items that were 'esteemed amongst the scarcest in the language'. The prices were vastly below those achieved in the heady days of the bibliomania. At the Roxburghe Sale, Linschoten's *Voyages to the East Indies* (1596) had sold for £10 15s. Davies' price for the same copy was 12s 6d. Davies sold Oldys' 1640 edition of Shakespeare's poems for a shilling. A large quantity of early quarto plays were knocked down as a job lot.

Like a police line-up, the main characters in Shakespeare's world—and future authorship controversies—appear in John Fry's publications: monarchs, aristocrats, literary giants, contemporaries, editors, printer-publishers, forgers. In *Pieces* and *Bibliographical Memoranda*, Fry quoted Sir Francis Bacon— 'Some books are to be tasted, others to be swallowed, and some few to be chewed and digested'—then précised Bacon's thoughts on nobility, scholarship, discourse, beauty, brotherly love and the greatness of kingdoms. He explored Sir Walter Raleigh's incarceration and its impact on his poetry. And he reproduced (from Howell's *Familiar Letters*, sixth edition, 1688) early anecdotes about Ben Jonson's method and egotism, such as this one.

I was invited yesternight, to a solemn supper, by B[en] I[onson]…there was good Company, excellent chear, choice Wines, and jovial welcome ; one thing intervened, which almost spoiled the relish of the rest, that B[en] began to engross all the discourse, to vapour extreamly of himself, and by villifying others to magnifie his own Muse. T[homas] C[arew] buz'd me in the ear, that though B[en] had barrell'd up a great deal of knowledge ; yet, it seems, he had not read the Ethiques, which among other precepts of morality forbid self commendation, declaring it to be an illfavour'd solecism in good manners.

Wrangham owned a large collection of Dibdin's works, including his unpublished 'Specimen of an English De Bure' (1810), 'only 50 copies'; Dibdin's *The Library-Companion*; and, purchased from John Fry, Dibdin's *Bibliomania*. For Fry, Dibdin began as an inspiration and ended as an antithesis. *Bibliographical Memoranda* criticises Dibdin's sloppy methods and recurring incompetence. Unlike Dibdin, Fry focused on English works, and was not dazzled by the bibliomania cult. Unlike Dibdin, he sought the humble, day-to-day books and manuscripts and pamphlets. That is where Shakespeare was to be found.

The work of Fry and his fellow Malonites was immediately influential. Among editors and bibliophiles, the network helped popularise the search for Shakespeare's library, directly influencing attempts by Nathan Drake and, later, William Hazlitt and John Payne Collier, to reconstruct 'Bibliotheca Shakespeareana'. By analysing the plays and poems to identify the romances, novels, poems and histories that Shakespeare was thought to have used, Drake helped answer, 'Of what extent was the library of Shakespeare?' Published in *Shakespeare and His Times* (1817), Drake's Shakespeare library included the original source manuscript for Fry's *The Legend of Mary, Queen of Scots*—and scores of other source books such as Roger Ascham's *Toxophilus* (1545), Thomas Wilson's *Arte of Rhetorique* (1560), Puttenham's *Art of English Poesie* and Florio's *First Fruits* (1578).

William-Henry Ireland's bogus library catalogue was a crude but not altogether alien preview of Drake's Shakespeare library, and the two editions that followed it: *Shakespeare's Library*, by Collier (1840–43), and Hazlitt's second edition with the same title (1875). In essence, these three latter compilers 'catalogued' Shakespeare's library using the same methods Ireland had employed to assemble the handlist that impressed his father and conned literary London.

Wrangham bought copy number 86 of *Pieces*. He also bought Fry's *The Legend of Mary, Queen of Scots* and had it bound into a composite volume alongside Dibdin's *Bibliomania* and John Davors' *Secrets of Angling*. He became one of Fry's best supporters and friends; a father figure who chided him over his lifestyle and his frequent bouts of illness. 'If at three or four and twenty the health begins to feel the effect of nightly lucubration, it is indeed the first of duties by consulting it to guard against the unavailing remorse of a disoccupied and exhausted old age.' There was no question, though, of the bookseller suffering into old age. In 1822, at the age of thirty and just over a decade after his 'premature' edition of Carew, John Fry died. Wrangham grieved the loss of a young man who possessed a 'rare union of talent and industry' that should have borne 'rich and lasting fruits'.

A self-made bookman, Fry had learned by finding and handling important books, and by cultivating friendships with the foremost collectors and litterateurs of the era. Copies of his books held in libraries today feature warm inscriptions to his friends and supporters. *The Legend of Mary, Queen of Scots* in the New York Public Library is warmly inscribed by Fry to the editor of the *Examiner*.

More grounded than Dibdin, more honest than the Irelands, more sane than Steevens, and faithful to the methods modelled by Malone, Fry performed a preservative function that is invaluable for modern scholars. Looking back over the history of Shakespeare studies, it is remarkable how many Shakespearean documents have been found and analysed, only to be lost again. Infamous examples include the papers Malone used to prove Shakespeare lived in Southwark, near the Bear Garden, in 1596, and maintained multiple London residences until 1608. Thomas Greene, the Stratford town clerk, referred to two letters he had written to 'Shakspeare' about the enclosure of fields at Stratford; these, too, are now lost. Perhaps the most intriguing piece of missing evidence is John Shakespeare's 'Spiritual testament'.

Just six small leaves stitched together, the document appeared to be a Catholic 'will' bearing the name of John Shakspear—along with the name of his patron saint, 'Saint Winefride'. Poet and antiquarian John Jordan claimed the bricklayer Joseph Moseley found the will in April 1757 between the rafters and the roof tiles when retiling a Henley Street house owned by descendants of Shakespeare's sister Joan. Passing through the hands of inter-mediaries, the document reached Malone around 1789. Jordan had been implicated in more than one forgery, and the spiritual will was greeted with scepticism. After much deliberation, Malone published the testament as genuine in his 1790 edition of Shakespeare's works, but then had second thoughts, concluding in 1796 that it 'could not have been the composition of any one of our poet's family'. The will's authenticity is still the subject of debate, and the debate is likely to continue: no one since Malone has seen the document.

In his friends' libraries, Fry studied and recorded poems, prose works and documents whose original versions have since been lost. Today, he is the sole source for notable verse fragments and details of early book collections. Without Fry and his league of bibliophiles, much more would have perished.

Wrangham lived for two more decades, long enough to complete the epic catalogue of his library. When Dibdin visited in 1838, the archdeacon's figure was 'inclined at a gentle angle', his step was 'hesitating', but he was still engrossed in his library, and in planning its fate. Wrangham gifted a collection of ten thousand pamphlets, including many not in the British Museum Library, to Trinity College, Cambridge. Bound in a thousand volumes at the time of their delivery, they are still there today. Sotheby's auctioned most of his other books in 1843 at a sale lasting twenty days. Wrangham's treasured books nourished libraries around the world.

Francis Freeling did so well at the General Post Office that the King made him a baronet. Late in his life, he spent as much time as possible in his library. 'Many were the hours of weariness and suffering in his latter days which were thus happily soothed.' After Freeling's death in 1836, the Roxburghe auctioneer Robert Harding Evans sold, at an auction extending over nine days, 'the Curious, Choice and Valuable Library of the late Sir Francis Freeling, Bart. F.S.A.' Dibdin dedicated to Freeling his 1836 memoir, *Reminiscences of a Literary Life*.

Fry's discoveries about Shakespeare's sources and Greene's 'Shake-scene' attack would be crucial evidence in the authorship debate. In this and other respects, Fry accomplished much in his shortened life. He became one of the world's most diligent searchers for Shakespeare's library; unlike Drake and Hazlitt, who traced textual sources, Fry sought actual books. His legacy supplied new pictures of Shakespeare. The book-loving scholar-librarian. The anti-censorship activist. The radical gentleman.

If Fry had lived longer, there is little doubt he would have outshone Dibdin, and bibliography would have made greater progress. Fundamentally, though, in the search for Shakespeare's library, Fry and his network failed. The significance of some of their discoveries is not yet fully understood, but they never found a verifiable Shakespeare manuscript or association copy. Measured against the standards set by Malone, the network never found a single book or document that has been directly, authoritatively linked to Shakespeare's library.

Now one of several nineteenth-century searchers whom history has largely forgotten, John Fry nevertheless leaves us at a telling point in our quest. He had free access to the major libraries of his era. And he found none of Shakespeare's books. This conclusion has led many people to question whether there were any such books to be found in the first place.

Part II

THE HERETICAL SEARCHERS

CHAPTER 9

The Musikbibliothek

Bear pit. War zone. Mad house. My first serious contact with twenty-first-century Shakespeare studies was during my doctorate at Monash University. Rumour had it that the Clayton campus was the main recruiting ground for Australia's spy agencies. It was also a hotbed of Shakespeare scholarship—mostly unorthodox and not confined to the English department.

I met at Monash an 'experimental pathology' professor who studied coded messages in Shakespeare's sonnets. In another faculty, a philosophy professor studied the same sonnets to trace arithmetical, musicological and Platonic patterns. Across the university there were Shakespeare scholars whose backgrounds looked like an implausible case study in multidisciplinarity: law, geography, medicine, nursing, mathematics, French Renaissance studies, commerce, music history, librarianship, drama therapy. In every department and every cafe, it seemed there was a scholar with a new take on Shakespeare and his work.

In this milieu I encountered several breeds of Stratfordians (those who accept the standard Shakespeare biography) and a multitude of anti-Stratfordians (those who reject it): Baconians, Oxfordians, Marlovians, Derbyites, Rutlanders, Groupists. One sub-species was especially well represented. Monash was home to the world's richest concentration of Nevillians: people who think Sir Henry Neville wrote Shakespeare's plays and poems. Landing in this parallel universe of unorthodoxy was an unsettling experience. Finding out you're surrounded by Shakespeare sceptics is like discovering all your friends are Scientologists, or swingers.

At Monash I absorbed the doctrinal distinctions that define the Shakespearean sub-groups, just as hair-splits and sore points separate Trotskyites from Leninists. A Baconian offshoot, for example, claimed Sir Francis was the bastard son of Queen Elizabeth and the Earl of Leicester. An Oxfordian splinter claimed Henry Wriothesley was the lovechild of busy Lizzie and the Earl of Oxford. Quickly I worked out which topics were taboo, which researchers were on friendly terms, and which were on 'no speaks'. I acquired the jargon of Shakespeare heresy. Already able to tell my Folios from my Florios, I learnt to speak in shorthand about Quiney, Looney, 'Wrizzley' and Knollys, and to cite from memory the Tower Notebook and the Northumberland Manuscript.

Though the heretical factions have little regard for each other, they are united in their belief that 'Shakspere' of Stratford cannot have written Shakespeare's plays and poems. Each faction has a defining affiliation with one or more 'true author' candidates.

The Marlovians believe Christopher Marlowe wrote the plays and poems, possibly after faking his own death in 1593. The Oxfordians stand with Edward de Vere, Earl of Oxford (and are known to throw the best parties). The Baconians, the most respectable heretics, attribute the works to Sir Francis Bacon. Different varieties of fence-sitting Groupists postulate sundry scenarios of joint authorship. Through this unorthodox minefield, I had as my guide John O'Donnell. Modest to the point of introversion, brainy to the point of genius, John was the hub of the Nevillian sect, the only member on polite terms with all the others.

When I first met John, he was the university's organist. By the end of primary school John could play and conduct all nine Beethoven symphonies. He wrote concertos and symphonies, performing them in his uncle's amateur orchestra. John won a music scholarship to a school where Shakespeare's plays and Bacon's essays were central to the curriculum. By the end of high school John could recite from memory *Julius Caesar*, *The Merchant of Venice*, *Twelfth Night* and *The Taming of the Shrew*.

After he graduated from university John stayed on to specialise in deep analysis of early musical documents. He made dozens of trips to the libraries and music rooms of Germany, Austria and Italy. From disparate and forgotten fragments he was able to piece together, and then perform, some of the first operas. This work took John to the top of his field. Becoming head of music at the Victorian College of the Arts was the high point of his career. John, though, was never more content than when teaching and performing. Specialising in sixteenth- and seventeenth-century music, John mastered and taught 'sight singing', the highest level of choristry.

Precise and diligent as a musician and as a scholar, John discovered that seventeenth-century musical printings were unreliable. He also found that games and puzzles were central to the creation of classical music; the mathematical squares embedded in Bach's works were an example. These discoveries laid a foundation for entry into Shakespearean scepticism, a field to which John brought a unique perspective. He heard the music in the writing.

John first paired off with his future wife, a musician and masters student, at a surrealist ball. Surrounded by clawed hands, marble sushi, tomato throwers and dry ice, John and Jacky had their first kiss. The ball's organiser would later initiate university changes that became a lightning rod for discontent with the local version of modern academia. A new breed of academic took over the music school. When I met John and Jacky, they were almost émigrés from an academy they felt had turned its back on excellence.

John and Jacky's neighbourhood north of Melbourne was a place of danger. Bushfires regularly threatened the district. On the main road, reckless kangaroos jumped precipitously into the path of cars. In 2015 John survived two separate high-speed collisions with eastern greys. Shunning these external dangers, the interior of John and Jacky's home was a refuge. It housed a Shakespeare reference library and a sixteenth-century *Musikbibliothek*, including volumes of musicology, early music and the largest collection of early keyboard instruments outside Europe.

Despite his status as an academic exile, John continued to travel regularly, visiting libraries, playing French and German church organs, and otherwise studying and performing. Several trips were made as part of John's lifelong search for the Monteverdi opera *L'Arianna* (1607–08). The opera's libretto survives but the music is lost. Partly to fill this gap, John and Jacky named their daughter Arianna. In Arianna's first year at high school, her English teacher announced that the class would study Shakespeare. Did anyone in the class know anything about him? Brought up from birth as an anti-Stratfordian, and recently converted to Nevillism, Arianna was ready with the answer. 'He was illiterate,' she declared, 'and he died in 1615.' At home that evening, she recounted the exchange to John, who brimmed with pride.

Over many meetings and glasses of Heathcote shiraz, John tutored me on the Shakespeare authorship controversy and the Nevillian heresy. Sir Henry Neville is a recent addition to a list of aristocratic author candidates that includes three monarchs and eight earls, plus Sir Francis Bacon, Sir Walter Raleigh, Sir Anthony Sherley and William Seymour, the 'illegitimate son' of Lady Catherine Grey and the Earl of Hertford.

Courtier, politician and diplomat, Henry Neville was born with an impeccable pedigree. His great-great-great-grandfather was Ralph Neville, First Earl of Westmorland and husband of Joan Beaufort, the daughter of John of Gaunt. Henry's noble ancestry also stretched back to Gilbert de Neville, steward to William the Conqueror, and possibly to Alan de Neville, chief forester of Henry II. He grew up at Billingbear House in Berkshire. His tutor at Merton College, Oxford, was the brilliant but autocratic Henry Savile. Between 1578 and 1582 Neville accompanied Savile on a Continental tour that took in France, Italy and Germany. The Queen's Secretary of State, Sir Robert Cecil, introduced Neville at court. Neville served as Berkshire's High Sheriff, and sat in Parliament at different times as the member for New Windsor, Sussex and Berkshire. After the 1597 election he was MP for Liskeard in Cornwall. Two years later he took up an even more distant posting: ambassador to the Court of Henri IV, King of France.

Neville abhorred his ambassadorship and tried many times

to get out of it. When eventually he returned to England he was caught up in the disastrous Essex Rebellion of 1601, a bungled attempt to depose the aged Queen. The leader of the rebellion, Robert Devereux, Second Earl of Essex, had previously enjoyed the Queen's favour and a lucrative royal monopoly on the sale of sweet wines. After the rebellion fizzled, Elizabeth had Essex executed. Neville escaped that fate 'only with difficulty'. Imprisoned with Henry Wriothesley, Earl of Southampton, in the Tower of London, Neville was stripped of his position and fined ten thousand pounds (later reduced to five thousand, payable in convenient instalments). He had to wait for the Queen's death before he could hope to be released.

Once free, and having already alienated one monarch, Neville set about antagonising King James by advocating for a powerful House of Commons. As a consequence, Neville was overlooked for the position of Secretary of State. When offered the position of Treasurer of the Chamber, he turned it down, possibly out of pique. He did enjoy, however, the royal right to collect a twelfth of the tariff on imports of indigo.

Portentously, the *Oxford Dictionary of National Biography* suggests that Neville was a more important figure than he seems. If he did indeed write Shakespeare's plays and poems, then that suggestion is certainly correct.

The first direct expression of the Nevillian authorship case was *The Truth Will Out* (2005) by Brenda James and William Rubinstein. Like all Shakespeare heretics, James and Rubinstein had to prove two things: first, that Shakespeare did not write the plays and poems; and second, that a specific someone else did. Shakespeare's missing library was key to how James and Rubinstein answered the first question. The co-authors could not believe Shakespeare was a playwright yet no one in his Stratford household had retained a book, playscript or other document from his literary career.

The Nevillian answer to the second question rests on four pillars, plus one 'smoking gun' and much circumstantial evidence. The first pillar is chronological. Unlike those of Edward de Vere, who died in 1604, and Christopher Marlowe, who died in 1593, Henry Neville's dates align very closely with Shakespeare's. James and Rubinstein put forward plentiful evidence that the published plays and poems closely reflect the sequence of Neville's foreign travels, business affairs, relationships and achievements.

The second pillar rests on an interpretation of the cryptic dedication in the 1609 edition of Shakespeare's *Sonnets*:

TO THE ONLIE BEGETTER OF
THESE INSVING SONNETS
MR W. H. ALL HAPPINESSE
AND THAT ETERNITIE
PROMISED
BY
OVR EVER-LIVING POET
WISHETH
THE WELL-WISHING
ADVENTVRER IN
SETTING
FORTH

T.T.

James announced she had deciphered a coded message in the dedication. She further claimed to have explained the dedication by linking it to Neville's investment—the 'adventure'—in the new American colony of Virginia.

The third pillar is the so-called Northumberland Manuscript. Discovered in 1867, it is a curious document that features the names of Neville, Shakespeare and Bacon, along with the Neville family motto, the names of two plays, a line from *The Rape of Lucrece*, a version of the mysterious long word—honorificabilitudinitatibus—from *Love's Labour's Lost*, and much else seemingly of relevance to the Authorship Question. The manuscript may date from as early as 1596.

The fourth pillar is also documentary. Dated 1602, the Tower Notebook is an anonymous manuscript, nearly two hundred pages long, possibly completed by Neville during his imprisonment. It describes Anne Boleyn's coronation in phrases that James and Rubinstein believe are precursors to the coronation scene in *Henry VIII*. James and Rubinstein also claimed to have found a 'smoking gun' that sealed their proof of Nevillian authorship: the identification of Malvolio in *Twelfth Night* as a caricature of the womanising nobleman, William Knollys (more about that later). Based on all this evidence, James and Rubinstein concluded Shakespearean authorship was a 'conspiracy' and an 'elaborate hoax'.

James and Rubinstein are not without academic credentials. Brenda James was an occasional lecturer at the University of Portsmouth, where she pursued her interest in Rosicrucian and Cabbalistic symbology. After completing postgraduate studies then lecturing on English and Civilisation, she left her occupation to pursue Neville. 'I was embarking,' she said, 'on a trail of long-envisaged, very independent research.'

An adjunct professor at Monash University, James's co-author Bill Rubinstein was well placed to collaborate in the unmasking of a conspiracy. He had already written on two mainstays of the conspiracy movement: the Kennedy assassination and the Jack the Ripper murders. On Kennedy, Rubinstein's thesis was that Oswald did shoot the President, but was aiming at Texas Governor John Connally.

James and Rubinstein's collaboration was uneasy from the start. Impatient with each other's boundaries, the authors ended their collaboration not long after *The Truth Will Out* appeared in print. During the processes of research and writing, James worked largely in secret. When the writing was mostly finished, Brenda gingerly admitted a fellow lecturer into the circle—David Jenkins—to help with a few things. She later thanked him for his trustworthiness, and for his knowledge of 'esoteric symbolism'.

Rubinstein's role in the project is fairly clear. He was both co-author and structural editor. After receiving Brenda's 'over-long manuscript' he removed much of the padding (the resulting three hundred pages are still hard going). James and Rubinstein disagreed on fundamental points of fact and method. How should their case be presented? Could evidence from ciphers be taken seriously? What constituted sufficient evidence? The negotiated resolution of many of these questions failed to satisfy either author. After *The Truth Will Out*, Rubinstein would collaborate again. With Dr John Casson, a 'retired psychotherapist, dramatherapist and psychodrama psychotherapist', Bill published *Sir Henry Neville Was Shakespeare*. Brenda's subsequent books, though, would all be solo projects.

Rubinstein seems to have been the main author of several parts of *The Truth Will Out*, especially the introductory chapters that locate the Nevillian thesis in the broader context of Shakespeare scholarship and heresy. The British Library catalogue, though, puts Brenda as the principal author. The book's imprint page states that the copyright rests solely with her. In both the hardback and paperback prefaces, she claims the book and the initial discovery as her own.

Many heretical tomes have appeared under little-known imprints and with the look of self-publication. A surprisingly high proportion, though, have been produced by well-known publishers. Shakespeare heretics complain that British universities maintain an embargo on heretical works, but major trade publishers abide by no such constraint. Literary agents sold the James–Rubinstein manuscript to Pearson Longman, now part of the Penguin Random House group. Pearson is a serious publisher, and the book demands to be taken seriously. Though it contains many typos, the book has a feel of quality production. Adding to the sense of weight, the endmatter stretches for 142 dense pages. Unexpectedly, the book became a bestseller.

John O'Donnell's scepticism about Shakespearean authorship had been building for decades. He could not believe spontaneous natural genius was enough to catapult the son of a provincial tradesman into the pantheon of poets and playwrights. John drew analogies from his musical studies. Bach and Mozart possessed ample reserves of genius, but also enjoyed wonderful musical educations; both had people in their lives who steered the evolution of their talent. Pure, natural genius, John thought, was not enough for someone to author Shakespeare's works. Knowledge and training were also prerequisites. John turned his sceptical eye to Shakespeare's Stratford grammar-school education. Certainly the curriculum there could not explain Shakespeare's trajectory.

Even more damaging for the Stratfordian case was John's conclusion that Shakespeare probably did not attend the school at all. When young William was of an age to attend grammar school, only one in two boys from his Stratford cohort did so, and Will's parents were broke. Illiterate John Shakespeare had risen in the Stratford community, becoming an alderman and an important local figure. If he could do that without a school education, John O'Donnell asked, then why send his son to grammar school?

O'Donnell's musical studies taught him how to gauge the personality behind the music. He could do the same with writing. Reading Bacon alongside Shakespeare, he concluded Bacon's was neither the same personality nor the same mind as Shakespeare's. The Earl of Oxford also left behind published work that John could compare with Shakespeare's. (Henry Neville did not publish at all, but left plentiful letters.) O'Donnell went online and ordered the foundation texts of the Oxfordian case. Then he read some of de Vere's own writings—and he cancelled the book order. 'This man is nothing like Shakespeare,' he said. 'Wrong voice, one dimensional, whereas Shakespeare is multi-layered.' (De Vere's odious character traits—the casual murders, the paedophilia—were further reasons to rule him out.)

O'Donnell considered other candidates. On paper, Mary Sidney had a lot going for her. She came from a literary family. She had estates on the Avon. Spenser dedicated a poem to her. She was well educated and beautiful. In Bill Bryson's words, 'All that is missing to connect her with Shakespeare is anything to connect her with Shakespeare.' So, too, for the other candidates. Every one had a fatal flaw.

And then John O'Donnell read *The Truth Will Out*. Bells rang. Pennies dropped. He could see the book's shortcomings, but was sufficiently convinced to delve deeper into the Nevillian case. He re-read the plays with Neville in mind. 'Everything began to fall into place,' he said. The other contenders had nothing on Neville. He was the state-of-the-art candidate.

O'Donnell wrote to local and international Nevillians and

other anti-Stratfordians. He formed heretical friendships with Neal Platt (as 'Neal Roberts', author of the *New York Times* bestseller *A Second Daniel: A Tudor Intrigue* (2015)) and Dr John Casson (author of *Enter Pursued by a Bear* (2009), in which he claimed to have attributed to Shakespeare another poem, another comedy and two tragedies).

At Monash, John O'Donnell befriended Mark Bradbeer, and Brenda James' co-author, Bill Rubinstein. A series of Nevillian soirees followed. At one landmark dinner in Melbourne in 2015, six heretics gathered to celebrate the four-hundredth anniversary of Neville's death. Having agreed that de Vere and Bacon suffered from 'glaring deficiencies', the diners drank the first of two toasts: to Neville as the most viable author of the Shakespeare œuvre.

The second toast acknowledged what the Nevillians were getting into. Infused with everything bad about academic politics and art-world politics and small committee politics, the field of modern Shakespeare studies is toxic. (There were bad vibes from the very start: when Garrick led the Shakespeare Jubilee, querulous literary scholars queried why an actor was in charge.) Vitriolic antipathy stands between the Stratfordians and anti-Stratfordians, and within and between the anti-Stratfordian sects. As Reginald Churchill noted in 1958, the number of authorship candidates exceeds the total number of plays and poems. There are more Shakespeare claimants than there are variant spellings of his name. The proliferation of heretical species pleases the Stratfordians: division makes the other side appear more vulnerable; and the Stratfordians like to imagine each flavour of heretic belonging to its own tailor-made compartment of Hell.

The diners raised their glasses, to 'swimming in shark-infested waters'. That year would be a good one for the cause. John Casson collaborated with Mark Bradbeer to write *Sir Henry Neville Alias William Shakespeare* (2015), a work focused on evidence in the history plays. Rare-book dealer Malcolm Moncrief-Spittle called it 'an excellent book. It seems to me that the case for Henry Neville as author is proved beyond reasonable doubt.'

John O'Donnell had already decided to swim with the sharks. He delved into authorship studies and conducted his own Nevillian research. Naturally, John adopted a musical perspective. I was at John's home in the giddy moment when he first learned that Neville had owned a lute, and may have had lute lessons in Italy. As Bill Bryson noted, the author of Shakespeare's plays knew that 'lute strings were made from cowgut and bowstrings of horsehair'.

John announced his findings at a stately mansion on Mount Macedon. (The mansion's previous owner was at the centre of a spy scandal; the building was said to be bug-wired throughout.) Interspersed with musical interludes, John's speech summarised the Nevillian case: the inadequacy of Shakespeare's education; the missing library; hints at secret authorship; the decryption of the sonnet dedication; Neville's foreign travels; the many mentions of his ancestors in Shakespeare's works; and Neville's frequent use of hendiadys, also common in Shakespeare.

Other thrilling moments would follow, such as when John shared the discovery that Neville was among the first to use the word 'refrigeration'. The most exciting moment of all, though, was when John announced the Nevillians had found a library. Neville's library. Shakespeare's library.

CHAPTER 10

Alias William Jones

The work of Bill Rubinstein and John O'Donnell on Sir Henry Neville places them in an Australian tradition of heretical Shakespearean research that stretches back well into the nineteenth century. George Caldwell achieved a world first in Melbourne when his 1877 pamphlet on Sir Walter Raleigh proposed the famous adventurer as the surreptitious poet and playwright. In the same city the Baconian Dr William Thomson produced a series of major books about the Authorship Question. His *On Renascence Drama, or History Made Visible* (1880) quoted Bacon's attitude to drama thus: 'It is a thing indeed, if practised professionally, of low repute; but if it be made a part of discipline, it is of excellent use: I mean stage-playing.' Arrogant, superior, cranky, Thomson possessed a unique ability to annoy people. He died from a kick he received from a patient. Despite his personality, he attracted in his life a devoted following of Baconian professionals, all of whom were convinced that Bacon wrote publicly as a philosopher and privately as a playwright.

In *Hits! Skits! and Jingles!* (1899) the comic balladist William Thomas Goodge produced a humorous rebuttal of the Baconian case:

> Shakespeare's the author, I'll vow,
> And nothing my faith can be shakin',
> For it would be ridiculous, now
> If we talked about 'Lamb's Tales of Bacon'.

The Melbourne-based spiritualist and distiller Hugh Junor Browne arrived at the same destination via a very different route. Browne's supernatural findings appeared in 1888 as *The Grand Reality*, followed by the 1898 pamphlet *The Baconian Authorship of Shakespeare's Plays Refuted*. The latter work included the surprising revelation that Shakespeare had composed his plays while under the control of a band of poetic spirits, led by a chief called Busiris. Thus controlled, Shakespeare could not 'blot a line'—because he lacked the skill to edit the spirits' writing.

Using the paranormal apparatus of séances, automatic writing and intermediating 'sensitives', Browne conversed extensively with Shakespeare. Revelations came thick and fast. According to Browne, the Bard spent 'his younger days on earth'

> slaughtering sheep and delivering the meat to customers, and...often in those days his hand would be controlled to write all over the skin of the sheep he had just skinned, but from his not understanding, as I and others do now, about

automatic writing through sensitives, he placed no value on what had thus been written, consequently, he added, many plays probably almost equal to any written through him in after years were in this way lost to the world.

This adds a grotesque new dimension to the authorship problem and the missing manuscripts. John Aubrey's gossipy *Brief Lives* contains a less colourful but equally doubtful farmyard anecdote. In Aubrey's tale, John Shakespeare was a butcher and young William followed in his father's trade. Whenever William killed a calf, 'he would do it in a high style, and make a speech. There was at this time another butcher's son in this town that was held not at all inferior to him for a natural wit...but he died young'. Apart from making unprecedented findings about Shakespeare, Browne also described how Mozart wrote under the control of 'spirit musicians'.

The tradition of Australian Shakespearean heresy continued into the twentieth century. The *Bulletin* magazine published heretical articles. The 'Scope' radio program hosted heretical debates. Germaine Greer's *Shakespeare's Wife* (2007) expressed a new variety of unorthodoxy, as did Christina Montgomery's *Shakespearean Afterglow* (1942), which argues that Shakespeare was a talented Latin scholar. Heretics took up Montgomery's thesis to help prove the true author must have had more than just a provincial grammar-school education.

The number of radical and unorthodox works produced in Australia seems disproportionately high. For some reason, Australians have been more willing to entertain ideas of fake authorship, misleading title pages, unscrupulous publishers; more willing to believe 'William Shakespeare' might just be an 'allonym', a brand or a catch-all for works authored by someone else, or by multiple other someones. Melbourne and Sydney are almost as far from London and Stratford as a traveller can get without leaving planet Earth. Perhaps the extreme distance permits greater neutrality, more freedom to countenance heresy. There is probably another reason as well. When it comes to authorship mysteries, Australia has seen this kind of thing before.

For a period in the 1780s, George Barrington was a principal actor in a Glasgow company. He played the male leads in *Romeo and Juliet* and *The Beggar's Opera*—until his fellow actors discovered he'd been stealing from their wardrobe. Barrington skipped town with Miss H, the young actress who'd been Juliet to his Romeo and Polly to his Macheath. On Barrington's arrival in London he resumed a prior career, that of theatrical pickpocket. We know this because several volumes of Barrington biography were published in the eighteenth and early nineteenth centuries. He became so famous that Thomas de Quincey wrote of him in *On Murder Considered as One of the Fine Arts*, likening him to Autolycus in *The Winter's Tale*, 'a snapper up of unconsidered trifles'. This would not be Barrington's only brush with Shakespearean fame.

Of all the eighteenth-century enthusiasts, the actor David Garrick was most responsible for the Incredible Growing Shakespeare. His 1769 Shakespeare Jubilee was intended as a gala event to celebrate the Bard in the town of his birth. (Baffled Stratford locals reportedly feared the event had something to do with the controversial 'Jew Bill'.) James Boswell attended the gala, mainly to have an excuse to miss an appointment for the treatment of his venereal disease. In 1776, Garrick was still riding high when he and his inseparable Viennese wife, Eva Marie, celebrated the Queen's birthday at the Royal Levee. Eva Marie wore artificial flowers and real diamonds. The Earl of Mexborough was wearing diamonds, too, in the insignia of his Order, until Barrington, disguised as a clergyman, robbed him of it in Garrick's presence. Barrington later sold the loot to a Dutch fence for eight hundred pounds.

Though Barrington sometimes stole at such special events, and at celebrated places like St Paul's Cathedral and the Houses of Parliament, London's theatres were his main hunting ground, and Covent Garden was his favourite. An unsympathetic observer described that theatre as 'swamped with thieves and prostitutes'. Barrington was one of the thieves, plying his trade in the foyer, the pit and the two-shilling gallery.

Garrick jointly managed another favoured Barrington haunt: the Drury Lane theatre where *Vortigern* had had its world premiere. Barrington was especially busy there whenever the glamorous Mrs Siddons played Lady Macbeth. In 1776 the King and Queen attended a performance at Drury Lane; at the same time, down in the pit, Barrington stole a young woman's purse. At a Haymarket opera in 1784, Barrington picked the pocket of a baronet. A year later, Barrington was apprehended after another theft during another performance of *Macbeth*. Two years later he was back at Drury Lane, where, during a performance of Sheridan's *School for Scandal*, Barrington robbed Alderman Paul Haviland le Mesurier in the presence of Major George Hanger, the social campaigner and lech who championed polygamy as an antidote to prostitution.

One of Barrington's richest prizes was a Russian snuff-box decorated with miniature pictures and large gemstones. Barrington stole it outside Covent Garden Theatre, from Count Orlov, a visiting Russian nobleman. Arrested and placed before the Bow Street magistrate, Barrington claimed to be a surgeon and a native of Cork. He denied stealing the box, which was said to be worth a stunning forty thousand pounds. Acquitted of the theft, Barrington was again apprehended two years later—after a Humane Society event—with three watches hidden in his 'well dressed' hair.

During a career in which he committed scores of other known offences, and probably hundreds of unknown ones, he seems to have partnered up with Miss Elizabeth West, a femme fatale and Fagin-like figure in London's underworld. She became his paramour and is said to have taught him much about picking pockets, and even more about the 'tender civilities' of the night. In the daylight hours she may have introduced him to high-tech tools like the whalebone drag, the ring with springs, the knife with three joints, and an ingenious variety of other keys and snags and jerks. Barrington and West's affair came to an abrupt and tragic end after she was arrested outside the Drury Lane playhouse, having stolen a watch 'after the *Oratorio*'. Locked up in the notorious Newgate prison, she caught 'gaol fever' and died just two weeks after the end of her three-year sentence.

Barrington's conduct at his frequent court appearances earned him the reputation of the 'genteelest thief'. He adopted the clothes and the demeanour of a gentleman and made *extempore* addresses to the court in a clear, eloquent and seemingly sincere manner. His theatrical training served him well: he cried real tears on demand, displayed all sorts of other dramatic flourishes, and conducted himself 'with the greatest propriety'. In the newspapers, he published ardent though spurious letters in his defence, and came to be known popularly as the 'Macaroni Pickpocket'—a reference to the flamboyantly foppish fashion adopted by the voguish young men of the day. Like the bookbinder Charles Lewis, George Barrington always dressed upward.

His trials were at least as entertaining as Covent Garden's dramatic performances. Throughout his career, his exploits were closely followed by the *Morning Post, Morning Chronicle, London*

Chronicle, London Magazine, Daily Universal Register, Gazetteer and New Daily Advertiser, Public Ledger and *World*—and were widely reported outside London as well. He was enough of a household name to earn a mention in the comic opera *Fontainebleau*. His name was also linked to a political scandal. During the grubby general election of 1784, he appeared on the satirical frontispiece of a parodic work, *The Oriental Chronicles of the Times*, written for the Whig MP Charles James Fox, whose vigorous supporter, the Duchess of Devonshire, was accused of 'trading sexual favours for votes'. Compounding the insult, the conservative *Morning Post* claimed that Barrington voted for Fox, 'at the earnest solicitation' of the Duchess.

Barrington's oratorical skills won his acquittal many times, but not every time. In a seventeen-year criminal career he spent seven years in prison. Towards the end of his career, his flamboyant ruses and excuses were wearing thin. As the heat closed in, he appeared at his second-last trial under the alias 'William Jones'. Things came to a head when Barrington was arrested after picking the pocket of Henry Hare Townsend at an Enfield race meeting. In September 1790 he was sentenced to be transported far away to the new penal colony at Port Jackson in New South Wales.

Two years after Barrington set sail, a delectable snippet reached London: the pickpocket had become a policeman. And not just any policeman, but 'Head Constable' at the satellite settlement of Parramatta. The notorious Barrington was, it seemed, one step away from becoming the new colony's chief of police! The news may have been exaggerated, but Barrington's appointment was far from impossible in a colony where former and serving convicts occupied many official positions. Whatever the truth about the anecdote, it became the catalyst for Barrington's fame as an author. The publisher H. D. Symonds issued in 1795 a work by Barrington entitled *A Voyage to New South Wales*. The book was a great success. Publishers such as 'M. Smith, Opposite Fetter-Lane, in Fleet-Street' and 'A. Swindells, Hanging Bridge' also issued Barringtonian accounts.

Writing in 1930, Barrington's biographer R. S. Lambert detailed the former pickpocket's transformation into the chronicler of Botany Bay. Barrington, Lambert wrote, 'had some skill in observation of detail, and some power of describing particular episodes [but] no talent for composition and arrangement as a whole'. It was up to Symonds in London to paper over the cracks; he did so, efficiently, and in the book's preface Barrington promised a further volume, on Norfolk Island. Plentiful Barringtonian accounts of the antipodes would follow. His literary talents extended not just to books but also pithy epigrams, and an ode, of passable poetic merit, 'to Light', and a verse prologue, 'Spoken by George Barrington, on Jan. 16, 1796, at the opening of the Theatre at Sydney, New South Wales'. Printed as a broadside in 1802, the prologue contains the oft-quoted lines, 'True patriots all—for be it understood, / We left our Country for our Country's good'.

Though uneven, Barrington's writings are vivid and engaging. Moving deftly between different styles and genres—the life story, the travel memoir, the adventure romance, mysteries, histories—Barrington produced works that appeared under such titles as *The History of New South Wales* and *The Life and Extraordinary Adventures of George Barrington, Now Transported to Botany Bay*. Some were mere pamphlets, others expensive octavo volumes with colour plates. The books were the means by which many people in England received news of the infant settlement on the other side of the globe. Barrington helped feed the huge appetite for books about natural history and the expanses of the Empire.

An important document for the birth of Sydney, Barrington's 1802 *The History of New South Wales* contained the first colour illustrations of the settlement, and one of the first printed images of a kangaroo.

John Ferguson's *Bibliography of Australia* informs us that Barrington's books made it into many of the world's great libraries. There is a copy of the 1802 *The History of New South Wales* in the Bodleian, and other volumes are held by the Mitchell Library, the British Library, the National Library of Australia and nearly every other significant collection of Australiana.

Despite these holdings, and Lambert's biography, Ferguson had his doubts. His *Bibliography* labelled nine Barrington titles 'pseud.', indicating that he thought the author's name was most likely pseudonymous. Ferguson also expressed suspicions about Barrington's authorship of the 'True Patriots All' prologue. (These were shared by Lambert, who concluded that the lines were actually written by Henry Carter.) Finally, in a separate note headed 'GEORGE BARRINGTON', Ferguson brought his findings together:

> There is little doubt that Barrington had no connexion whatever with the many publications listed, except, possibly, to a slight extent, with *A Voyage to New South Wales*, published in London in 1795, with a dedication written (allegedly) at Parramatta in 1793. His name was used by literary hacks to help sell their chap-books, and Barrington is said to have expressed indignation at the liberties taken with his name.

In *Australian Rare Books*, Jonathan Wantrup cast an even more sceptical eye, and reached a conclusion that went further than Ferguson's. 'There is no question,' Wantrup wrote, 'that all the books ascribed to Barrington are completely fraudulent and that he had no share in them.'

Thanks to the work of Ferguson, Wantrup and a young scholar named Nathan Garvey, we now know what was going on with the Barrington books. Close textual analysis shows that the books stole flagrantly from the 'foundation volumes' of Australian history—such as David Collins' *An Account of the English Colony in New South Wales* and John Hunter's *An Historical Journal of the Transactions of Port Jackson and Norfolk Island*—but also from descriptions of China, Africa and the South Pacific. To produce the Barrington books, piratical publishers adopted a crude method. Slabs of text lifted from these genuine sources were knitted together with fanciful episodes—a boy lost in the bush; a man sleeping on an ant hill; Barrington's amours with his new Juliet, a sexually curious Eora woman named Yeariana. In his Ireland *Inquiry*, Edmond Malone decried this 'modern mode of making books' in which earlier sources are 'properly sliced and hashed and stewed' before being 'served up in a late work, without any acknowledgment where the ingredients of the literary mess were found'.

Over time, the Barrington piracies became more elaborate and grandiose in their marketing and presentation. The Barrington legend grew in proportion. Nourished by injections of more and more colourful narrative twists, Barringtoniana continued to appear for another forty years. Publishers in Amsterdam, Paris, New York, Philadelphia, Moscow, Dublin and Cork issued editions of the *Voyage* and its sequel. The Russian edition, entitled *Puteschestivie w Botani-Bai*, bore the august imprint of the Moscow University Printer. Barrington the author had become world famous.

We know a lot, too, about the men behind the Barrington books. Dwelling on either side of the law, they dabbled not just in picturesque piracies but also in fantastical books on conjuring and the occult, practical books on farming and economics, and risky political volumes. The publisher-bookseller Henry Delahay Symonds—who produced the first edition of Barrington's *A Voyage to New South Wales*—was in prison when it came out. He'd been locked up for publishing radical and anti-aristocratic works. For pirates like Symonds, incarceration was no great setback. Inside Newgate they remained 'very busily employed… in the sale of books', even trumpeting their imprisonment in the advertisements for their wares.

The names 'Smith' and 'Swindells' may have hinted at specious publication, but Barrington's publishers used all the tricks in the book to make their volumes appear legitimate. One trick was to augment the texts with frontmatter and endmatter such as dedications, prologues, prefaces, appendices and indices, all of which helped create the impression of authority and authorisation. The 1802 Barrington book, *The History of New South Wales*, was the first such volume to be issued in parts; it was dedicated—speculatively, deceptively—to His Majesty, King George III, and it bore—shamelessly—the royal crest.

Relationships among publisher-booksellers, and between them and the state, were complex. Some booksellers entered joint ventures, or acted as retailers or wholesalers or fronts for others. To obtain literary properties, the booksellers and publishers shared with and stole from each other. Some partly clandestine publishers served useful political purposes by issuing polemics and importing and republishing foreign works that expressed convenient sentiments. Many publishers and booksellers engaged writers and editors who did the legwork of piracy. Part-time or full-time, settled or itinerant, criminal or just unscrupulous, all of them had a talent for fabricated narrative and literary fraud, and all belonged to a para-profession that had already enjoyed an extended history in England.

The Barrington scam, too, had a long run. Editions bearing his name and published in Boston (1832) and Lyons (1834) are, according to Garvey, 'the last known books published under Barrington's name'. By this point, Barrington had been dead thirty years, and 'further publication would probably have seemed ridiculous, even by the generous standards of the "Barrington" fraud'.

Though a vast amount has been written about Barrington's life, and though even more words have been published under his name, his true biography remains obscure. Possibly the illegitimate son of one Captain Barrington, he hailed from Cork, or Dublin, or somewhere else—perhaps Maynooth, on the edge of the picturesquely named Bog of Allen. In his youth, he may have been seduced out of an apprenticeship by a 'libidinous' young woman with the harmless-sounding name of Miss Ranby. Or perhaps he wasn't. Afterwards, he was variously said to have become a surgeon, a clergyman, a gambler, a merchant, a gamekeeper and a messenger—and it seems he adopted most of these personae as covers for his actual career.

The details of Shakespeare's early life are equally sketchy. Like Barrington's, the date and place of Shakespeare's birth are uncertain. Biographers of both men suffer from the problem of writing about people who lived long ago and were not aristocrats. Neither man was famous at birth, or during his childhood or youth, or in the early years of his career. (Shakespeare may not have been famous at any point in his lifetime.) Despite this challenge, though, we do know a few things about both lives. Curiously, there are many parallels between them.

Both men came from modest but aspirational backgrounds,

away from the metropolis. Both families were litigious and half respectable. John Shakespeare was famously fined a shilling for making a dungheap on the road outside his home. Apart from dealing in wool and leather, and piling up dung, he was an alderman and an ale-taster.

William Shakespeare's formal education, like Barrington's, was minimal and truncated. Both men fell in with groups of travelling players. Both went to London seeking fame, fortune and fun. Formidable and resilient characters, in London they moved in grimy and shady circles, changing their lodgings frequently. (What are the implications of this for Shakespeare's library? Did he send books to Stratford for safe keeping?) Both men brushed shoulders with the aristocracy, while at the same time consorting with publicans, usurers and pimps. Both established strong economic connections to the theatre. Each was accused of pretending to be a gentleman.

Barrington's criminality is well established, but Shakespeare, too, had credentials in that sphere. An ancestor, William Saksper, was hanged in 1248 for robbery. The popular tradition of young William Shakespeare the poacher has already been mentioned. In the Elizabethan social taxonomy, travelling players were grouped in the same class as vagabonds. Shakespeare consorted with many varieties of player, and knew real vagabonds as well. He had his own minor scrapes with the law, and encountered hardened criminals through known associates such as Robert Greene and George Wilkins, a playwright and brothel-keeper notorious for acts of brutal violence towards women.

Some authors have painted a thuggish and decidedly ungentle picture of Shakespeare. If accurate, that picture would explain why Michael Drayton waited a safe eleven years after Shakespeare's death before writing anything about him. When Drayton did write, he referred to Shakespeare's 'rage'. Other people, too, seem to have been genuinely worried that Shakespeare would beat them up. Though not entirely mad or bad, Shakespeare may have been dangerous to know.

Itinerant Barrington occasionally dropped off the grid: between 1773 and 1775, for example, his whereabouts are uncertain. He may have been in Dublin, operating at Rider's Theatre; by 1775, though, he was certainly back in London. Shakespeare, too, had many lost years; virtually nothing is known about where he was and what he was doing in the decade of his twenties, for example. At other times, Shakespeare like Barrington had a knack for being in two or even three places at once.

Both men were naturally talented with words and oratory; both are the subject of early anecdotes in which they are told to stop carping on. Ben Jonson remarked that loquacious Shakespeare 'had an excellent phantasy, brave notions and gentle expressions, wherein he flowed with that facility that sometimes it was necessary he should be stopped'. Both men had run-ins with unscrupulous publishers; the print culture of the late sixteenth century was even more shadowy than that of the late eighteenth. Like Barrington, Shakespeare allegedly complained about his name being applied to works he did not write. (He told Thomas Heywood, for example, that he was cross about *The Passionate Pilgrim* (1599), a book of mostly non-Shakespearean poems published by William Jaggard under Shakespeare's name.)

Both men contributed, indirectly, to the burgeoning concept of authorial copyright. Both men would eventually become famous authors, in part for writing poetry. At least one of the men was famous for poetry written by someone else.

Barrington and Shakespeare were very much alive above the ears and below the waist. They chased skirt, consorted with fallen women and were occasionally triumphant in love. Shakespeare's quasi-underworld colleague, Robert Greene, had a fully underworld mistress who rivalled Barrington's Miss West for illicit charisma. Then there is the youngish woman whom Shakespeare wooed with a chair and a bugle-bead purse.

According to the Bishop of Worcester's register, on 27 November 1582 William Shaxpere was granted a licence to marry Anne Whateley of Temple Grafton. The following day, a marriage bond was issued to William Shagspere and Anne Hathwey of Stratford. The Hathwey–Whateley difference is a puzzle. Are the two Annes the same person, the Hathwey–Whateley transformation yet another example of the Elizabethan versatility that permits Shakespeare / Shagspere / Shappere? Or were *two* women involved, in some sort of romantic intrigue? There is much speculation on this question—some authors have gone so far as to characterise one Anne as a nymphette and the other as a shrew—but no one knows for sure either way.

We do know that the marriage was ill-starred. Picture the match: William, aged eighteen-and-a-half; Anne, eight years older and three months pregnant. Two or three years after the wedding, Shakespeare moved to London. By all accounts he sowed his oats there to such an extent that he contracted more than one type of venereal disease, including syphilis, a frequent subject of his writings. (Jane Davenant, mistress of the Crown Tavern in Oxford, is one rumoured lover; her son William, the future poet laureate, inferred Shakespeare was his father in more than just a poetical sense.)

In the final years of both men's lives there would be doubts about their cerebral faculties. Scholars looking at the handwriting on Shakespeare's will noticed signs of mental, possibility syphilitic, degeneration. After Barrington's death in 1804, a newspaper announced the sale of his estate with the heading: 'Mr George Barrington, a Lunatic'. Death brought an end to neither man's publishing career.

In 2018, bibliographical scholarship has reached a point of utter certainty that Barrington was never an author, never a poet. The bookish Barrington was a phantasm constructed by the literary culture of the day. And yet, despite the efforts of Ferguson and Wantrup and Garvey, there are still pockets of belief in Barringtonian authorship. Booksellers and librarians occasionally take the books at face value. Internet sites still assign 'True Patriots All' to Barrington.

Some of the books that appeared under Shakespeare's name are universally regarded as 'allonymous'; he certainly did not write them, and unscrupulous publishers are accused of exploiting his name as a brand. The saucy *The Passionate Pilgrim* is an example of a work that suffers in this way from 'the Barrington Problem'. 'A Lover's Complaint' is another; it was included in Shakespeare's 1609 *Sonnets* but is thought to be by someone else (and is not a sonnet). In 1605 Nathaniel Butter published an unregistered play, *The London Prodigal*. Attributed to Shakespeare on the title page, the play is most likely the work of Thomas Dekker, John Fletcher, George Wilkins or Thomas Middleton. In 1608 Thomas Pavier registered and published *A Yorkshire Tragedy* under the name 'W. Shakspeare', though the play is widely thought to be by Middleton.

Unorthodox scholars, though, go much further and contend that *all* of Shakespeare's œuvre was allonymous; that, like Barrington, he authored *none* of the works; that his name was always merely a label behind which shady publishers, opportunistic compilers and secret authors lurked. Shakespearean heresy pivots on the extent to which the Barrington Problem applies to Shakespeare's works.

Shakespeare's library bulges and shrinks with the size of his authorial career. Barrington's author library was empty; if the heretics are right, Shakespeare's was empty, too. Machiavelli is mentioned three times in Shakespeare's works: in two of the *Henry VI* plays and in *The Merry Wives of Windsor*. Forgery is mentioned in *Hamlet* (remember the altered letter that dooms Rosencrantz and Guildenstern) and in *The Rape of Lucrece* ('To blot old books and alter their contents'). If Shakespeare was another Barrington—just an allonymous brand, just a gormless frontman—then there had to be a Machiavelli in the background—a cunning architect of an elaborate bibliographical hoax. How could such a thing be done? And what kind of person could pull it off?

CHAPTER 11

Emperor and Grand Lama

The story of Elizabeth Barrett Browning is one of the most touching in literature. The eldest of Edward Moulton-Barrett's twelve children, she taught herself the classics and published her own translations of Greek and Roman poetry. Forbidden by her father to marry, even in her adulthood, she fell ill—a broken blood vessel was blamed—and spent much of her life unwell and confined. When her eldest brother drowned at Torquay, she entered a long grief. At the age of thirty-nine she was still unwell, still grieving and still not allowed to marry when she began swapping letters with the poet Robert Browning. The pair met, a secret engagement followed, then a secret wedding. In 1846 they eloped to begin a new life in Italy. The lovers' fifteen joyous years of marriage ended when Elizabeth died in Robert's arms.

Recent literary historians have revised the story somewhat—Elizabeth's illness was not so severe, her father not such a tyrant, her marriage not so sublime. But the Brownings' love affair was demonstrably productive: during their courtship and marriage the pair wrote some of the most admired lines of English verse.

Shakespeare's sonnets are said to have circulated in manuscript for many years before their 1609 publication. An exceptional rarity in Shakespeare's day, the manuscript passed from reader to reader within Shakespeare's closest circle of friends. Today, the manuscript's whereabouts are unknown. It may not have survived the rise of Puritanism in the seventeenth century. One of the most magical missing books of all time, it would, if found, command a price well into the tens or even the hundreds of millions of dollars, and would be a prize perhaps second only to an autograph manuscript of *Hamlet* or *King Lear*.

Influenced by the 1609 *Sonnets*, and appreciating Shakespeare's raw passion, Elizabeth chose the sonnet form to express her love for Robert. Giving her sonnet sequence the title 'Sonnets from the Portuguese' to distract from their intensely personal character, Elizabeth had them published in 1850 as part of a collection of her poetical works. In the 1890s, further details of the sonnets' history came to light. The 1850 appearance was not, it seemed, the true first edition.

Literary heavyweight and occasional Shakespearean Edmund Gosse recounted in 1894 'a very pretty episode in literary history'.

[The young couple's custom was] to write alone, and not to show each other what they had written...One day, early in 1847, their breakfast being over, Mrs Browning went upstairs, while her husband stood at the window watching the street till the table should be cleared. He was presently aware of someone behind him, though the servant was gone. It was Mrs Browning, who held him by the shoulder to prevent his turning to look at her, and at the same time pushed a packet of papers into the pocket of his coat. She told him to read that and to tear it up if he did not like it; and then she fled again to her own room.

Mr Browning seated himself at the table and unfolded the parcel. It contained the series of sonnets which have now become so illustrious. As he read, his emotion and delight may be conceived. Before he had finished it was impossible for him to restrain himself, and, regardless of his promise, he rushed upstairs and stormed that guarded citadel. He was early conscious that these were treasures not to be kept from the world; 'I dared not reserve to myself,' he said, 'the finest sonnets written in any language since Shakespeare's.' But Mrs Browning was very loth indeed to consent to the publication of what had been the very notes and chronicle of her betrothal.

At length she was persuaded to permit her friend, Miss Mary Russell Mitford, to whom they had originally been sent in manuscript, to pass them through the press…Accordingly, a small volume was printed, entitled Sonnets / by E.B.B. / Reading / Not for Publication / 1847 / an octavo of 47 pages.

That little pamphlet became one of the most sought-after modern rarities. Collectors in Britain and America climbed over each other to own a copy from an impression that numbered as few as thirty. When copies came on the market in the first decades of the twentieth century, they changed hands for high prices—as much as US$1250 at auction in America. In his 1918 work, *A Bibliography of the Writings in Prose and Verse of Elizabeth Barrett Browning*, the eminent bookman Thomas J. Wise confirmed the

1847 *Sonnets'* status as the cornerstone of any Browning collection. Wise included in the bibliography the story of how he himself came to own a copy of the rare pamphlet.

> Dr W. C. Bennett, who had been Miss Mitford's intimate friend...disposed of some ten or twelve copies of the *Sonnets* which he had received from her hands. In one of these copies, evidently the one dedicated by Miss Mitford to her own use, was inserted a manuscript of *Future and Past*... This copy, with the manuscript sonnet inserted, I purchased from Dr Bennett; it is one of my most valued possessions.

A short and gouty Honorary Fellow of Oxford's Worcester College, Wise had climbed from humble origins to stand at the very top of the book world. Bibliographer of Ruskin, Swinburne, Tennyson, Coleridge, Wordsworth, the Brontës, Conrad, Keats and both Brownings. Collector of and dealer in Elizabethan and Jacobean plays. Member of the Roxburghe Club; Friend of the Bodleian; President of the Bibliographical Society; Secretary of the Shelley Society; devotee of the Browning Society.

Wise assembled a spectacular collection of books and called it the Ashley Library. With a scope that stretched back to Elizabethan times, the collection was widely regarded as the best library of English literature in non-institutional hands. Gosse called it 'the finest private library in the kingdom'. It was remarkably strong in literary manuscripts and the rarest printed editions. For people in the book world, Wise was a force to be reckoned with. Under the Ashley Library imprint he issued bibliographies and 'private printings of choice unpublished things' for connoisseurs and bibliophiles. His bibliographies were monoliths: unshakeably authoritative and eminently reliable. Ever-ready to call out bibli-ographical deceptions—'"fakes" are to him what rats are to a terrier', Gosse wrote—he jumped hard and fast on any upstarts who dared disagree with his bibliographical pronouncements and methods.

There was something fishy, though, about the 1847 *Sonnets*. Despite the personal content and the romantic backstory, not one of the copies was inscribed by the author. All the copies looked remarkably crisp, and recent. Supposedly circulating since the middle of the century, they lacked any kind of sale record before the 1890s. And they bore a family resemblance to other first-edition pamphlets in recent circulation, all of them with early dates, none with the expected inscriptions or bookplates or signs of age. Those pamphlets included works by other respected nineteenth-century authors: Matthew Arnold, George Eliot, William Morris, Algernon Charles Swinburne, John Ruskin, Lord Alfred Tennyson. Even though Wise had endorsed the 1847 *Sonnets* by including them in his Barrett Browning bibliography, the young bookseller John Carter heard rumours that cast doubt on the *Sonnets'* credibility. He asked about the volume at Quaritch's bookshop, and received the reply: 'It is a book we don't much care for.'

With his bookseller colleague Graham Pollard, and using Malone-like rigour and methods, Carter embarked on a thorough investigation of the 1847 *Sonnets*. Carter and Pollard studied the book's typography, paper, provenance, contents, publication history and sale history. In 1934 the booksellers published their electrifying findings under a consciously Malonite title: *An Enquiry into the Nature of Certain Nineteenth Century Pamphlets*. The 1847 edition of the *Sonnets*, they discovered, was just one part of an audacious program of forgeries.

The method of production was ingenious. Using unsuspecting mainstream printers such as Richard Clay & Sons, the forger or forgers selected well-known texts, then re-set and re-printed them with falsely dated title pages and with bogus publishing imprints. The false dates created 'pre-firsts' that cashed in on the Dibdin-inspired appetite for first editions. The scam was more sophisticated than Ireland's, and much harder to detect, though easier to repeat. The falsely dated new editions could not be compared to 'genuine' examples, because there were none. To help legitimise the books, the forgers placed them in major institutional collections such as the British Museum, the Cambridge University Library and the Bodleian.

The *Enquiry* ignited an explosive exposure. Not only were the books forgeries, but the perpetrator was none other than the great bibliographer himself, the Ashley Librarian, the doyen of literary society, Thomas Wise. Seemingly respectable Wise was in fact as much a thief as Barrington. The Marquess of Blandford would not be the only Roxburghe member to bring disgrace on the Club.

Wise had perpetrated the fraud with a co-conspirator, Harry Buxton Forman, the author of another Barrett Browning bibliography, *Elizabeth Barrett Browning and Her Scarcer Books* (privately printed, 1896). At the beginning of their fraud, the forgers experimented with a variety of scams and formats before settling on their method. Their very first forgery—*Galatea Secunda*, by the manqué poet and Shakespeare editor Richard Hengist Horne—was a broadside with a fake Melbourne imprint. Up to a hundred Wise–Forman forgeries followed, many with equally false imprints. The forgery of Matthew Arnold's *St Brandan*, for example, identifies its publisher as 'E. W. & A. Skipwith' and its printer as 'J. S. Seaton & Co.' Both firms were entirely made up. Statements of rarity were also falsified. The editions were not so small as claimed; copies of the 'rarest' Wisean pamphlets turn up surprisingly often.

A key part of Wise and Forman's M.O. was to include the forgeries in their bibliographies. Reading them now, and seeing how prominently the forgeries appear there, it is hard not to think that the bibliographies were produced for the sole purpose of furthering the scam.

Typographical analysis played a large part in the exposure. Carter and Pollard noticed that many of the circulating modern pamphlets had been printed in the same typeface, and that one piece of type was a misfit: a broken-backed 'f', which showed that the different volumes, supposedly produced by different printers over a span of decades, had actually been made at the one printery. The crime writer Dorothy L. Sayers suggested an alternative title for the *Enquiry*: 'The Case of the Crook-backed F'. To the typographical evidence Carter and Pollard added a forensic analysis of the pamphlets' paper; it contained esparto grass and 'chemical wood', not used in papermaking at the purported dates of many of the pamphlets.

Wise tried to defend himself in a letter to the *Times Literary Supplement*. He also changed his story about the 1847 *Sonnets*, in an attempt to shift blame towards Buxton Forman, who had died in 1917, and away from Dr Bennett, whose family were close to the formidable bookman Sydney Cockerell.

> I will now consider the theory of unauthorised printing. With whom could this have originated? One name must be cleared out of the way at once:...In the introduction to 'A Browning Library,' 1929, writing forty-three years after the event, I told the story of a visit to W. C. Bennett in 1886, and said that I acquired my two copies of the 1847 book from him... What I actually brought away with me was his own sonnets, 'My Sonnets,' privately printed at Greenwich in 1843. The confusion of two such books may seem incredible, even after

thirty-six years. It is to be explained by the subjects of our conversation: his friendship with Mary Russell Mitford, our common interest in the Brownings, Mrs Browning's association with Miss Mitford and the presence among his poems of two sonnets, one on Robert and the other on E. B. Browning, and the mention of both of them in yet another sonnet. In size and outward appearance the two books are almost identical.

My two copies came to me not from W. C. Bennett but from Harry Buxton Forman. From whom did he obtain them? Neither I nor his son Mr Maurice Buxton Forman can tell with any certainty.

Wise's squirming revision drew ridicule. Writing as 'Richard Gullible', Richard Jennings produced new versions of Wise's account and retraction.

I had agreed, one memorable evening, to dine with my dear old friend, Clem Stunter, whom you may remember as the author of *Banjo Ditties* and *Odes for Bargees*. Clem, I well remember, lived on the banks of Thames Reach near Rotherhithe. So, immediately after the opening of the pork shops in Whitechapel Highway, I picked up Clem not far from Clink Street and we made our way merrily enough— for the gin palaces were then not closed at fixed hours—to my old friend's neat villa down Wapping Stairs. After a savoury meal of tripe and onions, washed down with a mug of double Bass, I saw Mrs Clem, who was bending over the washer, taking something out of her hair. 'Curl papers, mother?' said my dear old pal laughingly. And in high good humour his faithful wife untwisted from her head this very poem which I now transcribe...'Why, Clem,' I remember saying, 'this may be Browning.' 'It might be blacking for all I care,' he jovially answered, and added: 'How much?' He had no bank account, hadn't Clem; so, placing a sovereign on the kitchen dresser—we were of course on the gold standard in those days—I came away the proud possessor of what I am convinced is an unpublished poem by the Mark Tapley of English verse.

Jennings added a Wisean postscript:

Since I communicated the poem to Mr Carter I have become increasingly uncertain whether I did, in fact or fiction, receive this most interesting copy of verses from the late Mr Stunter. More and more vividly, as I sit thinking of it, it comes over me that all I bought of my good friend Clem, in those days or nights, was a limited issue—an issue limited, I think he told me, to 10,500 copies—of my dear pal's lively volume *Crumpets for Crimps*. This was a sizeable tome illustrated with colour plates by my aged Chum's 'Old Dutch' as he used to call her...I had much difficulty in squeezing the volume into the capacious pocket of my Macfarlane, as I made my way home to tell my fellow-collectors the good news. From whom then—you may ask—did I receive the poem by R. B.? It was (if an old man's memory may be trusted) from a friend of a friend of the late Sir Edmund Gosse's friend of the Poet. His name escapes me. But in those jolly days we were all friends together.

Giving a false account of *Sonnets from the Portuguese* was one of several ways in which Edmund Gosse became embroiled in the Wise affair. He was entangled to such an extent that American writers would accuse him of being a primary co-conspirator with Wise and Forman in the forgeries.

Some years after the *Enquiry* was published, a letter came to light that supplied the final, definitive proof of Wise and Forman's guilt. Now referred to as the Pforzheimer Document, the letter captures an argument in which Forman accuses Wise of being dishonestly vague about the number of copies of his semi-legitimate Ashley Library publications. Wise answers, 'Quite so. And we print "Last Tournament" in 1896, and want "someone to think" it was printed in 1871! The moral position is exactly the same!'

Wise's deception seems shocking in its scale, and even more so against his respectable veneer. But Wise was just the latest version of a criminal type. He was the latest update of John Payne Collier.

In 1806, at the age of seventeen, Collier bought a Third Folio in Baldwin's Gardens. 'I fancied it the First Edition and a great prize,' he later wrote. In 1808 he joined his father as a reporter at *The Times*. A friend of John Keats and other famous poets and authors, Collier was doing well at *The Times* until he misreported a parliamentary speech. This and other missteps led him to move to the *Morning Chronicle*. A law reporter by day, in the evenings he pursued his love of books.

Inspired by Drake's *Shakespeare and His Times*, Collier published *Poetical Decameron* (1820) in which he opined on Elizabethan and Jacobean literature, including Shakespeare's sources; he analysed Barnaby Riche's *Farewell to Military Profession* as a source for *Twelfth Night*, for example. The public largely neglected his writings until, in 1831, he issued *The History of English Dramatic Poetry to the Time of Shakespeare*. Collier's ambition, like Steevens', was to outdo Malone. The *History* was well received; the Duke of Devonshire liked it so much he gave its author a hundred pounds and appointed him paid curator and adviser to the library at Devonshire House.

Collier was now respectable. He joined the Garrick Club and the Society of Antiquaries, and co-founded the Shakespeare Society. He met a legion of aristocratic bibliophiles. The Earl of Ellesmere gave him unfettered access to the collection of Elizabethan and Jacobean papers at Bridgewater House. Some of the papers were still in bundles last tied up in the seventeenth century. For Collier, equipped with such new friends and new income and old documents, Shakespearean discoveries were inevitable. In 1835 he published *New Facts Regarding the Life of Shakespeare*, in which he thanked the Earl for having 'laid open the manuscript stores of his noble family with a liberality worthy of his rank and race'.

The revelations in *New Facts* were many: precise details of Shakespeare's first decade in the theatre, even details of his wardrobe and shareholdings; a letter from Henry Wriothesley to an Ellesmere ancestor; a royal patent for a children's theatre. Further Collier publications would follow, some of them auspiced by the Shakespeare Society and all containing new insights and titbits.

By now, the pattern is sounding appallingly familiar, echoing not just Wise but also William-Henry Ireland. Collier was of course a fraud, more competent than Ireland but no less devious. The Shakespeare Society was a legitimate-seeming front for sundry criminal enterprises. Small and large falsehoods filled Collier's *History*, *New Facts* and subsequent editorial efforts. Frustrated, like Ireland, by the lack of Shakespearean documentary evidence, he had manufactured it. There were multiple strings to his forger's bow. The children's patent and some of the letters were written from scratch on leaves removed from old books. (Hugh Junor Browne was one of the dupes taken in by Collier's Wriothesley–Ellesmere letter.) Other letters were original but with new interlineations.

James Halliwell issued his *Observations on the Shak̰sperian Forgeries at Bridgewater House* in 1853. This denounced Collier's discoveries but stopped short of accusing Collier of forgery. The end for Collier's credibility came when people looked more closely at the Perkins Second Folio.

Supposedly bought for thirty shillings from a country library sale, the book contained thousands of annotations that looked to have been made at an early date. The book was incomplete, dog-eared and dirty; stained by 'wine, beer and other liquids'; burned here and there by 'the lighted snuff of a candle, or by the ashes of tobacco'. Speculating that the book had been owned by a careless descendant of Richard Perkins, who acted in Marlowe's *The Jew of Malta* in 1632, Collier suggested that the many annotations were made by someone with access to early, 'purer' versions of Shakespeare's plays, perhaps manuscripts prepared for performances in the Bard's lifetime. Here, then, was a hint as to the use and perhaps even the whereabouts of Shakespeare's library.

Literary detective Andrew Brae was unconvinced, and he said so, naming Collier in an 1855 public letter entitled 'On Literary Cookery'. Collier sued for libel, swearing that he had not inserted 'a single word, stop, sign, note, correction, alteration or emendation' that had not been added soon after the Second Folio's publication. The legal action petered out but further problems soon arrived. Sir Frederic Madden, the foremost palaeographer of the era, took a look at the Folio. For Madden, the chicanery was obvious immediately. Not only was the handwriting wrong, but he could see, partly erased, the modern pencil marks that the forger had laid down to guide his pen. Chemical testing by a mineralogist confirmed that the pencil marks were beneath the ink notes, and that the ink was not ink at all but a modern watercolour formulation.

Madden and his assistant, Nicholas Hamilton, were now sure that Collier had written both the pencil notes, which were clearly in his handwriting, and the final annotations. Collier's jig was up. In another homage to Edmond Malone, Hamilton published the results of his and Madden's research as the 1860 *Inquiry into the Genuineness of the Manuscript Corrections in Mr J. Payne Collier's Annotated Shakespeare, Folio, 1632; and of Certain Shakespearian Documents Likewise Published by Mr Collier.*

Unlike Carter and Pollard, Hamilton named the forger in his *Inquiry*. Collier's conduct after his exposure followed a pattern painfully similar to Wise's. Make hopeless counterblows. Issue ridiculous and elaborate defences. Call on a dwindling number of influential friends for support. Fire barbs at deserting former friends. Do not repent.

Just as some of Shakespeare's earliest books suffer from the Barrington Problem, so, too, some suffer from the Wise Problem.

In 1619, three years after Shakespeare's death and just four years before the First Folio, William Jaggard printed a collected edition of Shakespeare's plays. Only ten plays were included: *Henry V*; *King Lear*; *The Merchant of Venice*; *The Merry Wives of Windsor*; *A Midsummer Night's Dream*; *Pericles, Prince of Tyre*; *Sir John Oldcastle*; *A Yorkshire Tragedy*; and *The Whole Contention Between the Two Famous Houses, Lancaster and York*—the latter a joining of two playtexts, the early versions of *II Henry VI* and *III Henry VI*.

Not all of the plays are strictly Shakespearean. *Sir John Oldcastle* appeared in the second printing of the Shakespeare Third Folio but is currently thought to be a collaborative work, executed by several authors, none of whom was Shakespeare. *A Yorkshire Tragedy*, too, belongs to the 'Shakespeare Apocrypha';

as already noted, it is thought to have been written by Thomas Middleton. *Pericles, Prince of Tyre* is now regarded as at least partly Shakespearean, though it was excluded from the First Folio. George Wilkins was probably the play's principal co-author.

In the production of the 1619 edition, Jaggard seems to have collaborated with the stationer Thomas Pavier to print the plays in a large quarto format. This seemingly benign project was actually an extremely curious one. In a mysterious Wisean move, Jaggard and Pavier printed six of the ten plays with false title-page dates: not 1619 but 1600, 1608 or 1609. Jaggard and Pavier also used false imprints: four of the plays were falsely attributed to other named stationers. For these reasons, the 1619 collected edition is known as the 'False Folio'. (At least one edition of *Venus and Adonis* also appeared with a false title-page date. Burton's copy, now in the Bodleian, purports to be an edition from 1602, but was in fact printed in 1607 or 1608.)

What were Jaggard and Pavier up to? Falsely dating the plays may have been a way to more safely print content that the publishers did not own. It may have been a ruse to make the plays seem more authoritative, more antiquarian, closer to the author—perhaps in a pre-Dibdinian exercise in first-edition mongering. The false imprints may have been an attempt to make the new quartos look more like the originals. Or the whole thing could have been a stunt to stoke interest in the forthcoming First Folio, which Jaggard would soon print and publish. (Jaggard had already printed the allonymous, Barringtonian *The Passionate Pilgrim* as Shakespeare's in 1599 and again in 1612, and had printed at least one genuinely Shakespearean quarto play.)

Today, only two complete copies of the False Folio are known to have survived; they are held by the Folger and the Special Collections of Texas Christian University. Other libraries, including the British Library, hold individual Jaggard–Pavier quartos. At the start of the twentieth century, Shakespeare scholar and Keeper of Printed Books at the British Museum Alfred William Pollard was the first to analyse the False Folio in any detail. He, like everyone since, could not provide a satisfactory answer as to what was going on.

Fake first editions were not Thomas Wise's only scam. Unlike Ireland, Wise never tried to forge a Jacobean play; instead, he tore out leaves from genuine editions.

After Wise died in 1937, the British Museum purchased the Ashley Library from his widow for £66,000. The Museum had for many years been aware of thefts from its holdings of seventeenth-century plays—plays such as Middleton's *Family of Love* (1608), Jonson's *The Case Is Alter'd* (1609) and John Webster's *The Devils Law-case* (1623). The Ashley copy of *The Case Is Alter'd* gave the game away. Four leaves at the end had been inlaid and repaired. One of the two Museum copies lacked precisely those four leaves, and had been cropped precisely where the Ashley copy was restored. A title leaf in the Museum copy had also been stolen; that leaf, with the same pattern of restoration, was also found in the Ashley copy.

This discovery was the catalyst for a wider search of the Ashley acquisitions. In 1956 bibliographer D. F. Foxon announced the results of the search: a substantial number of leaves stolen from early seventeenth-century plays in the British Museum had been found in the Ashley Library copies of the same plays.

For this part of his scam, Wise's method was crudely simple. Alfred W. Pollard was Wise's friend and fellow bookman. Pollard authored an introduction for a volume of Wise's magnum opus, the eleven-volume *Ashley Library Catalogue* (1922–36).

The following year he wrote to Wise, praising him as the 'One Provident Man who has been buying and buying the right things'. In his role as Keeper of Printed Books, Pollard accepted Wise's forged modern pamphlets into the British Museum's collections, thereby helping to legitimise them. He also gave Wise privileged access to the same collections. 'Trusted readers' of Wise's apparent standing were allowed to keep books out on a reserved desk; no one checked to see if Wise took the books home overnight. Overawed junior members of the Museum's staff left him alone in the alcoved 'Large Room'.

Using these privileges, Wise stole leaves and added them to plays he already owned. Some of the stolen leaves enlarged and improved the Ashley Library's holdings; some helped to make up copies for sale to Wise's main American customer, John Henry Wrenn; and other thefts enhanced copies for sale to other collectors. Thus engaged in a commercial operation, Wise mistreated his customers as much as he mistreated the books. The most inferior leaves—those that were stained, creased, cropped, wormed or worn—ended up in the Wrenn copies, while the cleaner and crisper leaves were used in the Ashley copies. The wreckage was devastating. Pristine, complete and exceptionally rare copies were cut up and blended together to make mongrel editions. Wise added, for example, a third-edition title page to a rare first-edition play because the later title page was cleaner. In this way, he destroyed the books' bibliographical integrity.

Today, retracing and unravelling Wise's vandalism requires a delicate effort of matching: lining up torn pages like a seventeenth-century jigsaw puzzle; matching stains; matching 'stab holes' from where pamphlet pages were sewn together with thread; matching ancient worm-holes, an infallible method due to the idiosyncrasy of the holes. Different plays were printed on different paper, as evidenced by watermarks and 'chain lines'. When making up composite volumes, Wise did not attempt to match paper. Today, mismatched watermarks and lines are another giveaway of Wise's handiwork, and another guide for the curators who try to make restorative matches. Mixed feelings confront those curators: each mating is a happy reunion, but also painful proof of the scale of Wise's crimes.

Of the 206 leaves first discovered as stolen from the Museum's early quartos, eighty-nine were found in Ashley copies and sixty in Wrenn copies. These numbers have continued to rise as more of Wise's thefts have come to light.

Just as Wise had antecedents as a forger, he also had them as a thief.

James Halliwell was an accomplished Shakespearean scholar and antiquarian. In 1848 he published a *Life of Shakespeare*. Other projects included his limited folio edition (150 copies) of Shakespeare's works; his *Descriptive Calendar of the Ancient Manuscripts and Records in the Possession of the Corporation of Stratford-upon-Avon*; a *History of New Place*; and his campaign to buy Shakespeare's 'home' (a nineteenth-century counterfeit of the sixteenth-century original) for the Stratford municipality. A bit-part player in Collier's exposure, Halliwell made an appalling return to the stage when he himself was exposed as England's most deplorable nineteenth-century thief of valuable books and manuscripts.

Like Wise, Halliwell had enjoyed privileged access to the best libraries—until people started noticing things going missing. Invited at the age of twenty-one to visit the wonderful library of the great bibliophile Sir Thomas Phillipps, Halliwell was as impressed by the library as he was by Phillipps's daughter

Henrietta. Or perhaps Halliwell thought marriage to Henrietta would be a way to win both prizes.

An engagement quickly followed. But when Phillipps learned that Halliwell had been accused of stealing manuscripts from Trinity College, Cambridge, the horrified bibliophile refused to bless the marriage. (An anonymous letter challenged Phillipps to ask Halliwell 'where those valuable books came from that were sold by Sotheby two years ago, to save him from a prison'.) The couple eloped; Henrietta was cut off irrevocably; and Phillipps launched a sadistic public campaign to destroy what remained of Halliwell's reputation. Halliwell, though, had a mad streak as well, and did much to darken his own name. On the way out of Sir Thomas's mansion he seems to have taken away not just the baronet's daughter but also his most valuable book—a first printing of *Hamlet* (1603), one of only two known copies. Halliwell sold the *Hamlet* to the British Museum, but not before mutilating it by removing its title page. In Halliwell's career as a thief, he stole thousands of books and manuscripts.

In 1932 E. V. Lucas recalled how Halliwell, in a candid moment at the age of about sixty, elucidated his attitude to rare books and documents: 'If he ever chanced to see anything in anyone else's house or in a museum that he thought he was more worthy to possess…he had no scruples about taking it.' Halliwell also had a grievous habit of cutting up seventeenth-century books and pasting their dismembered parts into scrapbooks. He did this hundreds of times. For librarians and curators and scholars, Halliwell's crimes pose a reunion challenge that is even more dispiriting than Wise's.

The book world struggles with the Wise case. In some circles, an interest in Wise's productions is frowned upon. They make bibliographers and booksellers nervous. They are difficult to catalogue. Booksellers feel leery about knowingly selling forger-ies. Uncomfortable reminders of a dark episode, the books show how frothy and precarious the book market can be, especially the market for 'first editions'. They also show up the fallibility, even the gullibility, of 'experts'. Some booksellers refuse to deal with the books at all. The book trade's convulsions and conniptions about Wise and his forgeries are a small taste of how the trade would react to proof that Shakespeare's works were a colossal hoax.

A surprisingly high number of booksellers, though, still approach the Wise pamphlets naively, buying and selling them on the basis that they are what they say they are. This presents an opportunity for book dealers because, perversely, the forgeries are now worth much more than the real thing. Who wants to pay good money these days for a Matthew Arnold first edition, for example, or a Ruskin? But a Wise forgery, now that's interesting. When I was a graduate student, that wrinkle in the market was very welcome. Wise's creation of bogus imprints is a boon on the internet, where books can be searched by publisher or printer. Worth more than ten times the books they purport to be, bargain-priced forgeries are only a keyword search away.

In their early decades, the forgeries conspicuously lacked a sale record. They certainly have one now. In 2005 John Carter's own copy of the 1847 *Sonnets* sold at Christie's for US$19,200 against an estimate of US$5000 to US$7000.

For the search for Shakespeare's library, the lessons from the Wise case are salutary. Don't take at face value any book's cover, endpapers, dedication, title page, imprint page, preliminary matter, contents, endmatter or provenance. Beware of book-world bullies and blowhards. Scoundrels like Wise, Forman, Collier and Halliwell set back the search for Shakespeare's library, but also equipped us with new tools and sharper eyes. The outing of Wise as a fraudster enabled a new generation of book detectives to take Edmond Malone's investigative methods to a whole new level.

Editor Wilfred Partington called Wise the 'Emperor and Grand Lama of Forgers'. Collier, Halliwell and Wise vie for the title of Most Audacious Nineteenth-Century Book Fraudster. If Shakespearean authorship is a hoax, men such as these, and those behind the Barrington fraud, reveal the possible mentality of the hoaxsters, and hint at how the fraud might have been executed. The Pforzheimer Document set a new benchmark of proof for all bibliomysteries, including the Shakespeare Authorship Question and the mystery of his missing library. Will someone one day come forward with a succinct and authoritative document that gives away a Shakespearean conspiracy? Brenda James and Bill Rubinstein believe they have done just that.

CHAPTER 12

The Conspiracy

The success of *The Truth Will Out* filled the Nevillian camp with confidence. A dozen books followed, all of them further detailing the compelling case for Neville authorship. Brenda James launched an online Neville–Shakespeare journal for scholarly papers and updates on Nevillian research. One after another, the Nevillians found books, letters and manuscripts that buttressed their case and showed Neville's hand in the creation of the greatest works of literature.

The *Sir Thomas More* manuscript, with additions evidently not by Shakespeare but by Neville, was a key discovery. Other treasures from Neville's library at Billingbear reveal his facility with living and dead Continental languages: a 1518 volume of Ovid that contains *Ars Amatoria* and a commentary in Latin; a volume of Dionysius of Halicarnassus on Roman history (1546, in Greek, annotated by Neville in his youth); Giovanni Tommaso Minadoi's *Historia della Guerra Fra Turchi et Persiani* (1594, in Italian); Jorge de Montemayor's *Diana Enamorada* (1574, in Spanish); and a copy of *Ptolemiæi Astronomi* (1538, annotated by Neville in Latin and Greek).

Highlights from Neville's collection of English books and manuscripts reveal a sound literary sensibility and strong literary connections. A handwritten copy of the banned 'Leicester's Commonwealth'. A copy of Thomas Mille's *Catalogue of Honor*, printed by Jaggard, 1610 (Neville's copy appears to be a proof version with pre-publication corrections). A rare manuscript of John Lydgate's *Fall of Princes*. Sir Thomas Hoby's translation of Baldassare Castiglione's *The Courtier*, 1561 (Hoby married Neville's aunt). Edward Hall's *The Union of the Two Noble and Illustre Families of Lancastre and Yorke*, 1542. And in all likelihood another key Shakespearean source, Holinshed's *Chronicles*, 1587, edited by John Hammond, Thomas Randolph and Sir Henry Killigrew (Neville's father-in-law).

Nevillians such as Mark Bradbeer, John Casson and Bill Rubinstein shared the priceless, exultant experience of handling the books that were used to write Shakespeare's poems and plays. The authenticity of that experience, though, depends on the case for Nevillian authorship. *The Truth Will Out* announced that the case was made; that the Authorship Question had been answered in favour of Neville. The announcement was premature.

Aristocratic. Born out of wedlock. Overweight all his life. The Henry Neville who emerges from James and Rubinstein's book is an English archetype: the fat bastard. A key plank of the Nevillian case is that Sir Henry's life aligns closely with the contents of Shakespeare's plays and the sequence in which they were written: 'The known facts of Neville's life consistently match the accepted chronology of Shakespeare's works in a way which is so precise, and so helpful in illuminating why the works of "Shakespeare" were written, that they simply cannot be coincidental.' In more than one important respect, that claim is false.

After four centuries of scholarship and speculation, the chronology of Shakespeare's plays is still unsettled. There are good reasons for this. Each play went through multiple performed versions, and often multiple printed versions. Pinning a play to a specific moment in time is difficult, if not impossible. Shakespeare's liberal use of literary sources further complicates things. Some of his sources were prior plays whose performance histories blended into those of the Shakespearean versions. To date the plays, editors and scholars look for references to trials, rebellions, invasions, shipwrecks, tempests. Such references are only partly helpful: many are cryptic, supporting diverse readings.

From contemporary documents it is possible to assemble a record of when the plays were performed, but that record, too, is imprecise. Dutch and Swiss tourists are among the audience members who penned some of the best evidence about what was performed when. The brief information they left behind—play titles, venues, impressions—is helpful but inconclusive. Different playwrights used the same titles for different plays, for example, so it is hard to tell if a note about 'Hamlet' is referring to a Shakespearean performance or not.

The publication record of Shakespeare's plays is also sketchy. To squeeze the best performance value from the playtexts, owners typically delayed publication by a matter of years. Nineteen of the thirty-six First Folio plays did not appear in print at all during

Shakespeare's lifetime. (*Othello* first appeared in print in 1622, six years after the Bard's death.) When quarto editions did appear, not all of them were registered with the Stationers' Company. Some were produced in small numbers and may have circulated privately. There are intriguing hints that lost quarto editions— books that have not survived to the present day—pre-date the earliest known copies. None of these facts helps us to lock down the chronology.

Despite this uncertainty, James and Rubinstein pretend the chronology is final and fixed. They then proceed to align a version of it with the details of Neville's biography. More than once, the purported alignment is delightfully wacky.

A passage in *Macbeth* (act 1, scene 6) refers to weather and birds:

Duncan: This castle hath a pleasant seat; the air
Nimbly and sweetly recommends itself
Unto our gentle senses.
Banquo: This guest of summer,
The temple-haunting martlet does approve.

The sweet mild air, so the co-authors argue, is a real but unexpected feature of Scotland; to know about it, the writer must have travelled there. Neville certainly did so. James and Rubinstein think, more-over, that the reference to a martlet is telling: 'It is…typical of a Neville to notice birds—his father even made a specific point of mentioning his falcon in his will, while over the centuries Neville's descendants kept birds which they had stuffed because they could not bear to part with them when they died.' This last sentence about Nevillian bird noticers and stuffers breaks every rule of evidence. Another arresting example: Neville was lame, had gout and knew people who had the plague; *Measure for Measure* refers to sciatica of the hip and other unnamed diseases; ergo Neville must have written it. This style of anti-logic is emblematic of the book as a whole.

James and Rubinstein are at their weakest when they attempt literary readings of the plays. Their main takeaway from *The Merchant of Venice* is that 'business and friendship can be mixed together successfully'. To that idiosyncratic interpretation they append a quaint coda: 'This was a typically Nevillian stance in real life too.' Later, they mount a similar argument about Neville and Horace. They quote the 1974 *Encyclopaedia Britannica* on how 'Horace's fame rests chiefly upon the likable person revealed in his works...As time went on he became convinced that the good poet must first be a good man and useful to the community as educator and civiliser.' At the end of the quotation, the co-authors state: 'It is startling that everything written above applies so exactly to Neville.' Astrologers and fortune-tellers invented this technique. Horace provides a horoscope that fits Neville exactly: he is a good person, but under-appreciated.

Often, the purported alignment between Neville and the plays is absent altogether. In Neville's lifetime, the Puritans became more and more powerful. An austere offshoot of the Church of England, they despised the theatre, seeing 'the daily and disorderly exercise of a number of players and playing houses' as both a cause and a symptom of moral degradation. London's Lord Mayor agreed, writing to the Archbishop of Canterbury in 1592:

[The city's youth are] greatly corrupted and their manners infected with many evil and ungodly qualities, by reason of the wanton and profane devices represented on the stages... To which places also do usually resort great numbers of light and lewd disposed persons, as harlots, cutpurses, cozeners, pilferers and suchlike, and there, under the colour of resort to

those places to hear the plays, devise divers evil and ungodly
matches, confederacies and conspiracies.

Like many people connected with the theatre, Shakespeare
opposed Puritanism with his pen and in his bones. In *Measure
for Measure* he attacked the excesses of Puritanical extremism.
Sir Henry Neville, in contrast, was called 'a great puritan' by a
contemporary detractor, and sided with the Puritans whenever it
was politically to his benefit.

Other apparent contradictions are equally stark. Neville was
still grieving when, three months after the death of his father,
the long Shakespearean love-poem *Venus and Adonis* was registered with the Stationers' Company. Conservative in spirit,
Shakespeare's plays convey a patriotic respect for royal institutions
and authority; yet Neville was implicated in the Essex Rebellion.

Awkwardly for James and Rubinstein, *The Merry Wives
of Windsor* was registered while Neville was imprisoned in
the Tower. The co-authors describe Neville's internment as a
harrowing experience in which he was 'depressed and conceivably suicidal'; and yet elsewhere they characterise it as a period
of 'leisure time' in which he was disposed to write comedic plays
and romantic verse. Such clashes are no obstacle for James and
Rubinstein. They power on, turning contradiction into confirmation. The imprisoned Neville indulged in a kind of gallows
humour: 'Conceivably, Neville wished to escape his misery with
ribald, subversive, slapstick comedy, although facing the prospect
of being hanged, drawn and quartered.'

Many of the Shakespeare plays were written in the 1590s
and 1600s. When Neville was supposedly busy as a clandestine
playwright, he had a lot of other things on the go. We know
this because Neville's biography is well documented and firmly
established. From the mid-1590s he was lord of an estate; he

was playing a prominent national role; and he was beginning to figure, too, in international affairs.

Neville's duties as a member of parliament in various parts of England have already been noted. In addition to those duties, he was active as a Justice of the Peace, and performed other official and civic functions. He was often preoccupied with managing the affairs of a large household in which he had eleven children. More than once he was forced to move that household, such as when plague made Billingbear dangerous. All the while, Neville managed extensive business interests including a foundry that manufactured artillery. He held shares in the London Virginia Company, which became for him 'a central obsession'.

In France, Neville was a busy if incompetent ambassador. Clumsily he went in disguise to the funeral of the King of Spain, and was later blamed for the failure of the treaty with England's principal rival. Confronted with this failure, James and Rubinstein put on a brave face, describing the ambassadorship as 'partially successful'; a diplomatic curate's egg. Neville's humpty-dumpty diplomacy failed to earn him any favour at court.

James and Rubinstein claim Neville wrote *As You Like It*, *Twelfth Night* and possibly *Much Ado About Nothing* during his failed ambassadorship. Noticing an obvious problem here, the co-authors make a concession: 'Even for the greatest author in history, writing two or three plays as an Ambassador is asking quite a lot.' Such biographical misalignments are graver than the ones that made people doubt Shakespeare's authorship.

Apart from these specific infelicities, the attempt to align Shakespeare's works with Neville's life suffers from a fundamental problem. Reading the plays and poems biographically is an error, a Romantic fallacy. Why? Because the contents of the plays and poems were dictated by fashion and context as well as by the author's personality and experiences; because Shakespeare borrowed plots, style and language from earlier authors who, if the biographical approach is to be taken seriously, would have left behind traces of their own biographies; because parts of the plays were produced by co-authors and editors who also brought along their own biographies; because all of the plays' authors were engaged in writing fiction, at a time when writers of fiction did not think to write autobiographically; and because, even if a given piece of fiction were partly inspired by and reflective of its author's biography, the biographical and non-biographical threads are impossible to disentangle.

This critique applies to every attempt to match the works to any historical person, whether it be Henry Neville, Edward de Vere, Francis Bacon or 'William Shakspere' of Stratford. Pretty well any conception of Shakespeare's biography can be supported by his works. Sheepskins, for example, are mentioned in *Hamlet*; surely a hint of the wool and hides in which John Shakespeare dealt during William Shakespeare's youth? Other traces point to close familiarity with more exalted occupations and spheres, such as the royal court and the law courts. (Unlike many heretics, James and Rubinstein argue that Shakespeare did *not* train as a lawyer. Neville, needless to say, was not a lawyer.) Reading biography into such traces is untenable. How can we ever be sure that a word or phrase is 'biographical' or not? What number of 'biographical' words and phrases is enough to establish a strong connection? These questions can never be answered in a useful way.

Authorial arguments that depend on biographical match-ing suffer from other logical problems as well. Two things can happen at the same time without one having caused the other. The first meeting of the International Rosicrucians may have coincided with the beginning of Shakespeare's London career, and the second may have coincided with his death, but this doesn't make his career a Rosicrucian plot. Then there is the problem of subjectivity. When heretics detect an 'aristocratic attitude' in Shakespeare's plays, they are really just perceiving a twenty-first-century, upper-middle-class idea of what an Elizabethan aristocratic attitude might have been like.

Much of the Nevillian enterprise involves searching the plays for references to Neville and his relatives. Such references, though, do not support a conclusion about authorship; they do not even withstand a common-sense critique. What number of references is a lot? The Nevilles were a famous family. Plays that speak of kings and lords and diplomats will inevitably bring Nevilles into the picture. How can we be sure that the references are not inadvertent? Every reference can support multiple hypotheses, all of them equally impossible to prove. A playwright who filled his plays with Nevilles may have done so because he admired them, or because he thought his audience admired them. An infinite variety of such stories can be told. The upshot is this: we cannot claim that a person wrote a play just because it refers to or resembles that person's life, especially if the person was famous and from a famous family.

Another mass of Nevillian work focuses on matching Shakespeare's and Neville's expressions and vocabulary. The language fallacy—whereby common use of words, grammar and phrases is taken incorrectly to mean common authorship—has already been discussed in connection to 'Shakespeare's dictionary' and similar entrepreneurial 'discoveries'. The fact that Neville and Shakespeare sometimes used the same language and turns of phrase does not make Neville the author of the plays.

~

Neville's Virginia venture is central to the second pillar of James and Rubinstein's case. The Nevillian movement started, so the story goes, when James 'decrypted' the *Sonnets* dedication. That was a recent example of how the hapless dedication has been sliced, diced, shuffled, quartered and abused in every way. It has been read at séances and through intoxicating hazes of absinthe, opium and laudanum. It has been read backwards, upside down, along the diagonals and around corners. Searchers have looked for telluric currents, anagrams, palindromes, acrostics, snakes and ladders.

Theories of the dedication abound. Many relate to the third line, 'MR W. H. ALL HAPPINESSE'. Perhaps that was a typographical accident and 'Mr W. H. All...' was meant to read 'Mr W. Hall'. No one knows, though, who Mr Hall might be. Perhaps 'Mr W. H.' was meant to be 'Mr WSH', for William Shakespeare. Maybe 'W. H.' is 'Walsing-Ham'. Or perhaps he is Henry Wriothesley, Earl of Southampton, his initials erroneously or affectionately reversed. Perhaps the Mr is Willie Hughes, the beautiful boy-actor; William Hall, cousin of Anthony Munday; William Herbert, Earl of Pembroke; Sir William Harvey, third husband of the Dowager Countess of Southampton; William Holme, a recently deceased associate of the sonnets' publisher; William Hatcliffe, Prince of the Purpoole at the Gray's Inn Revels; William Hathaway, a Shakespeare in-law; William Henry Ireland, the elder; or, an expedient solution, 'William himself'.

James and Rubinstein claim Neville wrote and dedicated the sonnets to Henry Wriothesley, Earl of Southampton, allegedly his prison lover and certainly his fellow member of the council of the London Virginia Company. Why 'W. H.' and not 'H. W.'? Because, in the Tower, 'stripped of their titles...they would have referred to each other as Mr H. N. and Mr H. W. Or, even more likely...Neville reversed his friend's initials so that there was no confusion as to which Henry was meant.' (With all those Henries in such a confined space there was bound to be confusion.) Southampton, so the argument goes, was the 'onlie begetter' because he inspired Neville to write the sonnets. The phrase 'all happinesse' echoed the dedication from *The Rape of Lucrece*, which wished Southampton 'long life still lengthened with all happiness'. The timing of the *Sonnets'* publication was significant: 'It was, quite plainly, occasioned by the granting of a royal charter, three days after the official registration of the work, to the second London Virginia Company.' That is why the dedication ends with 'the well-wishing adventurer in setting forth'.

There is much to dislike in this pillar. The H. W. / W. H. reversal, for example, really doesn't sound very likely. The deepest problem with James and Rubinstein's theory, though, is that the *Sonnets* dedication is not a secret code. It is not even relevant evidence. We know from centuries of book history that preliminary and endmatter in books is frequently put there by the publisher, not the author; often the material is there to help sell the book; often it is irrelevant to the body text. (In 1568, William Turner complained to Queen Elizabeth that a 'crafty, covetous and Popish' stationer had issued one of Turner's books with the author's preface replaced by the stationer's.) In the case of the 1609 *Sonnets*, the dedication is signed by T. T., uncontroversially the book's publisher Thomas Thorpe, which makes it clear that the dedication is not in the author's voice. If the dedication is nevertheless read authorially, several parts make no sense, such as the references to 'our ever-living poet', which is a way to refer to someone who has died. The biggest furphy of Shakespeare studies—a field remarkably rich in furphies—the dedication is of no evidentiary value for any important questions, including the Authorship Question.

In *The Truth Will Out*, Brenda James is cagey about the precise timing and circumstances of her 'decipherment' of the dedication and her consequent 'discovery' of Nevillian authorship. The Eureka moment probably occurred when she came across an old work, Charles Mills Gayley's *Shakespeare and the Founders of Liberty in America* (1917). Gayley's book is an implausible piece of wartime propaganda aimed at strengthening the trans-Atlantic anglophone alliance during the First World War.

> In this period of conflict, the sternest that the world has known, when we have joined heart and hand with Great Britain, it may profit Americans to recall how essentially at one with Englishmen we have always been in everything that counts. That the speech, the poetry, of the race are ours and theirs in common, we know—they are Shakespeare. But that the institutions, the law and the liberty, the democracy administered by the fittest, are not only theirs and ours in common, but are derived from Shakespeare's England, and are Shakespeare, too, we do not generally know or, if we have known, we do not always remember.

Gayley predicts much of the Nevillian case. He notices how Shakespeare's and Neville's circles overlapped; he scrutinises the mysterious Northumberland Manuscript; he notices that Shakespeare, like Neville, displayed an interest in the Virginian settlement; and he suggests that Shakespeare had inside knowledge of Sir Thomas Gates' experiences as administrator of the settlement and the enterprise in which Neville owned shares. Indeed, Gayley is so assertive of a Shakespeare–Neville connection that, to the extent the Nevillians have come upon any kind of 'discovery', the discovery arguably belongs to Gayley.

The authors of *The Truth Will Out* downplay the importance of decipherment in the Nevillian case. They also distance themselves from the most enthusiastic cipher-hunters. At the same time, though, they allow that 'some encryption might be legitimate', and then embark on the clumsiest anagram hunt this author has ever seen. A poem by Leonard Digges appeared in the First Folio's preliminary matter. Searching for secret messages in the poem's last line, 'But crown'd with Lawrell, live eternally', James and Rubinstein detect, 'But crown'd with all Law't reely neville'. They repeat the same childish trick with the last line of Hugh Holland's First Folio sonnet: 'The life yet of his lines shall never out', becomes, 'The life yet of his lines has Nevell rout'. Claiming that Neville turned to writing sonnets after his ambitions at court were thwarted, James and Rubinstein hit rock bottom when they find 'an echo of Neville's bitterness in the lamenting Sonnet 111 (perhaps representing I, I, I)'.

Volumes of nonsense have been written on the subject of Shakespeare's hetero, bi and multivalent sexuality. In their attempt to explain the apparent homosexuality of the sonnets, James and Rubinstein perpetrate a good example of the nonsense: 'It is possible that, while confined [to the Tower], Neville had some kind of homosexual relationship with Southampton, although Neville, with eleven children, was obviously heterosexual under normal circumstances.' The words 'some kind of' and 'obviously' are wonderfully quaint—and wonderfully ambiguous, especially as James and Rubinstein note elsewhere that Neville enjoyed conjugal visiting rights while in the Tower. With similar vagueness, James and Rubinstein also announce that Francis Bacon 'was, apparently, a homosexual'. Like Edward de Vere and

Henry Neville, Francis Bacon has therefore been accused of two clandestine Elizabethan activities: writing Shakespeare's plays, and buggery.

In addition to modelling the biographical, chronological, crypto-graphic and language fallacies, James and Rubinstein offer documentary evidence in support of Neville authorship. They have especially high hopes for the Northumberland Manuscript, a big name for a small document. Even calling it a 'manuscript' is a stretch. The item in question is 'a scrap of torn paper that seems to be part of the cover of a folder'. What the folder contained is a matter of debate. James and Rubinstein propose the folder was 'used to hold or catalogue some sixteenth-century literary works'. The word 'catalogue' here makes the document seem more choreographed than it is. In reality the manuscript is a page filled from edge to edge with chaotic scribbling, like an exercise in writing practice or an Elizabethan doodle pad. Multiple scribes seem to have been doing the doodling, mostly in the secretary hand. The Nevillian argument relies on the inclusion of two names: Neville and Shakespeare. The manuscript, though, does not say '*Henry* Neville'; the identity of the Neville in question is unclear. Shakespeare's name appears several times; the Nevillians suggest that the scribbler was 'practising Shakespeare's signature'. That is probably not true; even if it were, it would not help the argument. The Stratfordian case does not depend on evidence from signatures; and writing or even forging someone's name is not the same as executing a colossal literary identity fraud.

Much of the writing, including Shakespeare's name, is unclear. James and Rubinstein present a 1904 transcription of the Northumberland Manuscript into modern handwriting. The transcriber, Frank Burgoyne, seems to have done a large amount of subjective tidying up, and a small amount of converting text into what he hoped to find. The sequence, 'By mr. ffrauncis Bacon / Essaies by the same author / William Shakespeare', arguably involves a deliberate selection to support a deliberate inference. That part of the text could support a dozen other readings.

The 'manuscript' is problematic in other ways, too. Its chain of provenance is weak. To connect the document to Henry Neville, James and Rubinstein posit a complex scenario involving dukes, earls and a distant Neville relative. Henry may have owned the document, or he may not have. He may have written some of the scribbles, or he may not have. The manuscript's date is also unclear and debatable. It could be from 1596, or it could belong to a much later date.

The contents of the Northumberland Manuscript are even more of a 'word salad' than the *Alvearie* leaf, and this time the salad is rotten. The Nevillians are not the only sect to take it up; it has also been used to advance the claims of Sir Francis Bacon and the Earl of Derby. If a hundred such documents were found, they would not strengthen the Nevillian case.

The fourth pillar is the so-called Tower Notebook. As an early seventeenth-century document, the Notebook is interesting, though quite routine and, for the Authorship Question, essentially irrelevant. But the authors of *The Truth Will Out* bend over backwards to link it to Shakespeare's plays.

A single one of the Notebook's two hundred pages describes positions of honour at Anne Boleyn's coronation in 1533. James and Rubinstein characterise that page as something like an early draft of act 4, scene 1 of *Henry VIII*, which has Anne in procession to the coronation ceremony.

In the play, elaborate stage directions are given. They were lifted from Holinshed's *Chronicle*, a well-known Shakespeare source that provided material for many other parts of *Henry VIII*. The Tower Notebook has only two details in common with the play: one relating to the role of the Mayor of London in the ceremony, the other to the carrying of a canopy. Several authors have pointed out that the *Chronicle* provides these details perfectly adequately, in a manner that aligns with the play much more closely than the Notebook does. As a 'source' for the play, therefore, the Notebook is redundant; another furphy, another effort by the co-authors to make nonsense sound like evidence.

The Notebook suffers doubly for its weak link to the plays and its weak link to Neville. Reprising the Northumberland formula, James and Rubinstein propose a doubtful provenance hypothesis that links the Notebook neither to Shakespeare nor to Neville (they concede the Notebook is not in Neville's handwriting). The hypothesis requires leaps of logic and one eleven-year leap of chronology: according to James and Rubinstein, *Henry VIII* was not written or performed until 1613, eleven years after the date of the Notebook.

Another difficulty for James and Rubinstein is that *Henry VIII* was probably co-authored with John Fletcher. James and Rubinstein turn this problem into a virtue by pointing out, misleadingly, that Fletcher, with Francis Beaumont, dedicated a play to Neville. The suggestion is that Fletcher was somehow in on the whole thing—but that only makes the 'conspiracy' even less plausible.

The Truth Will Out uses tricks to enhance its veneer of authority. The long appendices have already been mentioned. Spurious exhibits are another technique: the bogus 'family tree' is a classic of its kind. Infused with truthy rhetoric—'the truth from primary sources', 'the true background of the Tower of London prisoners'—the book in fact contains very little truth. In the face of uncertainty, the co-authors are ever ready to assert certainty. Neville 'unquestionably' wrote the sonnets in the Tower (this is very questionable). He 'certainly authorised' their publication (that is far from certain). The conspiracy covering up Shakespeare's authorship 'must have occurred' (it very likely didn't).

Paring back all the false confidence and wishful thinking leaves one bare fact. James and Rubinstein provide no evidence of any relationship, arrangement, undertaking or conspiracy between Henry Neville and William Shakespeare. For the claimed conspiracy to work, during Shakespeare's lifetime there must have been a deep and binding understanding, and probably a commensurate financial relationship, between Neville and Shakespeare. Yet there is no evidence of any arrangement, deep or shallow, between the two men. Nor is there evidence of a connection between Neville and the plays and poems that bear Shakespeare's name. Neville predeceased Shakespeare by nine months; what arrangements were in place to keep Shakespeare's mouth shut after Neville exited?

For Neville, a hidden life as a dramatic author makes no sense. Why would a busy aristocrat—MP, courtier, entrepreneur, diplomat—spend such time and vigour on such an extensive yet secret œuvre? Ambitious and thwarted in politics and at court, he seems to have craved fame and favour. During the reign of James I, Neville had a strong incentive to disclose his authorship of plays that were sympathetic to the King, and upon which the King looked favourably. And yet, according to the Nevillian theory, he kept quiet, as did everyone else who was in on the conspiracy.

In laying out their theories and evidence, the co-authors evade the most important questions, the ones supposedly the subject of their book and their 'discoveries'. 'How Neville became Shakespeare' is something about which 'we can only surmise'. Why did Neville and his family wish to keep the real authorship a secret? That 'remains a mystery', the co-authors state, before floating a convoluted and unconvincing theory about a Hungarian humanist, Baltic trade routes, Shakespearean soliloquies and Lord Abergavenny. In their concluding chapter the co-authors ask why Neville's secret authorship was not revealed by co-conspirators during his lifetime or after his death. Why did the First Folio editors, who knew both Shakespeare and Neville, decide to publish thirty-six plays under Shakespeare's name after both men had died? This, the co-authors say, is just one of the 'many mysteries' we are left with, mysteries that will probably never 'be completely resolved'.

The reader will remember that James and Rubinstein also claimed to have found 'smoking-gun' evidence of Nevillian authorship: the inclusion in *Twelfth Night* of William Knollys as Malvolio. Not surprisingly, this sub-argument is as flimsy as it is tortuous. Not a gun, no smoke. The paperback cover of *The Truth Will Out* attempts to align the faces of William Shakespeare and Henry Neville. The jarringly misaligned eyes and foreheads serve as metaphors for the misalignment of Neville and Shakespeare. Manifesto and mothership for the Nevillians, *The Truth Will Out* does them great harm.

There is insufficient room here to list every flaw in James and Rubinstein's argument. But the main defects bear importantly on the question of whether Neville's library was Shakespeare's. *The Truth Will Out* exemplifies many species of impaired logic and method. It rests on four Swiss-cheese pillars. The goal of rigorous analysis is to avoid fixing on random and spurious correlations. Many unorthodox theorists are 'noise traders', finding meaningless patterns in the randomness. It is useful to call out their fallacious methods, to better equip us when looking at future arguments.

The Nevillian Authorship case made a strong start. To the extent that the case is founded on James and Rubinstein's collaboration, however, we can be certain Neville's library is not Shakespeare's. Though no doubt genuinely felt and voraciously savoured, the Nevillians' experience of handling Shakespeare's books was not authentic.

When I finished *The Truth Will Out*, one thought was foremost in my mind. My next meeting with John O'Donnell would be awkward.

CHAPTER 13

The Country Bumpkin

During Shakespeare's lifetime, editions of his poems and plays found their way into the libraries of his fellow Elizabethans and Jacobeans. We know this because the book buyers recorded their purchases, and wrote notes in the books themselves. In 1593 Richard Stonley made the earliest known acquisition of a Shakespearean book. The printer-publisher Richard Field had registered *Venus and Adonis* with the Stationers' Company on 18 April; less than two months later, Stonley recorded his purchase of 'Venus and Adhonay per Shakspere'. For Stonley, who accumulated a library of more than four hundred books, things would soon take a turn for the worse. A Teller of the Exchequer, he was convicted of stealing more than £12,000. Stonley went to prison and his library was dispersed to pay his creditors.

At the high point of Shakespeare's writing career, Scipio Squyer was a student. He went on to work for a judge before becoming Deputy Chamberlain of the Exchequer. In the course of his London career he assembled a creditable library of well-cared-for books and manuscripts. On the title pages he wrote his name and the date of acquisition. He also wrote, in 1632, an inventory of his library. Extending to almost seven hundred titles, the list included Shakespeare's *Venus and Adonis*, *Pericles*, *Romeo and Juliet* and *The True Tragedy of Richard Duke of York*, an early alternative title for *III Henry VI*. The Squyer copy of *Pericles*, now in the Elizabethan Club at Yale University, is annotated on the title page, 'Scipio Squyer. 5. Maij 1609', and includes early textual corrections.

Gabriel Harvey had an even richer library. In his copy of Thomas Speght's 1598 *Chaucer* (now in the British Library), Harvey added a useful note: 'The younger sort takes much delight in Shakespeares Venus & Adonis: but his Lucrece, & his tragedie of Hamlet, Prince of Denmarke, haue it in them, to please the wiser sort.' The note is as mysterious as it is useful: Harvey made the note in 1600 or thereabouts, but the earliest known *Hamlet* edition was not published until 1603. Did Harvey take his information from the stage, or from an as yet unknown edition, perhaps unregistered?

Discovering a lost first-edition *Hamlet* quarto would be almost as exciting as discovering a *Hamlet* manuscript. It is quite plausible that whole editions of Shakespeare plays and poems have been lost. Some of the surviving editions do so only in very few copies, in some cases as few as one copy.

Venus and Adonis is an example. Frances Wolfreston was the most important early female collector of Shakespeare. Her library of nearly a thousand books included at least ten Shakespeare quartos and the only surviving copy of the first edition of *Venus and Adonis*, now in the Bodleian. Despite the efforts of collectors like Wolfreston and Squyer and Harvey, the average Elizabethan and Jacobean reader regarded plays as ephemeral entertainments and low literature, just as readers in the 1950s thought of 'pulp' magazines as fodder to be read and thrown away. Whole editions, printed cheaply and in modest quantities, could simply have been trashed.

It is also possible that unknown early editions will be discovered in the future. Things do turn up. In 2015 Dutch authorities found a chest that contained 2600 unsent seventeenth- and eighteenth-century letters. In 2005 a copy of Mandrop Torst's exceptionally rare 1701 voyage account—a twenty-four-page pamphlet found bound with other pamphlets in a composite volume—was sold in Melbourne for $768,900. Early plays are among the books being unearthed. In 1904 the only surviving copy of the first quarto of *Titus Andronicus* was found—wrapped in a pair of lottery tickets—among items inherited by a Swedish postal clerk. A lost play by Ben Jonson, *The Entertainment at Britain's Burse* (1609), was rediscovered as late as 1997.

Hamlet is not the only Shakespeare play that may have existed in an early edition that is now lost. Also in that category are pre-1600 editions of *Othello*, pre-1598 editions of *Love's Labour's Lost*, and all editions of *Love's Labour's Won*. Hints point to the existence of at least one unknown early *Othello*. In 1600, Edward Pudsey recorded in his commonplace book passages from his favourite texts. They included eight plays by Shakespeare: *Hamlet, Othello, Romeo and Juliet, The Merchant of Venice, Titus Andronicus, Richard II, Richard III* and *Much Ado About Nothing*. Here, *Othello* is the odd one out because the earliest known quarto edition dates from 1622, well after the date of the commonplace book. Pudsey seems to have owned all seven of the other plays in early quarto editions; perhaps he also owned an early *Othello*, now lost. Or, better still, hiding somewhere.

Shakespeare and his work were also mentioned in plays, poetry and prose written by his contemporaries. An example is the reference in *Returne from Parnassus* (1606), 'acted by the Students in St John's College in Cambridge'—racy Shakespeare enjoyed cultish popularity among the students. Francis Freeling owned this play, and John Fry studied it, focusing on the now famous line, 'Why heres our fellow Shakespeare put them all doune, I and Ben Johnson too'. Early poetical references to Shakespeare include the 1603 poem in which John Davies of Hereford expressed admiration for Shakespeare and Burbage.

Shakespeare's epic poem *The Rape of Lucrece* was first published in 1594. Later in the same year, a popular book of poetry appeared. Purportedly by Henry Willobie, *Willobie his Avisa* includes the line, 'And *Shake-speare* paints poor Lucrece rape'. The book also includes a reference to 'W. S.', who was once infatuated with lovely Avisa, but then changed his mind.

In 1598 Richard Barnfield lauded *The Rape of Lucrece* and *Venus and Adonis*:

And Shakespeare thou, whose honey-flowing Vein
(Pleasing the World), thy Praises doth obtain.
Whose *Venus*, and whose *Lucrece* (sweet, and chaste)
Thy Name in Fame's immortal Book have placed.

In the same year, *Palladis Tamia: Wits Treasury* appeared. Produced by a clergyman named Francis Meres, the book is a collection of quotations, sayings and anecdotes with as much originality as the hodgepodge Barrington volumes. One section, though, is of much interest. Meres listed the greatest classical writers, then matched them to Englishmen of comparable talent. He put Shakespeare with the authors 'best for Tragedie' and 'best for Comedie'. He then expanded on Shakespeare's achievements, providing priceless information about the Bard's work and how it was regarded:

> As the soul of Euphorbus was thought to live in Pythagoras, so the sweet witty soul of Ovid lives in mellifluous and honeytongued Shakespeare, witness his 'Venus and Adonis', his 'Lucrece', his sugared sonnets among his private friends, etc.
>
> As Plautus and Seneca are accounted the best for Comedy and Tragedy among the Latins, so Shakespeare among the English is the most excellent in both kinds for the stage; for Comedy, witness his 'Gentlemen of Verona', his 'Errors', his 'Love's Labour's Lost', his 'Love's Labour's Wonne', his 'Midsummer Night's Dream', and his 'Merchant of Venice'; for Tragedy, his 'Richard the 2', 'Richard the 3', 'Henry the 4', 'King John', 'Titus Andronicus' and his 'Romeo and Juliet'...

This passage confirmed *Love's Labour's Won* was not just an alternative title for *Love's Labour's Lost*. Further evidence on the *Love's Labour's Won* mystery would also be found. A fragment of a bookseller's list of items sold in 1603 included 'marchant of vennis', 'taming of a shrew', 'loves labor lost' and 'loves labor won', suggesting that the latter play was indeed printed.

Meres's text also confirmed that Shakespeare was known at a relatively early date as both a poet and a dramatist. The fascinating statement that Shakespeare's 'sugared sonnets' were circulated 'among his private friends' is of immense value, as is the attribution of plays such as *Titus Andronicus* to Shakespeare.

England's Parnassus (1600) included ninety-five Shakespeare quotations, along with 386 by Spenser and 225 by Drayton. Apart from quoting and praising his writing, Shakespeare's contemporaries left behind hints about how he worked. Francis Beaumont knew something of Shakespeare as a playwright; he had co-authored plays with John Fletcher, who in turn had collaborated with Shakespeare on plays such as *Henry VIII*, *The Two Noble Kinsmen* and *Cardenio*. Beaumont wrote to Ben Jonson a manuscript verse-letter that praised Shakespeare for creating admirable lines 'by the dim light of Nature', without 'Learning'. Shakespeare's 'natural wit' was remarked upon by many people in the seventeenth century. According to Gerard Langbaine, 'His Natural Genius to Poetry was so excellent, that like those Diamonds, which are found in Cornwall, Nature had little or no occasion for the Assistance of Art to polish it'. Similar remarks would appear in the First Folio's preliminary matter and in later reflections on Shakespeare's creative achievements.

Another recurring theme was darker: Shakespeare's use of other writers' work. In 1610, John Davies called him 'our English Terence'. Comparing Shakespeare to a classical author sounds like praise, but the comparison had a sharp edge. An impoverished Roman writer, Terence was rumoured to have published under his own name lines he did not write. Davies wrote of Shakespeare:

Some say good *Will* (which I, in sport, do sing)
Hadst thou not plaid some Kingly parts in sport,
Thou had'st bin a companion for a *King*;
And, beene a King among the meaner sort.
Some others raile; but raile as they thinke fit,
Thou hast no rayling, but, a raigning Wit:
And honesty *thou sow'st, which they do reape*
So, to increase their Stocke *which they do keepe.*

These and other lines are ambiguous, but they have been read as an accusation that Shakespeare used, improperly, the work of others. Furthering that theme, Thomas Freeman's 1614 *To Master W. Shakespeare* again linked Shakespeare to the 'borrower' Terence:

> Besides, in plays thy wit winds like Meander,
> When needy new composers borrow more
> Than Terence doth from Plautus or Menander.

These battle lines had already been laid down much earlier, in the works of Robert Greene.

Accused of being constitutionally unreliable, Greene is a puzzle for modern researchers. His claims about his university education, Continental travels, love affairs, offspring and record of authorship are hotly contested and at least partially fabricated. So, too, the circumstances of his death, which, at the age of thirty-two, was hastened by wine and pickled herring. In his last days, so the story goes, he looked back over what he saw as a failed career, and concluded that others were to blame for his failure. He had been robbed of his authorial legacy, and the worst robber was a ruthless young upstart in the theatre world.

Greene captured these reflections in a deathbed pamphlet: *Groats-worth of Wit, Bought with a Million of Repentance, Describing the Follie of Youth, the Falsehoode of Makeshift Flatterers, the Miserie of the Negligent, and Mischiefs of Deceiuing Courtezans.* The book is divided into four parts. The first is a fictionalised tale of Greene's alter-ego 'Roberto', a promising young scholar who, after being cheated by a prostitute, fell into disgrace. Then he met a rich-looking stranger—a successful actor who could also write plays. The stranger needed a writing assistant for his theatre company. Roberto signed on, but dissolution and depravity followed. The book then changes gear and voice. The non-fictional second part of *Groats-worth* is a repentance and a list of life lessons and precepts. The third part is also factual: a letter to three of Greene's fellow scholar-dramatists (probably Christopher Marlowe, Thomas Nashe and George Peele) in which he warns them about a dangerous man preying on dramatists.

> Yes, trust them not: for there is an upstart crow, beautified with our feathers, that with his *tiger's heart wrapped in a player's hide* supposes he is as well able to bombast out a blank verse as the best of you; and, being an absolute *Johannes Factotum*, is in his own conceit the only Shake-scene in a country. O, that I might entreat your rare wits to be employed in more profitable courses, and let those apes imitate your past excellence, and never more acquaint them with your past inventions. I know the best husband of you all will never prove an Usurer, and the kindest of them all will never prove a kind nurse: yet whilst you may, seek you better Masters; for it is pity men of such rare wits, should be subject to the pleasure of such rude grooms.

There is a lot going on in this passage. The target, evidently William Shakespeare, employed actors and also dabbled in acting and writing. Greene accuses him of usury, plagiarism and bad dealing. The 'crow' reference is one of the several charges of literary theft: in classical fables the crow is a thieving bird, stealing the finer plumes of others. 'Johannes Factotum' is the man-of-all-trades; the sense here is that Shakespeare is not a real playwright, nor much of an actor, but an over-confident dabbler who believes he can out-write and out-act the true men of the stage.

The line, 'tiger's heart wrapped in a player's hide', was adapted from York's outburst, in *III Henry VI*, against his captor, Queen

Margaret: 'O, tiger's heart wrapt in a woman's hide!' Greene's pun accomplishes a few things. Most importantly, it reinforces the symbolism of cruelty and double-dealing, and links the passage to Shakespeare's writing, or possibly to writing he filched from someone else. Though *III Henry VI* first appeared in print in the First Folio under that title, earlier versions of it and of *II Henry VI* circulated and were performed in Greene's lifetime. Sidney Lee claimed in his *Life of William Shakespeare* that Shakespeare had not originally written the three parts of *Henry VI*, but had revised and expanded them.

Greene's *Groats-worth* concludes with a fable about an Ant and a Grasshopper. The accusations against Shakespeare are repeated, with the bad Bard now appearing as the heartless Ant, a miserly profiteer whose 'thrift is theft'. Greene's image of Shakespeare aligns well with much of the documentary evidence. Shakespeare owned shares in theatres, and would therefore have been involved in the business side of the theatre world, including the employment of actors. The Clayton loan and other financial and legal documents confirm Shakespeare lent money for profit. Collectively, his business interests were lucrative, enabling him to buy not only New Place but also other real estate in Stratford and in London. In 1611 and 1614 he took legal steps to protect the returns from his property investments.

Greene left behind a poignant document: a dying man's bitter reflections on a benighted life. The confessional deathbed memoir has been a literary device for more than four centuries. In this convention, the author speaks with unusual candour and authority; he has no earthly thing to lose by plain speaking. The *Groats-worth* pamphlet's fatal veracity is stressed in the preface, 'To the Gentleman Readers', and on the title page: 'Written before his death and published at his dyeing request'. In practical terms, though, the deathbed author is at a disadvantage. Deathbeds are not good places to write. Imminent mortality makes seeing a book through the press difficult. A severely ill Greene supposedly wrote this and other longish pamphlets in the last weeks of his life. It is likely that Greene did no such thing. (Another problem: the time of a future death from illness is hard to predict. How embarrassing to publish a deathbed pamphlet and then linger on or, worse still, recover.)

Apart from being a literary device, the deathbed reflection is also a convenient cloak. As soon as the pamphlet appeared, Greene's contemporaries saw through it: other writers had used Greene's death as an opportunity to denounce Shakespeare in print. Greene was the ideal front. He had earned a reputation as a perspicacious observer and a snipey exposer of bad conduct. Behind their Greene cloak, the true authors could say what was on their minds.

Groats-worth's denunciation of Shakespeare caused a stir. The three living men implicated in the book's production—Thomas Nashe, William Wright and Henry Chettle—took great pains to disown it. Nashe, an author and an addressee of Greene's open letter, angrily denied having written the pamphlet. Wright, the publisher who registered it, claimed he did so 'upon the peril of Henry Chettle', who was therefore responsible. Chettle, a printer, author, typesetter and book-trade all-rounder, issued a florid and panicked apology, in which he admitted to having edited Greene's work but desperately denied having done more than that.

[In *Groats-worth*] a letter written to divers play-makers is offensively by one or two of them taken, and because on the dead they cannot be avenged, they wilfully forge in their conceits a living author. [At] the perusing of Greene's book, [I] struck out what then in conscience I thought he in some displeasure writ, or had it been true, yet to publish it was intolerable...To be brief, I writ it over, and as near as I could, followed the copy; only in that letter I put something out, but in the whole book not a word in, for I protest it was all Greene's, not mine nor Master Nashe's, as some unjustly have affirmed.

The apology is as cryptic as the offending passages. 'Because on the dead they cannot be avenged' seems to confirm Greene was used as a front for others. Chettle names none of the aggrieved parties. They were probably Marlowe, Nashe and Peele, the notional addressees of the *Groats-worth* letter. But Shakespeare, the subject of Greene's original accusations, may too have been aggrieved, and his reaction may account for a share of Chettle's apparent contrition.

The Greene–Chettle imbroglio is of immense value for what it says about Shakespeare's gossipy, backstabbing milieu. Powerful people, 'divers of worship', were somehow involved in the affair. At least one wounded party had friends in high places. Chettle's apology again indicates that Shakespeare, like Marlowe (a secret service agent who died a violent death) was not a man to annoy.

The Bard is thought to have had the last laugh on *Groats-worth* when, in *Twelfth Night*, he depicted Robert Greene as the roly-poly, Falstaff-like character, Sir Toby Belch. The feud with Chettle, though, continued. Upon the death of Queen Elizabeth, for example, Chettle criticised Shakespeare, as 'Melicert', for not writing a tribute.

Since finishing James and Rubinstein's book, I had worried about my next meeting with John O'Donnell. The meeting, though, was just as friendly and enlightening as all the others had been. John was unperturbed by my reaction to *The Truth Will Out*, which he knew was not the best advertisement for Nevillism. We talked through some of the holes in James and Rubinstein's case, then discussed some of the weaker thinkers on the orthodox side. We shared a joke about the flimsy scholarship and weighty pomposity of the celebrated Shakespearean A. L. Rowse. John gave me another book, Diana Price's *Shakespeare's Unorthodox Biography* (2001). This, he said, would end my neutrality and bring me over, once and for all, to the unorthodox side. I delved into it that very night.

According to Price's published résumé, she has lectured at Shakespeare's Globe, the Smithsonian Institution, the University of Tennessee Law School, California State University and the University of North Carolina. Her style and methods differ strikingly from those of *The Truth Will Out*.

Devoting much of her book to the Greene–Chettle controversy, Price argues that Greene's hidden authors spoke of Shakespeare mostly as a theatre investor, playbroker and businessman; not in any sense as an actor or playwright. John O'Donnell had made a similar point at our meeting. Shakespeare, John said, was an actor merely in the way that the owner of a circus might erect the tent, drive the truck and occasionally appear before the audience as a clown.

Shakespeare's missing library is central to Price's argument. How could he have been a writer, Price asked, if all his surviving documents were non-literary? This, she concluded, was not only 'bizarre', but 'statistically impossible'. To formalise her conclusion, Price set out ten criteria and used them to score Shakespeare and twenty-four of his literary and para-literary contemporaries. She explained her approach in Darwinian terms: 'Just as birds can be distinguished from turtles by characteristics peculiar to the species, so writers can be distinguished from doctors, actors or financiers, by the types of personal records left behind.'

Five of the ten criteria are about Shakespeare's library and those of his peers. Price gave Ben Jonson a winning score of ten out of ten. Edmund Spenser scored a creditable seven, Robert Greene a middling six, Thomas Kyd a sorry four, and William 'Shakspere' a devastating zero. No one else scored worse than four on Price's ten-point scale.

Price provided other evidence and arguments that reinforced Shakespeare's nugatory performance. She argued that the Shakespeare hyphen revealed the name as pseudonymous. She argued that the plays must have been written much earlier than is typically thought, and too early for Shakspere of Stratford. With these and complementary arguments, Price answered the first of the two heretical questions: Did Shakespeare write the poems and plays? No, he did not; he was a barely literate bumpkin; a money-hungry playbroker, of mediocre intellect; merely a user of others' material; an ambitious commercial man, not respected by his literary associates, and not a literary man himself at all. Shakespeare's authorial library was empty.

On the second question—Who wrote the poems and plays?— Price refused to endorse any particular candidate, except to say that the author must be 'a gentleman of rank'.

> The idea that 'William Shakespeare' was the pen name of an Elizabethan aristocrat is ultimately less fanciful than ascribing to an alleged grammar school dropout the most exquisite dramatic literature in the English language.

Garrick had pumped Shakespeare up. Price did her best to deflate him.

Though *Shakespeare's Unorthodox Biography* has been adopted as a core text of the Nevillian movement, Price's arguments are kryptonite to the Nevillians' Superman. Neville's dates are almost identical to Shakespeare's. If Shakespeare's are too late, so are Neville's. After Price, the best thing Neville had going for him turns into his Achilles' heel.

At my next meeting with John I pointed this out, and we debated Price and her conclusions. John and I agreed her arguments were fascinating and her methods displayed admirable, even Malonite, rigour. She helped set out the unorthodox case, fair and square. And she painted a novel but realistic picture of Shakespeare, some of whose features were certainly convincing—his acumen, his ambition, his worldliness.

At the same time, though, both of us could find flaws in Price's reasoning. Her scoring of Shakespeare against her criteria was subjective and indubitably harsh. (Price's ten criteria also echo unhappily the bogus nine that J. Thomas Looney used to 'prove' Edward de Vere wrote Shakespeare's works.) Both of us could think of ways to rebut Price's conclusions. She was wrong to claim that none of Shakespeare's associates referred to him as a writer. She was wrong, too, about the age of the plays: most of them were too fresh, too imbued with topical references—Holofernes as Florio, the 'dead shepherd' as Marlowe, and Macbeth as a Gunpowder Plotter—to have languished in the theatrical refrigerator. (R. C. Churchill called Hamlet's melancholy 'a fashionable, *fin de siècle* mental disease'.)

The fraught latter years of Elizabeth's reign were dangerous for playwrights. In 1593 alone, Thomas Kyd was tortured on the rack and Christopher Marlowe was murdered. Being the frontman for a secret aristocratic playwright would have been exceedingly perilous. If the writer offended the powers of the day, the frontman himself would be in danger, and could readily betray the true author. 'William Shakespeare' was not just a disembodied pseudonym; it was the name of a real person with diverse interests in London's theatre world. As a cloak for a secret author, that name was unsuitable and unsafe.

To solve these problems, Price put forward a solution that took Shakespearean heresy in a bold new direction. The identity of the true author, she argued, must have been a collective conspiracy on an epic scale; an Elizabethan and Jacobean 'open secret' which, under a 'code of silence', Londoners maintained out of respect for the aristocrat and the aristocracy:

> ...which scenario is more plausible: A code of silence that prevented or obscured written references to an aristocratic writer, or an inexplicable conspiracy to eradicate *all* the personal literary paper trails for the commoner William Shakspere?

Though intellectually courageous and intriguing, this expedient is fatal to Price's argument. The theatre in Shakespeare's day was not respectable. An easy way for an aristocrat to lose favour at court would be to write plays secretly-openly as an absent-present author. Moreover, there are many routes through which an open secret could reach us today. Private letters from the period have survived, as have notes in private diaries and logbooks. In these documents, though, the secret was never recorded, never revealed. Many owners of anonymously and pseudonymously authored books wrote the true authors' names on the books' title pages. Where is the quarto with 'William Shakespeare' struck through and replaced by the true author's name or initials or watchword? If such a quarto existed, Malone would have found it. Fry would have found it. Probably even Dibdin would have found it.

George Buc worked at the Revels Office licensing plays. Though he owned many books, including at least fifteen plays, we do not know if any were by Shakespeare. We do know, however, that Buc was familiar with the Bard and his work. Some time after 1599, Buc asked Shakespeare if he knew who wrote the play *George a Greene, the Pinner of Wakefield*. Shakespeare could not recall the author's name, but he remembered that the author was a minister and had acted in the play, in the role of the pinner. Buc recorded the information on the title page of his copy of *George a Greene*. Further inquiries followed. Edward Juby told Buc that the author was Robert Greene. Did Shakespeare know this and feign ignorance? Was he still cross about *Groats-worth*? Greene was notorious for his dissolute ways. Was the 'minister' answer a Shakespearean joke?

Another book with a contemporary annotation is now in the library of Balliol College. It is a copy of *Rimas* by the 'Shakespeare of Spain', Lope de Vega. Leonard Digges inscribed the book with a personal note; it refers to Shakespeare as an author. William Drummond owned the second edition of *Romeo and Juliet* (1599), and he wrote Shakespeare's name on the title page. Late in the seventeenth century the Anglican clergyman Richard Davies made a private note about Shakespeare: 'He died a papist'.

One thing is clear: Buc and other book owners left behind notes and inscriptions that did not disclose, or even hint obliquely at, a secret Shakespearean author. No one struck out the printed name on a quarto or otherwise blew the secret, even in their personal books in their private libraries.

Other parts of the documentary record also contradict the secret author theory. No evidence has been found of a person pulling Shakespeare's strings. Henry Wriothesley, Earl of Southampton, is often referred to as Shakespeare's patron. Southampton's papers, though, confirm he was not. Shakespeare's *Venus and Adonis* and *The Rape of Lucrece* include dedications to Southampton, but these, like the *Sonnets* dedication and the spurious and prospective Barrington prefaces, are part of the publisher's clothing of the author's text; they lend cachet and help make the books seem authorised and authoritative. Many contemporary dedications were built on clouds, with no underlying patronage relationship. Like the body texts, preliminary matter cannot be read naively for biographical content.

Price's 'open secret' theory warrants a short Nevillian detour. James and Rubinstein have their own version of the theory, arguing that many of Neville's associates must have known about his authorship of the plays. Francis Bacon supposedly knew, and Queen Elizabeth supposedly suspected. This argument stretches to breaking point at the time of the Essex Rebellion and Neville's arrest and trial for treason. The co-authors' argument degenerates into a hyper-fiction that makes the idea of a conspiracy of silence ridiculous: 'A reasonable inference is that those who knew of his authorship, such as Francis Bacon (one of the government prosecutors) and Southampton did not wish to give away the secret, which would probably have meant a certain death sentence for Neville.' This is a big ask: Southampton was in grave danger himself. Imprisoned and on the brink of execution, he had little love for Neville (notwithstanding the amorous picture painted by James and Rubinstein) and no reason to keep such a secret. In the case of Bacon, he was a *prosecutor*, loyal to the monarch. And yet these two men are supposed to have protected Neville–Shakespeare.

Perhaps the strangest part of the Nevillian case is the identification of Henry Neville as Falstaff. According to James and Rubinstein, Neville based the lovable, rotund, punning, bumbling Falstaff on himself. The co-authors make much of this link: 'Falstaff,' they claim, 'was a deliberate and central component of [Neville's] persona.'

The Shakespearean character Sir John Falstaff was originally named 'Sir John Oldcastle', after the eponymous nobleman and Protestant martyr who died in the fifteenth century. Until about 1598, the Oldcastle character appeared in performances of the *Henry IV* plays. Outraged by this disgraceful depiction, Oldcastle's surviving relatives petitioned for the character's name to be changed. Falstaff was the new name, but the changeover was imperfect. In the published version of *I Henry IV*, Prince Hal calls Falstaff 'my old lad of the castle' (act 1, scene 2). In the 1600 quarto edition of *II Henry IV*, one of Falstaff's speech prefixes was left uncorrected as 'Old' instead of 'Falst'.

James and Rubinstein claim Oldcastle is a pun on Neville's name: 'New-ville' is the counterpoint of 'Old-castle'. (Other hyphenators take this argument two steps further, interpreting 'Fal-Staff' as 'Shake-Speare'.) If true, what was Neville thinking? Certainly Falstaff is lovable at times. Only someone with a very perverse sensibility, though, would build an autobiographical bridge to one of literature's most grotesque characters, whom Victor Hugo called a swine-centaur, and who took his name from Sir John Fastolf, a man remembered by history as a greedy coward.

James and Rubinstein explain Neville's rationale thus: 'As Neville participated more and more in high political circles [and] he himself increasingly appeared destined for a prominent place in such circles, the mood of personal optimism and self-esteem allowed him to bring to the fore an almost diametrically opposed element in his complex character, that of a buffoon and comic.' There is much perversity here. The Nevillians characterise Shakespeare as a real clown, and Neville as an aspiring one.

The Falstaff argument makes the Nevillian conspiracy even less tenable. A clandestine aristocratic author, embroiled in politics and eager to win favour at court, would have written for edification, not ridicule or disgrace.

Openness of the Shakespeare authorship secret is important to, and at the same time destructive of, Price's unorthodox thesis. The most powerful counterargument, though, to her conclusions—and the most powerful evidence for Shakespearean authorship—is the subject of the next chapter. That evidence is Shakespeare's library.

CHAPTER 14

The Inbetweener

My Fair Lady (1964), the much-loved cinematic realisation of George Bernard Shaw's play *Pygmalion*, centres on an idealised version of a scholar's library. Shaw also assembled a real library, one whose 1100 volumes were not entirely unlike those of Henry Higgins. In the late 1940s Shaw was aged in his nineties and struggling under the burden of Britain's post-war taxes. He told his friend Sydney Cockerell that he was 'out for money: HARD... for the rest of the year my name is Harpagon'. The solution was to sell his library through Sotheby's. Shaw settled on a way to turbocharge the sale: he would enhance the marketability of his largest and rarest books by adding long, handwritten notes and inscriptions.

As Oscar Wilde had done, Shaw disparaged throughout his life the pastimes of autograph hunting and association-copy mongering. In the 1920s, the young Allen Lane approached Shaw in the street and asked for his signature. The playwright's reply was blunt: 'Young man, if, instead of wasting your time asking people like me to give you their autographs, you were to spend those valuable moments learning more about your own business, you would soon find that your own signature would be as much sought after as mine appears to be.' (After that let-down, Lane lobbed his autograph book from Westminster Bridge into the Thames.) Shaw's dire nonagenarian straits, though, caused a change of heart. In volumes such as his deluxe edition of *Hamlet*, published by the Cranach Press, and his facsimiles of the Shakespeare Folios, published by Methuen, Shaw added autobiographical, critical and trivial manuscript notes on the endpapers, below his book label, '*Ex Libris* Bernard Shaw'.

At the auction on 25 July 1949, the enhanced copies attracted great interest. Actress Gertrude Lawrence ran up the facsimile Folios to £163. Apart from Shaw's additions, the First Folio volume included manuscript notes by the children's author Edith Nesbit. Shaw explained:

> Edith, the wife of my Fabian colleague Hubert Bland, began her career by writing verses for *The Weekly News* and being paid half a guinea a week for them. The verses were good enough to qualify her as a poetess; but she did not achieve worldly success until she took to writing fairy tales, which made her famous.
>
> Meanwhile a craze had set in for proving that Shakespear was somebody else, and that the First Folio…is full of ciphers to that effect. This was an easy game; for as there are only 26 letters in the alphabet, and 35 [sic] plays in the volume, the

titles alone, taking their letters in order, will spell the name of anyone on earth, including my own.

Edith, caught by this craze, borrowed this volume from me and stuck her bookplate into it. She then covered the opposite flyleaf with her cipher-seeking calculations, which disfigured it horribly.

This craze had curious origins. In 1893, a Detroit physician by the name of Orville Ward Owen authored a modest pamphlet that had massive reverberations. Written in a style that mimicked legal proceedings, *A Celebrated Case, Bacon vs. Shakespeare* argued that Francis Bacon not only authored Shakespeare's works, but also implanted secret messages in the texts. And he left behind, so Owen claimed, an instruction manual, expressed in verse, which a future decipherer could use to read the embedded messages via a word code that employed syntactic keys. The manual told Owen to build his cipher-reading machine, the Wheel of Fortune, which was specifically calibrated to detect the hidden words in a thousand-foot-long collage of the works of Shakespeare, Bacon, Greene, Spenser, Marlowe, Robert Burton and George Peele. Thus guided, Owen embarked on a unique program of research that blended intuition, inspiration and rotation.

The doctor's charisma, such as it was, enabled him to assemble in Detroit a circle of followers—the assistants and disciples, mostly women, who would join him in his search, help prepare his publications, and crank the handle on his Wheel. With this help, Owen extracted a text that was nothing short of revelatory: an entirely new Shakespearean history, epic in its breadth and enthralling in its drama. Issued in five volumes (a sixth was prepared but not published) between 1893 and 1895, *Sir Francis Bacon's Cipher Story* had everything. A secret royal birth. A cheated royal heir. Homicide. Fratricide. Regicide.

One of Owen's discoveries was the cue for Shakespeare studies to enter the realm of real-world adventure. It turns out that Bacon's original manuscripts—the primeval, handwritten nucleus of 'Shakespeare's library'—had been placed in iron boxes and then buried at a secret location. Their whereabouts could only be revealed with a new cipher, called the King's Move. A helpfully flexible utensil, the King's Move cipher is read by beginning at an anchor letter before moving left, right, up or down to find the next character in the sequence. The new cipher bore immediate fruit in the form of a specific location: a castle near the junction of the Wye and the Severn. Difficult, muddy excavations followed, but to no avail; all that the dig revealed was 'an abandoned cistern and the remains of a Roman bridge'. Owen and his adherents turned their attention to sites elsewhere in southern England, and back to the plays themselves.

Using a 'biliteral cipher' that divined imperceptible (and possibly imaginary) changes in typeface, Elizabeth Wells Gallup made a unique discovery in the search for Shakespeare's missing plays: they were present all along in the printed versions, buried as codes nested inside the text. Reading those codes enabled Gallup to write down plot summaries and extracts from hitherto unknown Shakespearean texts. In 1899 she published *The Bi-literal Cypher of Sir Francis Bacon*. Public interest in the search for Shakespeare's iron boxes was already intense. Gallup's findings turned that interest into a full-blown fad.

Bestselling books were among the several dividends for Owen and Gallup. An enlarged edition of Gallup's *Bi-literal Cypher* appeared in 1900, and a third edition soon after. Impervious to sceptics and detractors, she served up discovery after discovery, just as Ireland and Collier had done. After decoding the whereabouts of a cache of Shake-Bake manuscripts, she set sail for England.

As we have already heard, Gallup's search of Canonbury Tower yielded a sum total of one suggestive lintel and zero papers. A subsequent search at the ruined Gorhambury Manor was no better.

Other disappointments would follow, but Owen and his cipher-hunting team left behind a fascinating legacy. While they discovered no actual evidence of Shakespeare's missing library, they helped turn the search into a popular pastime—the same parlour game that Edith Nesbit played in Bernard Shaw's First Folio facsimile.

Shaw's last-minute notes helped raise £2570 15s from the sale of his books. (The Cranach Press *Hamlet*, at £115, brought the fourth highest price.) He died fifteen months later.

Cryptographic, stylometric or otherwise, the field of modern Shakespearean scholarship is as schismatic as it is large. Occupying more or less entrenched positions, the factions fight passionately on multiple fronts. Despite all the drama and disputation, though, the mass of 'Strat' and 'Anti-Strat' scholarship has landed us in a good place. In their messy way, scholars have made sound progress in understanding what Shakespeare actually did in his career, and how his plays and poems came to be. Thanks to James Shapiro, Alan Nelson, Diana Price, Germaine Greer and their colleagues and competitors, we now know how confidently we can say Shakespeare was a writer who owned a writer's library.

Close bibliographical analysis of the plays—their content, publication history and print-culture origins—reveals much about how they were made. Contemporary sources—the words of men such as Robert Greene, John Davies, Thomas Freeman and Ben Jonson—also reveal much about Shakespeare and his work. The slightly disillusioning conclusion from all the sources and debates and controversies and analysis is this: Shakespeare occupied an intermediate phase in a dramaturgical production process. In the phase immediately before him, authors and poets and dramatists wrote source texts. That phase extended years and even centuries back in time. In the phase immediately after him, editors prepared playtexts for publication. That phase, though shorter, also spanned years and in some cases decades. Shakespeare's in-between job was to transform the source texts into topical, enjoyable, performable plays. His talent was a specialised one. He cultivated a knack for knowing what would work theatrically (evidently he spent many of his lost years in playhouses). Versifier, vitaliser, even vulgariser, he took prior content and made it sing, turning it into plays that delighted audiences and sated the popular appetite.

Sometimes working alone, sometimes in collaboration, he spotted and procured performable and entertaining content, then readied it for performance. Sidney Lee described Shakespeare's talent as 'a rare power of assimilating and vitalising' the works of others. John Manningham, recorder of the 'William the Conqueror' episode, was an early commentator on Shakespeare's use of sources. *Twelfth Night*, Manningham noted, 'was much like the *Comedy of Errors*, or *Menechmi* in Plautus, but most like and near to that in Italian called *Inganni*'. As Manningham suggested, Shakespeare ranged far and wide in his search for material. English, French, Italian, Spanish and Scandinavian texts. Classical, mediaeval and contemporary. Sermons, grammars, guidebooks, treatises, dictionaries, novels, poems, chronicles and other works of history, biography, science and literature. Shakespeare picked from some sources like a magpie; others he gulped down whole, appropriating entire plots along with ready-made characters, dialogue and settings. As Australian poet and scholar Archibald Strong observed:

Shakespeare…took most of his stories and many of his characters at second-hand, where he could most easily find them, and in transforming Thomas Lodge's pastoral romance (*Rosalynde; Euphues' Golden Legacy* [1590]) into the pastoral comedy [*As You Like It*], he took over for the most part Lodge's men and women, transfiguring them into the beings whom we know by the sheer Form of his genius and craftsmanship.

Not just the men and women, but also the plot and much of the exposition in *As You Like It* came from Lodge. Shakespeare found nearly all his principal characters in this way, from the second-hand store.

Shakespeare's key sources have already figured in our tracing of the search for his library. Boccaccio was a favourite, both directly and via Chaucer. Shakespeare also lifted whole lines and phrases from Marlowe, his occasional collaborator. (He is probably also credited with plays that Marlowe largely wrote.) He used Plutarch for *Antony and Cleopatra* and other Roman plays. He used Ovid's *Fasti* and Eliot's *Ortho-epia Gallica* for *The Rape of Lucrece*; Plautus' *Menaechmi* and *Amphitruo* for *The Comedy of Errors*; and John Florio's translation of Montaigne's 'Of Cannibals' for *The Tempest*. And he used a veritable library of other source texts.

Recent research by Dennis McCarthy and June Schlueter has shown that Shakespeare borrowed heavily from George North's unpublished 1576 manuscript 'A Brief Discourse of Rebellion'. North composed the work at Kirtling Hall, his family's estate in Cambridgeshire. Shakespeare used North's words when writing *Macbeth* (such as where Macbeth likens the different breeds of dogs to the various types of men), *King Lear* (the Fool's prediction about Merlin's prophecy) and parts of the history plays, including

Gloucester's opening soliloquy in *Richard III*, which begins with the famous line, 'Now is the winter of our discontent'.

The first part of Cervantes' *Don Quixote* was the basis for the missing play, *Cardenio*, thought to have been written by Shakespeare and John Fletcher. Let us savour that idea for a moment. What an amazing discovery a Shakespearean Quixote would be. Or, perhaps even better, a Shakespearean Sancho Panza! An English translation of Part I of Cervantes' epic tale appeared in 1612. Don Quixote and Sancho encounter Cardenio, the 'Ragged Knight' driven mad by betrayal. His beloved Lucinda has been tricked into marrying Don Ferdinand. Thanks to Don Quixote's intervention, all is set right: Ferdinand repents; Cardenio is cured of his madness and he reunites with Lucinda. The extent to which Shakespeare's play adhered to the original story is unknown. Over the past three centuries, people have claimed to have found parts of the play. All such claims remain to be proven, and the delight of finding a demonstrably genuine *Cardenio* remains to be relished.

Shakespeare based *Hamlet* on an earlier play, also called *Hamlet* and probably written by Thomas Kyd. Kyd's play was in turn based on a twelfth-century Danish saga by Saxo Grammaticus (printed in Latin in 1514). In the original saga, the character Hamlet was 'Amleth'. The plot elements are strikingly familiar: Amleth's uncle kills Amleth's father and marries Amleth's mother. The prince feigns madness while planning to avenge his father's murder. Prototype versions of Ophelia, Laertes and even Rosencrantz and Guildenstern appear in the saga. From this material, and probably a 1570 French version of the same story, Kyd scripted a drama that contained nearly all of what we appreciate in the Shakespearean version, including royal adultery, the ghost, the play within a play, and Hamlet's climactic death.

Shakespeare did add a few things: the character Fortinbras, and Hamlet's famous soliloquy, inspired by another source, Thomas Bedingfield's translation of *Cardanus Comforte*.

Many different verbs have been used to describe what Shakespeare was doing. He acquired, adapted, appropriated, converted, revised, synthesised, improved, borrowed, copied, co-opted, re-used, re-worked, re-packaged, stole. Let us again remember he worked at a time when authorship, plagiarism and copyright were differently conceived.

Shakespeare's extensive use of sources helps solve much that is mysterious about his life and work. Based on readings of the plays and poems, more than eighty occupations have been proposed for Shakespeare. He had, it seems, more careers than Barrington. What was Shakespeare doing in his 'lost years'? He may have obtained expertise in some of the named fields, but not in all or even many of them. There must have been another way for his writings to pick up such a diverse range of expert content. Collaboration and voracious borrowing explain the breadth of his writing and the depth of his erudition.

They resolve, too, other troubling points in Shakespeare's biography. Brokering and improving source texts explains how his crowd-pulling plays rapidly had an audience, and how he rapidly came to be known as a man of the theatre. The pillaging of sources also accounts for the early dates of several plays, and the fact that plays with confusingly similar names, plots and characters existed before Shakespeare could have written them.

Substantially freed from the need to conceive of scenarios, characters and plots, Shakespeare could focus on the writing, and the drama. People noticed what he was doing. During his lifetime he was known among his peers as a nimble vitaliser of others' content. Late in the sixteenth century, Langbaine's

Dramatick Poets quoted Edward Ravenscroft on the origins of *Titus Andronicus*:

> ...the Play was not originally *Shakespear's*, but brought by a private Author to be acted, and he only gave some Master-touches to one or two of the principal Parts or Characters: afterwards he boasts his own pains; and says, That if the Reader compare the Old Play with his Copy, he will find that none in all that Author's Works ever receiv'd greater Alterations, or Additions; the Language not only refined, but many scenes entirely new: Besides most of the principal Characters heightened, and the Plot much encreased.

This function did not command respect. The indictments from Davies, Freeman and Greene have already been noted. In a similar vein, Henry Crosse's *Vertues Commonwealth* (1603) damned 'copper-lace gentlemen', 'not few of them usurers and extortioners', who 'grow rich' and 'purchase lands by adulterous plays'. 'Crosse' was probably a pseudonym, behind which, Nashe-Wright-Chettle style, grumpy and aggrieved men hid. The author or authors of *Vertues Commonwealth* used similar language to Greene's Shake-scene passage; so similar that Shakespeare was almost certainly again the subject. Greene's reference to usurers, for example, is repeated, as is 'bombasting' out 'blank verse'. Crosse thought little of the literature produced by vitalisers:

> Oh how weak and shallow much of their poetry is, for having no sooner laid the subject and ground of their matter...but over a verse or two run upon rocks and shelves, carrying their readers into a maze, now up, then down, one verse shorter than another by a foot, like an unskillful Pilot, never comes nigh the intended harbor.

Such verbalists were not of the same class as poets like Chaucer, Gower and Lydgate.

The clearest description of Shakespeare's vitalising role, and others' reactions to it, appeared in 1616, the year of his death. Ben Jonson published a collection of epigrams, witty verses about contemporary figures. Shakespeare was probably the subject of 'On Poet-Ape':

Poor Poet-Ape, that would be thought our chief,
Whose works are e'en the frippery of wit,
From brokage is become so bold a thief
As we, the robb'd, leave rage, and pity it.
At first he made low shifts, would pick and glean,
Buy the reversion of old plays, now grown
To a little wealth, and credit on the scene,
He takes up all, makes each man's wit his own,
And told of this, he slights it. Tut, such crimes
The sluggish, gaping auditor devours;
He marks not whose 'twas first, and aftertimes
May judge it to be his, as well as ours.
Fool! as if half-eyes will not know a fleece
From locks of wool, or shreds from the whole piece.

Jonson tells a fascinating story. Poet-Ape began his theatrical career as a playbroker. Then he crossed lines of demarcation to become a reviser and repackager of others' work, which he passed off as his own. When the original authors complained, the vitaliser slighted them, arguing theatre audiences cared nought about who wrote this or that play. Jonson, though, and other real literary men could distinguish an authentic play from an 'adulterous' one cobbled from fragments.

Title pages of early quartos speak of Shakespeare as a converter.

The 1598 first edition of *Love's Labour's Lost* states it was 'Newly corrected and augmented by W. Shakespere'. Editions of *I Henry IV* were similarly 'Newly corrected by W. Shake-speare'. *Richard III* was 'Newly augmented, by William Shakespeare'. The 1599 edition of *Romeo and Juliet* was 'Newly corrected, augmented, and amended', as was the 1609 edition. Some of this correcting and amending and augmenting must have been of earlier Shakespearean versions. But some, too, was most likely of earlier non-Shakespearean plays. The quarto title pages announce for Shakespeare a role that is not simply an authorial one.

Years after Shakespeare had done his work to prepare playtexts for performance, they were transformed into printed texts. This next stage in the literary production process was multifaceted. Editors of the plays (and probably the poems) did what editors do today: tighten syntax, enrich vocabulary, improve structure and flow, enhance rhythm and rhyme, and beautify the whole. Shakespeare's editors—men like John Florio and Ben Jonson—were master polishers and serial neologists. The craft of Elizabethan and Jacobean editing was well developed: it employed techniques and traditions that pre-dated the birth of printing. Most or all of the work to prepare Shakespeare's texts for publication was undertaken by people other than Shakespeare. We know this for certain because the greatest early effort of editing Shakespeare's plays occurred after his death, during preparation of the First Folio. Many features that we see as intrinsically Shakespearean—such as his act and scene structures—were added at the editorial stage. He was not responsible for them.

When the plays appeared in print, they often included extra matter, inserted to enhance for book buyers the experience of reading and the perception of value. The long and tidy *Hamlet* versions we know from the second quarto and First Folio were probably not performed until at least a century after they first appeared, long enough for people to have forgotten that the reading version was much longer than the stage version. Plays on stage and plays in print served different purposes and offered different experiences for different, though overlapping, audiences.

Shakespeare's place in the plays' production line sheds light on the mysteriously uneven quarto texts. Modern readers are struck by the scrappiness of certain plays published in Shakespeare's lifetime. They are simply not up to Shakespearean standards. An example is the *Hamlet* quarto that Halliwell stole from his future father-in-law. In place of the famous soliloquy are these forgettable lines: 'To be or not to be. Aye, there's the point / To die to sleep, is that all? Aye all.' Instead of, 'O what a rogue and peasant slave am I!', there is the colourful, Stratfordian line, 'Why what a dunghill idiot slave am I!'

These versions are a puzzle. Many scholars assert Shakespeare had no role in the publication of the plays because so many of the published editions are so poor. Alfred William Pollard, the man who let Thomas Wise into the British Museum, sorted all the quartos into 'good' and 'bad' editions. His results appeared in *Shakespeare Folios and Quartos* (1909) and *Shakespeare's Fight with the Pirates and the Problems of the Transmission of His Text* (1917 and 1920). As the latter title suggests, Pollard's theory was that the weakest versions were piracies: unauthorised texts, scribbled down in theatres or reconstructed from memory and from filched fragments of playscripts.

Hamlet and *Romeo and Juliet*, for example, were published in multiple quarto editions. After comparing the 1603 and 1604 editions of *Hamlet*, and the 1597 and 1599 editions of *Romeo and Juliet*, Pollard designated the two pioneering quartos 'bad', and the subsequent ones 'good'. This paradigm became a common-place of Shakespeare scholarship. The best editions were those that most closely approached Shakespeare's original writings; the plays as they were performed, or the playscripts, 'foul papers' or prompt books that included his annotations. The worst editions were unauthorised bootlegs—'stolne and surreptitious copies'—more distant from Shakespeare's pen.

The problems with the binary taxonomy are plain to see: the subjective boundary between 'good' and 'bad'; the use of moral language that contains hidden judgements; and determining goodness and badness with modern criteria. Viewed in light of the production sequence, Pollard's paradigm looks arse about. Rather than being *furthest* from Shakespeare, the 'bad' texts could be the most original, the most like the performed versions, the *closest* to Shakespeare's pen. The versions we know today, especially those in the First Folio, have been subjected to post-Shakespearean editing. This would have made the plays more tidy, more literary, perhaps more sublime. It would have estranged them from their raw Shakespearean state. (Traces of the raw playscripts remain in the printed plays. Collier noticed that part of the 1600 quarto of *Much Ado About Nothing* gives the names of the actors Cowley and Kemp instead of their characters Verges and Dogberry.)

The resulting picture is one of gradualism and collectivism. Using whatever material he could find, Shakespeare composed topical, popular plays. Though suitable for performance, his playtexts were imperfect: syntactically jumbled, stylistically uneven, artistically mediocre; quite different from what we know as 'Shakespeare' today. In his lifetime, many of the plays were improved by the first editors. After his death, the mostly 'good' (edited) quartos, plus newly edited plays, formed the basis for most of the First Folio texts. Accepting this new paradigm requires us to drop prejudices: about Shakespeare's literary talent and sensibility; about the phenomenon of solo genius; and about the dynamics of Elizabethan and Jacobean literary production.

The paradigm suggests a decidedly different relationship between Shakespeare and his publishers. The 'bad' quartos might not have been so surreptitious, so unauthorised. Shakespeare knew his way around St Paul's Churchyard and other centres of the book trade. He could easily have dealt promiscuously with numerous publishers, including ones we would call disreputable. Sale of plays for publication could help explain much of his unexplained income, and indeed much of his involvement in the theatre *per se*.

The preface to the First Folio has actors John Hemmings and Henry Condell condemning earlier publishers as 'injurious imposters' who perpetrated 'frauds and stealthes'. From the Wise case and other book-world trickery, we know to treat such claims with great caution. Denouncing earlier editions is a hackneyed tactic of salesmanship, a way to claim the high ground and to signal authenticity.

The sequence in which the quartos were published supports the alternative picture of pre- and post-editing versions. Scores of changes were made to *Hamlet*, for example, to lift it from being a 'bad' to a 'good' quarto. One of the editors knew the culture and geography of mountainless Denmark. The first quarto's lines, 'But look, the morn in russet mantle clad, / Walks over yonder mountain top', become in the revised edition, 'But look, the dawn in russet mantle clad, / Walks o'er the dew on yon high eastern hill'. The second edition also contains corrected Scandinavian names such as Polonius (Plönnies), Reynaldo (Ranald) and Yaughan (Jörgen); authentic Danish words such as *Danskers* and *crants*; and accurate details of the Danish court.

The Shakespearean production line helps explain the mystery of the Shakespeare Apocrypha. This is the set of twelve plays, not part of the current canon, but published at early dates under Shakespeare's name, and thought by some scholars to be genuinely his. Verse texts such as *The Passionate Pilgrim* belong to an analogous poetical apocrypha; they are mostly not thought to be by Shakespeare, even though they were attributed to him in his lifetime. Some Shakespearean surveys also leave out works that display a markedly different style; 'The Phoenix and the Turtle' is an example. All these apocryphal and marginal Shakespearean texts may be analogous to the raw, 'bad' quartos; the unedited 'before', just waiting to be transformed into the edited 'after'.

There will always be a fuzzy edge to Shakespeare's body of work. But understanding how the plays and poems were actually created takes us a long way in the Authorship Question and the library mystery. From the collaborative, phased, production-line picture, a newly sized Shakespeare emerges. He is not so small as in Diana Price's universe, but neither is he so large as the 'genius' version. He is not the solo literary mastermind pictured by Victorian adulators, nor is he the disreputable clown or hayseed of recent portraits. His role is middle sized: much of the work that went into the published plays was done by prior authors, and much of it—parsing, shaping, tidying, tightening—took place after he had done his work.

In this sequential process there is no need, and indeed no room, for a secret author, aristocratic or otherwise. All that the middle stage requires is a workaday dramatist with a talent for converting prior content into performable and entertaining plays. (And one with the nerve to keep doing it when prior writers complained.) The size and shape of that person fits Shakespeare very well. He was not a detached, meticulous, uber-literary author. He was a practically talented, commercial man, in tune with audiences. He seems to have cared little about how perfectly he appeared in print, and how the world credited him for his work. He was more interested in becoming a wealthy burgher in a provincial town.

This is all a bit disappointing for the heretics. The unglamorous role of adapting prior content is not what they have in mind for their candidates, who are imagined as secret virtuosos writing inspired, immutable plays and poems from scratch. Compared to secret Neville and secret Oxford and secret Bacon, William Shakespeare is much more likely to have pillaged earlier work. Why would an aristocrat bother to construct an elaborate secret authorial enterprise, and then do so merely by adapting earlier content? Shakespeare's missing library was a boon for heretics like Diana Price and Brenda James. It underpins much of their reasoning. Shakespeare's library of sources, though, is the heretics' downfall. Candidates like Neville are non-solutions to a non-problem.

Nor was there a principal 'secret author' who provided Shakespeare with input to be vitalised. Most of the sources have been identified, as have most of their authors. As we have seen, the range of input was remarkably wide: classics, historical works, Italian novels, early poetry, recent plays. Only one scrap of hope is left for the unorthodox camp. Though aristocrats could not write for money and would rather not be connected to the theatre, they certainly did write; mostly poetry but also playscripts. For a small proportion of the Shakespearean œuvre, there is room for a jotting, dabbling aristocrat to have supplied secret literary input into the production process. If Shakespeare sourced some of his material in this manner, evidence may have been left behind; evidence that could explain the more credible hints and trails so convincing to Baconians, Oxfordians and others that their candidate was the 'real Shakespeare'.

I hoped this crack of unorthodox light would be enough for me to stay friends with the Nevillians, even though we were heading inexorably towards a critical disagreement. I was certain a silent aristocrat was not responsible for most or all of the œuvre. This is clear from the breadth of Shakespeare's sources, and from how they were used. Even if the heretics were to find an inscription on an early Shakespeare quarto that read, in the hand of Neville, Marlowe, Oxford, Bacon or Queen Elizabeth, 'I wrote this', that would not cede the whole œuvre to the inscriber.

Diana Price's picture of Shakespeare as a provincial dunce doesn't square with his astuteness. He came down to London to make his living, and he made a Stratford fortune. Agile and versatile in business, he was nobody's fool. The evidence about Shakespeare's portfolio of profitable projects accords precisely with what we know about the early modern book world. That world was at least as complex and entrepreneurial as the domain of Barrington's publishers. Elizabethan literary tradesmen sought income wherever they could find it: writing plays for performance; working as actors; investing as sharers in theatrical companies; and selling texts for publication. They also did whatever they could 'on the side'. In Shakespeare's case, he invested in theatres and other real estate, and lent money at interest. Many of Shakespeare's peers lived in poverty: the historian and martyrologist John Foxe nearly starved to death in St Paul's Churchyard; theologian Richard Hooker's children were 'beggars'; Thomases Nashe and Dekker were locked up in debtors' prison; Michael Drayton died broke. Examples like these, and Shakespeare's own humble, dungheaped origins, provided ample motivation for him to seek wealth and worldly comfort.

Documentary evidence supports the sequential, production-line picture of Shakespeare's work. He was certainly involved in the theatre. He was certainly implicated in the sourcing of plays, and in their production and performance. Title-page evidence, and the comments of his contemporaries, show him incrementally improving texts. Several Shakespeare plays were published anonymously before they appeared under his name; that pattern is hardly congruent with a covert enterprise in which 'Shakespeare' was a pseudonym. If anything, the pattern of publication indicates William Shakespeare himself was the anonymous author, first concealed and then revealed.

The mystery of Shakespearean authorship boils down to a question of scale. How big a part did Shakespeare play in converting early content into the plays we know today? To what extent were subsequent editors responsible for elevating and even inflating his œuvre? We will return to these questions in the discussion of the First Folio and Ben Jonson's library.

In the computer era, Shakespeare authorship studies embraced techniques even more analytical and numerical than those of Diana Price. The diverse field of 'stylometry' successfully transported a toolbox of practical math into English Literature departments. The field involves looking for statistical patterns in word use, vocabulary, grammar, sentence construction and punctuation. Metaphors, similes, neologisms, hendiadys and *hapax legomena* are mainstays of the stylometrist's kit. The use of stylometry in authorship studies is based on a simple hypothesis: every author leaves behind a unique linguistic signature that can be detected quantitatively, then used to match works or parts thereof to that author.

Scores if not hundreds of slogging scholars are now testing that hypothesis on Shakespearean and non-Shakespearean texts. Despite its popularity, though, stylometry can never be definitive for the reasons given in relation to the language fallacy and 'Shakespeare's dictionary': fashions in style and idiom; the possibility of an author experimenting with style; and the possibility of an author deliberately aping the style of another. Those objections apply regardless of how Shakespeare worked.

Over and above those objections, the 'inbetweener' Shakespeare presents intractable difficulties. The rich stylistic variation in Shakespeare's plays and poems poses a fundamental question: to what extent is the variation due to different source authors further up the production line, and different editors further down? The variance in Shakespeare's œuvre is wider than the differences between him and nearby writers. How, then, are we to tell, just from counting linguistic indicators, where his œuvre ends and another's begins? A common editor may have applied similar styles, grammar and punctuation to the work of multiple authors. The presence of collaborators poses a similar problem. If Shakespeare collaborated with and borrowed liberally from Marlowe, for example, how can stylometry separate their works? (Evidently it cannot: a major statistical study by the physicist Thomas Mendenhall analysed word length in the writings of Shakespeare, Bacon and their contemporaries. He found an exact match between the works of Shakespeare and Marlowe.)

Some Shakespearean poems and plays are stylistic misfits. 'The Phoenix and the Turtle' has already been outed as one of these. Other blatant outliers include *Timon of Athens*—seldom performed, not well known, certainly not popular. The Shakespearean production process, in which there were multiple sources and multiple hands at work, helps explain these misfits in particular and the variability of the texts in general. Viewed through this kaleidoscopic lens, Shakespeare the adapter becomes many men in one.

Apart from cruelling the pitch for statistical analysis, the 'inbetweener' picture is a disaster for stylometry's evil cousin, cryptography. The crooked backbone of anti-Stratfordian scholarship, the search for codes and secret messages suffers from chronic ailments. As Shaw noted, with enough letters and enough methodological leeway, any combination of words—every name, every anagram, every riddle, every confession—can be found in any text. Once you have the whole alphabet, you can make a text say anything. The problem of intention is another impairment for the code hunters. If a concealed message is found, like 'Bacon wrote this', it could be any one of a number of things: a decoy, a prank, an accident, or perhaps a gift from another author experiencing a moment of existential crisis. Decipherment cannot get us far without corroborative, non-cipher evidence.

Cryptographers face such difficulties routinely, but the Shakespearean production line is the cipher-hunters' endgame. If the texts reflect multiple sources as well as multiple editors working separately from Shakespeare, then who in this mix is making sure the secret messages are getting through? Editing and print production processes were subject to their own forms of chaos. Frequent changes were made to texts, even within a single impression. The remaining First Folio copies, for example, display much textual variety due to the resetting of type during printing. For the purposes of cipher-hunting, this variety is a wicked dilemma. Which is the 'true', decipherable text? Shambolic printeries and haphazard print production would ensure that any embedded codes became irretrievably garbled; like William Burroughs' heroin-fuelled cut-up technique, without anyone making sense of the shuffling.

The last resort for cipher-hunters is a spectacularly extreme position: the differences among the First Folio copies are themselves a deliberate part of an uber-cipher, meant to be read four or five dimensionally across and between different copies, lines, plays, fonts and even, as Owen claimed, between the writings of Shakespeare and his contemporaries. That level of secret complexity—a pan-dimensional googolplex of hidden messages—would paralyse even the most sophisticated and meticulous printery, and is beyond unlikely.

For Shakespeare studies and the search for his library, cipher-hunting was a massive methodological sidetrack. Stylometry, as applied to the Authorship Question, is probably another.

Evidence from non-Shakespearean libraries proves that non-Shakespearean authorship of the poems and plays was not an 'open secret'. And Shakespeare's own library of sources proves that there was never a secret author at all. In the Shakespearean production process, there is no need for a secret author, and nor is there room for one. We have identified the 'author' who reliably fed texts to Shakespeare. That author is the library itself, and the Authorship Question is in large part its own solution.

Over the past quarter-century, competition between the Stratfordian mainstream and the anti-Stratfordian heretics has dominated Shakespeare scholarship. Ostensibly and rhetorically, the camps remain polarised; a quick look at any online authorship forum will show how vehement and nasty the debate can be. Something interesting, though, is happening inside the roiling eco-system of Shakespeare studies. Though neither group would acknowledge any kind of momentum towards convergence, nor agree they might ever meet at some kind of middle ground, the camps have been inching towards this 'inbetweener' view. That landing point is not too far, for example, from Price's *Shakespeare's Unorthodox Biography*, and nor is it entirely alien to Jonathan

Bate's orthodox *The Genius of Shakespeare* (1997). Years, perhaps decades, will pass before the more rational partisans on both sides notice how much their principal disagreements have withered.

Where, then, have we got to in our search? We seem to be back on track. There is a prospect, albeit mostly a theoretical one, that the orthodox and unorthodox camps might one day bury their hatchets. We can say with confidence that Shakespeare had a hand in the plays and poems that bear his name. He was, at least in a limited sense, a bookman. In other words, Shakespeare wasn't Barrington. He would have owned copies of at least some of his many source books, which were so very important as suppliers of content. He would have owned manuscripts and papers, as well as finished copies of his books. In other words, he would have owned a library. The final phase of our search is concerned with the question: what kind of library?

Part III

VISIONS OF
SHAKESPEARE'S LIBRARY

CHAPTER 15

Bibliotheca Mitchelliana

Over the past few centuries, people around the world have attempted to recreate Shakespeare's library. They have done so in print, by assembling and making collections of books; and they have done so in timber, plaster and bricks, by constructing and restoring physical spaces. The best known of the latter are Henry Clay Folger's Shakespeare Library in Washington, and the Shakespearean buildings in and around Stratford, such as Nash's House, Hall's Croft, New Place and the reading room at the Shakespeare Centre on Henley Street. One of the most compelling attempts to recreate Shakespeare's library began in an unlikely time and place: nineteenth-century Sydney.

For bibliophiles, the idea of an antipodean Shakespeare

library has magical attractions, and early antecedents. James Cook made his first voyage to the east coast in the *Endeavour*, which carried, in the library of natural history artist Sydney Parkinson, a set of Shakespeare's works—probably Johnson's 1765 edition. A member of Sir Joseph Banks' scientific team, Parkinson drew delightful images of Australia's people, flora and fauna, but sadly perished on the return journey. Almost a century later, the last convict ship, *Hougoumont*, brought to Western Australia an unusually literate cargo of prisoners. According to one convict's journal, there were many entertainments during the voyage: 'A debating society, recitations from Shakespeare, nightly theatricals, and the publication of a weekly journal containing original poetry, critical articles, and a lively correspondence column.'

William Shakespeare lived in a culture electrified by the exploits of seamen like Francis Drake and Sir Walter Raleigh, and by the voyage books of Walter Bigge and Richard Hakluyt. In 1589 Richard Field published a Bigge book on Drake's West Indian Voyage. The first Englishman to circumnavigate the globe, Drake missed the Australian continent by a whisker, passing between Timor and the north-western coast. Though world maps showed Terra Australis Incognita from about 1490, and though Portuguese sailors may have visited the continent as early as 1521, Shakespeare never referred to it by name. He did, however, refer to the Antipodes. In *Much Ado About Nothing*, Benedick offers to 'go on the slightest errand now to the Antipodes'. (In *The Merry Wives of Windsor*, Falstaff declares he will make love to two women simultaneously: 'They shall be my East and West Indies, and I will trade to them both.') *The Tempest* pivots on the hazards of maritime exploration and commerce.

A vibrant Shakespearean scene established itself soon after European settlement. Informal and disorganised readings and performances were ways to pass the time and maintain civilisation in the isolated outpost. Probably the earliest 'commercial' Australian performance of a Shakespearean play took place only twelve years after the arrival of the First Fleet. In his limerick of a career, Robert Sidaway was a baker, a watch-case maker, a convict and a theatre owner. His Sydney theatre performed *I Henry IV* in April 1800. According to David Malouf:

> It was a proper theatre, Georgian in style, with a pit, a gallery and boxes. The price of admission was five shillings to a box, two and six to the pit, a shilling to the gallery. But patrons who had no ready cash could pay in kind, that is, in meat, flour or spirits.

A convict enterprise in the infant colony, the theatre 'established itself rather more easily than the first church'. The cast of convicts and ex-convicts strived to behave with all propriety, but the authorities soon judged the theatre a corrupting influence and closed it down.

The authorities' anxieties were well founded. An earlier playhouse, licensed by the Governor and erected at a cost of a hundred pounds, was managed by 'a group of the more decent among the convicts'. According to the Barrington biographer R. S. Lambert, 'No improprieties took place inside the theatre, but a number of convicts who stayed away from the second performance spent their time in breaking into the huts of those that attended it, and robbing them.' This is the theatre in which Barrington is supposed to have read his 'True Patriots All' prologue, which alludes to *Richard III*: '"Give me a horse," bawls Richard…We'll find a man would help himself to one.'

Shakespeare's plays were quickly a mainstay of the professional theatre that emerged in Australia in the 1830s. They permeated the culture in other ways, too. They were intermittently performed at benefits and other special events. Fancy-dress balls were held on the date identified by convention as the Bard's birthday. Audiences around the country enjoyed Shakespeare-themed pantomimes and operas. Faithful citizens erected statues in the Bard's honour. Entrepreneurs named pubs, theatres and racehorses after his plays and characters. Galleries collected Elizabethan and Jacobean art. Freemasons established Shakespeare Lodges. Shakespeare societies popped up in cities and even in country towns. Wagga Wagga's Shakespeare Society was active in 1895 and, in different incarnations, for many decades after that.

William Walker's 1890 *Reminiscences* recorded a perfor-mance of *Othello* at Windsor. An actor named Kemble 'painted one side of his face black and alternated his profile to play both Othello and Iago'. When the same actor performed in Hobart, 'enraged audiences' bombarded him with vegetables and other food. American, English and other foreign performers toured regularly and profitably during the nineteenth century and well into the twentieth. Oscar Asche's 'triumphal' 1909 tour lasted eighteen months and packed theatres in Sydney and Melbourne with performances of *The Taming of the Shrew*, *Othello*, *As You Like It* and *The Merchant of Venice*. In 1948 the Old Vic brought out Laurence Olivier and Vivien Leigh to perform *Richard III*. Led by Anthony Quayle, the Shakespeare Memorial Theatre Company toured in 1949. The programmes for the company's performances feature Shakespeare's coat of arms and showcase the best of Australian industry. Theatregoers were reassured that the actresses wore Australian-made, True-to-Type foundation garments: 'There's a superbly fitting BERLEI behind the scenes.'

Grandsons of a Cornish farm-worker, the five Tangye brothers of

Birmingham exemplified the Victorian ethic of self-help. From modest beginnings they built a company and a fortune supplying the industrial revolution with steam engines, pumps and chain hoists. Using his new wealth, Richard Tangye assembled a Cromwelliana collection whose rather mournful highlights were Cromwell's coffin plate, death mask, funeral escutcheon and Bible. He also sponsored, with his brother George, public institutions such as the Birmingham Library, the Birmingham Art Gallery, and Britain's first municipal School of Art.

And Richard travelled. In 1883 he published a book of his recent world tour, *Reminiscences of Travel in Australia, America and Egypt*. Daytime amusements on the voyage included 'quoits, a run with the hounds, jumping in sacks by moonlight, racing in sacks'. Evenings were brightened by 'concerts, recitations, and occasionally theatrical performances'. The township of Sydney was even more impressive. Tangye appreciated immediately the optimism and ambition of this outpost of Empire. 'Young Australia, like his cousin in America, has an unbounded confidence in the future of his country; he has even more in himself.' Tangye admired Sydney's Free Public Library, which had opened in September 1869 with twenty thousand volumes and was modelled in part on the Birmingham example. The principal librarian greeted Tangye with 'civility and helpfulness'. In 1885 the industrialist presented the library with a spectacular gift: a Shakespeare First Folio. In excellent condition and said to have cost Tangye five hundred pounds, the volume was quickly appraised at double that value by Sydney newspapers. In the burgeoning international trend of free libraries, the gift—the only First Folio in Australia—was among the foremost acts of public philanthropy. It was delivered in a purpose-built carved box made from Warwickshire timber.

David Scott Mitchell was born in 1836 in the officers' quarters of the old Military Hospital in Macquarie Street, Sydney. His father, James Mitchell, was surgeon-in-charge. David's mother, Augusta, was descended from Sir John Frederick, a wealthy seventeenth-century lord mayor of London. James had arrived in New South Wales in 1821 after serving in the Napoleonic Wars. By grant and purchase, he acquired more than thirty thousand acres in the Hunter Valley. Through an extraordinary stroke of luck, the land proved to be rich coalfields. Mitchell was suddenly a very wealthy man.

Augusta's mother brought her personal library to Sydney, and continued to acquire books until her death in 1840. Many of her books passed to her grandson, David. During his childhood, a copy of Shakespeare's works was always in the family home. David was taught to appreciate the Bard as an example of a self-educated man who overcame impediments, a quality that appealed as much to the Mitchells as it had to the Tangyes. (*Moore's Almanack* listed Shakespeare alongside other self-raised high-achievers such as John Jacob Astor and Benjamin Franklin.)

At the age of sixteen, David entered the University of Sydney as one of its first six undergraduates. A formidable whist player, he won scholarships in maths and prizes in physics and chemistry. His professors, though, formally censured him for 'gross and wilful neglect to his studies'. He nevertheless graduated BA with honours in Classics in 1856, and MA in 1859. Admitted to the Sydney Bar, he instead devoted himself to managing his father's estates.

An 1864 photograph shows Mitchell's penetrating eyes, high cheekbones, square-trimmed beard and slender build. Women found him charming, but his amatory ventures were disappointing. In 1865 he was rumoured to be engaged to Emily Manning, the daughter of a Supreme Court judge. Emily was nine years younger and, at a height of four foot ten, a good deal shorter than Mitchell. But the engagement was shorter still, and Mitchell never married her, or anyone else. He did, however, become close to his still younger cousin, Rose Scott. Reading *The Taming of the Shrew* at an early age inspired Rose to fight for social justice. 'The craven witch, to give in in that servile manner and worse still to turn the tables on her own sex! From that moment,' Rose wrote, 'I was a rebel against all injustice and wrong.'

After Mitchell inherited his father's assets, he retreated into an uneven kind of bibliophile seclusion, attended by his faithful housekeeper, Sarah, and venturing forth mainly to buy books or to go to his club. Apart from letters from Rose, most of his contact with the outside world was via booksellers or games of cards.

The strongest early influences on Mitchell's book collecting were Dibdin and the Shakespeare biographer Charles Knight. Mitchell owned the volumes that turned Dibdin into a proper bibliomaniac: William Beloe's *Anecdotes of Literature and Scarce Books* (1807–12) and Isaac Disraeli's *Curiosities of Literature* (1823). Without these, Dibdin wrote, 'he would despair of ever attaining the exalted state of *Bibliomania*'. Mitchell read in Beloe:

Perhaps there is no book in the English language which has risen so rapidly in value as the first edition [he meant the First Folio] of the works of our great natural Poet. I can remember a very fine copy to have been sold for five guineas. I could once have purchased a superb one for nine guineas. At the sale of Dr Monro's books it was purchased for thirteen guineas; and two years since, I was present when thirty-six guineas were demanded for a copy.

Mitchell also owned Dibdin's key works, including *Bibliomania* (1811, a heavily marked-up copy) and *Bibliographical Decameron* (1817). Under these influences, Mitchell's foremost passion was Elizabetheana. An early purchase was a Shakespeare Fourth Folio. At the same sale Mitchell bought Conolly's *A Study of Hamlet* (1863), a presentation copy to Charles Dickens. The rate of Mitchell's buying accelerated, and his home at 17 Darlinghurst Road began to bulge with all manner of books. A. H. Spencer, who early in his career visited the home as a messenger boy for booksellers Angus & Robertson, described it thus: 'Books, pamphlets, maps, pictures, newspapers, manuscripts, filling a vast amount of shelving and stacked upon the floor, tables and chairs in every room, and up the staircase.'

In October 1898, Mitchell offered to gift his collection to the Public Library of New South Wales, on condition that a new wing would house the collection and that the books would be made freely available for study. He granted seventy thousand pounds to maintain the bequest. In 1899 a special act of parliament was passed to facilitate the gift and to mirror the British Museum's collection policies insofar as that would make the collection accessible to students.

The Public Library already had significant strengths in Elizabethan and Jacobean drama. Apart from the Tangye First Folio, the collection included a Second Folio that had belonged to Essie Jenyns, a popular Australian actress in the 1880s. Four admirers presented Jenyns with the volume in 1887. She married one of the four when she retired from the stage the following year.

The task of moving the 'fortress of books' from Darlinghurst Road attained epic proportions. After packing the books into damp-proof metal boxes, carriers loaded them on drays and transported them to the vaults of the Bank of Australasia where they waited until the Mitchell Library stacks were ready. The final move was completed in April 1908, and the new building was officially opened in March 1910. Sadly, Mitchell had died three years earlier.

The Mitchells and the Tangyes supplied a new vision of Shakespeare's library, and a new vision of Shakespeare himself, as the self-made man, the worker-hero. Apart from the Tangye First Folio and Mitchell's collection of Shakespearean and Elizabethan books, the Mitchell Library now features a beautiful, one-to-one scale replica of Shakespeare's library—a physical reproduction of what his bookroom at New Place might have been like.

Planning for the 'New South Wales Shakespearean Memorial Library' began before the First World War as a way to celebrate the tercentenary of Shakespeare's death. As initially conceived, the library would house the more than 1300 special items of Shakespearean interest in the Mitchell Library. The Shakespeare Tercentenary Memorial Fund set a target of £25,000, which was to be raised through a public appeal. The war intervened, however, and the appeal raised only £1425. The Fund handed over the money to the trustees of the Public Library.

Plans were scaled back. There would be a Shakespeare Room instead, within the walls of the Mitchell. The room was completed in 1942, and it is just the right size, with just the right level of provincial Elizabethan opulence, for Shakespeare's library. Two whole walls and much of a third are lined with sturdy bookshelves. Over the entrance there is a fine carving of the Shakespeare coat of arms—this is, after all, a proper gentleman's library. Symmetrically, the inner lintel displays Queen Elizabeth's coat of arms. Her arms are repeated on the wooden cornice, alternating with those of the Earl of Southampton. The

Shakespeare arms are repeated, too, in the stained-glass doors of the Shakespeare Room.

The room was modelled on Cardinal Wolsey's closet at Hampton Court Palace. The ornate coffered plaster ceiling is striking, as is the extensive woodcarving in Tasmanian blackwood, treated to mimic English oak. Carved pillars stand inside the door, and the walls are decorated with elaborate, Tudor-style carving: intricate linen folds and other period motifs, rendered in blackwood by the master carver Charles Sherline. The stained-glass window, Arthur Benfield's 'Seven Ages of Man', depicts a speech from *As You Like It*. Beneath the window sits a handsome, mediaeval-style window seat. The room features Elizabethan relics: a chair made from Shakespeare's mulberry tree—an organism that seems to have produced a supernatural quantity of timber—and, in pride of place, the Tangyes' carved First Folio box, made from oak grown in the forest of Arden. The library's trustees published an artist's impression of the Bard in his new library—sitting on his mulberry chair, absorbed in a book.

Henry Gullett, former president of the Shakespeare Society of New South Wales, commissioned a complementary statue by the sculptor Sir Bertram Mackennal. Unveiled in 1926 in Shakespeare Place, between the Mitchell Library and the Royal Botanic Gardens, the statue features six bronze figures: Shakespeare, Hamlet, Portia, Romeo, Juliet and Falstaff. The inscription quotes Prospero's poignant speech: 'Our revels now are ended…we are such stuff / As dreams are made on, and our little life / Is rounded with a sleep.' In 1959 the statue was moved to make way for an expressway.

When planning began, in the first decades of the twentieth century, for Australia's purpose-built capital city, many names were mooted. Ugly compromises like 'Sydmelperbaneho' were quickly rejected in favour of three frontrunners. One was the mildly gynaecological 'Myola'. Another was 'Canberra', which, as every Australian schoolkid knows, means both 'meeting place' and 'breasts'. King O'Malley was the driver behind the other frontrunner. A member of parliament and an American by birth, he pushed for the capital to be named 'Shakespeare', after 'the greatest Englishman who ever lived'. David Garrick had erected a temple to Shakespeare in his garden. O'Malley would have turned the whole of Australia into a Shakespeare monument.

CHAPTER 16

Bibliotheca
Jonsoniana

In the latter half of the nineteenth century, copies of the First Folio were scarce. And yet a determined man or woman of modest means could buy one. Sir George Grey—explorer, politician and linguist—bought two. Grey became Governor of South Australia and then of New Zealand (twice) and the Cape Colony in South Africa. In 1861 he donated more than 3500 volumes to the South African Public Library, including a First Folio. In 1894 he bought from Bernard Quaritch, for eighty-five pounds, his second First Folio. After paying a further three pounds to London booksellers Ellis & Elvey to improve the copy by replacing missing pages with genuine leaves and facsimile ones, Grey donated it to the Auckland Public Library.

Even in the early decades of the twentieth century a First Folio could be obtained with no great difficulty. England's economy was changing. Aristocrats fell on hard times and had to sell artworks and volumes from those grand libraries that had harboured books since Shakespeare's day. By mid-century, though, the First Folio bubble was well and truly inflating. The only buyers with deep enough pockets to afford a First Folio were oil billionaires and public institutions, most of them in Japan and America. Roxburghe member Sir John Paul Getty Jr was one of the few private citizens with sufficient resources. In 2003, he bought a fine First Folio from Oriel College, Oxford, for £3.5 million. Values dropped somewhat with the global financial crisis, but have since crept upwards. Today, a copy might command as much as $6 million, depending on its completeness and how many 'flakes of pie-crust' it had received in the servants' hall. When the First Folio was first issued, it sold for a pound—a not inconsiderable price, though cheaper than Holinshed's *Chronicles*.

The precise number of copies printed is unknown. Estimates range between five hundred and a thousand copies. Today, only about 235 copies remain; the number is imprecise because some incomplete copies are debatable inclusions in the census. What happened to the hundreds of missing copies? That is one thing we know for certain. Time is a destroyer of books. The lost Folios were sunk, flushed, flooded, gutted, eaten, mislaid, thrown out, blown up, pulverised, stabbed, recycled, buried, diced and used as food wrapping. Some were simply read to pieces. Fires such as those at Stratford (1641), London (1666), Ashburnham House (1731) and New Zealand Government House (1848) accounted for an unknown but significant number of copies.

In 1904, on behalf of publisher A. H. Bullen, Frank Sidgwick set up a press at Stratford-upon-Avon to print an edition of Shakespeare's works in his birthplace. A local woman called at the printery; she had heard that 'the young gentleman was interested in old books'. From her shopping bag she produced a volume that lacked its cover. Her children had scribbled in the book and torn pages out. Enough of it remained, though, for Sidgwick to identify it as a 1632 Shakespeare Second Folio, in even worse condition than the dirty, dog-eared, beer-stained, candle-singed, tobacco-ashed Perkins–Collier copy.

As nearly everyone knows, the First Folio was prepared by Shakespeare's fellow actors John Hemmings and Henry Condell. Recognising their achievements in preserving Shakespearean texts, Bill Bryson called them the 'greatest literary heroes of all time'. They wrote the preface and other preliminary matter, edited the plays and oversaw the printing. Except they very likely did not.

Editorial attribution of the First Folio to Hemmings and Condell passes into and out of fashion. Today, the balance of evidence points away from their editorship. First of all, Hemmings and Condell were stage players, with no apparent editorial experience, and certainly no experience with a project of the First Folio's scale. They were comedic actors, and their inclusion as named editors could well be a joke. (Hemmings ended his life as a grocer; Condell, a publican.) More likely, the claim that they edited the Folio is a commercial exercise in branding; a way to confer theatrical authority on a book made by a printery, Jaggard's, known for its piracies. From our journey so far, we know to view such preliminary matter with scepticism, and there are blatant falsehoods in this particular case. Notwithstanding Bryson's generous words, it is likely Hemmings and Condell had as much to do with publishing Shakespeare as Barrington had with the eponymous voyage accounts. To identify the editors, we must look elsewhere.

The First Folio preface, 'To the great Variety of Readers', is followed by Ben Jonson's dedicatory verse to Shakespeare, and by three shorter poems, attributed to Hugh Holland, Leonard Digges and 'I. M.', identity unknown. Jonson provided a grandiose poem with a grandiloquent title-cum-dedication:

To the memory of my beloved,
The AVTHOR
Mr VVILLIAM SHAKESPEARE
AND
what he hath left us

Jonson also contributed a ten-line poem commending (with characteristic ambiguity) the Droeshout portrait. Jonson, it seems, had a stake in the success of the venture.

Shakespeare in his lifetime was probably not a famous playwright, but Jonson certainly was. He had written more than fifty plays and masques, many of which appeared in print, as did his epigrams and verse. In 1616 he republished nine of his plays, plus thirteen masques and six 'entertainments', as a collected edition of his *Workes*. In 1623, entering the later part of an accomplished career, he was a celebrated man of letters, exceptionally well connected in the literary world and at court. Many times in that career he had been implicated in Shakespeare's œuvre, and there are numerous hints that Jonson was also complicit in the First Folio.

A good case has also been made that John Florio performed an editorial role on the volume. Florio was a serious scholar and skilled translator. He had tutored at Oxford and taught languages privately in London. Among other publications, he produced an important edition of Montaigne's *Essays* (1603). That book confirmed Florio's reputation as a masterful editor and liberal provider of preliminary matter, 'whether in the form of elaborate dedications, addresses to the reader, or verses in praise of himself by his friends'—'His prefaces are masterpieces of pomp and decoration'. A similar liberality was of course also evident in the First Folio, on which Florio may well have worked alongside Jonson as a co-editor.

Without further documentary evidence, the division of labour among these and other editors cannot be pinned down. We do know Jonson had already edited and overseen the production of a folio volume of plays: his *Workes of Beniamin Jonson*, published in the year of Shakespeare's death. Jonson understood what was involved in such a project. He understood the market, and had borne the jibes of detractors who accused him of confusing work and play, and who saw the *Workes* as folly, treating low drama as high poetry. The only significant single-author collection of plays before the Shakespeare First Folio, the *Workes* were so much a precedent that the two volumes can legitimately be considered part of a single endeavour. Readers certainly saw the books as two examples of a category: folio editions of plays for serious private appreciation. One day in 1623, Sir Edward Dering purchased Jonson's *Workes* and two copies of the brand-new Shakespeare folio. Collector Humphrey Dyson was another early buyer who acquired both the 1616 *Workes* and the 1623 works.

The principal architect of the First Folio's prefatory matter possessed both literary acumen and a hunger for the venture to succeed. The prefatory verses pump up the plays and position them in a literary tradition as poetry worthy of serious regard. Jonson's commendatory poem speaks of Shakespeare in classical terms: 'And all the Muses still were in their prime, / When like

Apollo he came forth to warme / Our eares, or like a Mercury to charme.' Apart from this reference, Jonson's poem invokes the Muses three more times. Designed to encourage people to buy the book (and to accept the story of its author), the preliminary matter is overtly commercial; Shaw called the dedications 'Beggars' Petitions'.

Jonson was Shakespeare's contemporary. The two men moved in overlapping circles and certainly knew each other. On 4 August 1600, four plays were listed together in the Stationers' register 'to be staied': *As You Like It*, *Henry V*, *Much Ado About Nothing* and *Every Man in His Humour*. This grouping suggests the authors were associated, or that their plays had a common publisher or owner. Jonson and Shakespeare did indeed have publishers in common. Thomas Thorpe, for example, the publisher of Shakespeare's *Sonnets*, published Jonson at least four times. Books and plays provide further documentary evidence of Jonson–Shakespeare connections; the two are referred to as fellows, and are known to have used the same source books. In 1610, Shakespeare and Jonson were both supplying plays for the theatre company known as the King's Men. In his own writings, Jonson referred to Shakespeare's plays and characters; the 1614 reference to *The Two Noble Kinsmen* in *Bartholomew Fair* is an example.

By that time, Jonson had settled into another important role: Shakespeare frenemy number one. Adept at homing in on the vulnerabilities of his contemporaries, Jonson left behind remarks about Shakespeare that are frequently critical and remarkably inconsistent. He based depraved characters on Shakespeare, and made fun of him in poems and epigrams, such as 'Poet-Ape', probably written shortly after *The Poetaster*, the play in which he ridiculed Shakespeare's gentlemanly aspirations.

Six years after Shakespeare's death, William Basse wrote about the Bard's poetical stature:

Renowned Spenser, lie a thought more nigh
To learned Chaucer, and rare Beaumont lie
A little nearer Spenser, to make room
For Shakespeare in your threefold, fourfold tomb.

In the First Folio, Jonson rejected Basse's idea: Shakespeare did not need to join the other poets as he was 'a monument, without a tomb'. People have wondered ever since if that was an insult or not. It probably wasn't; in the First Folio, Jonson was on his best behaviour. But other lines he left behind are more obviously derogatory. And Jonson interspersed them, perversely, with praise.

A note he wrote in the 1630s was found after his death and was published in *Timber, or Discoveries Made upon Men and Matter* (1640):

I remember the players have often mentioned it as an honour to Shakespeare, that in his writing (whatsoever he penned) he never blotted out a line. My answer hath been, 'Would he had blotted a thousand,' which they thought a malevolent speech. I had not told posterity this but for their ignorance who choose that circumstance to commend their friend by which he most faulted; and to justify mine own candour, for I loved the man, and do honour his memory on this side idolatry as much as any. He was, indeed, honest, and of an open and free nature; had an excellent phantasy, brave notions and gentle expressions, wherein he flowed with that faculty that sometimes it was necessary he should be stopped...But he redeemed his vices with his virtues. There was ever more in him to be praised than to be pardoned.

In 1618 Jonson walked from London to Edinburgh, where he stayed with the poet and book-collector William Drummond, Laird of Hawthornden. Jonson made the journey as 'a large, portly gentleman in his forties'. He was soon testing his host's patience. 'He hath consumed a whole night in lying looking to his great toe,' Drummond wrote, 'about which he hath seen Tartars and Turks, Romans and Carthaginians, fight in his imagination.' The muttering playwright disparaged his fellows. Drummond wrote down Jonson's claim, 'That Shakspeer wanted arte...Shakspeer, in a play, brought in a number of men saying they had suffered shipwrack in Bohemia, where there is no sea neer by some 100 miles.' The reference to a Bohemian shipwreck is in *The Winter's Tale*, which Shakespeare wrote using Greene's *Pandosto*. Shakespeare's alleged want of 'arte' stands in stark contrast to the First Folio verse in which Jonson lauded Shakespeare in terms such as these: 'Thy Art, / My gentle Shakespeare, must enjoy a part; / For though the Poets matter, Nature be, / His Art doth give the fashion.'

Reverend William Beloe called the 1623 Shakespeare First Folio the 'first edition of the works of our great natural Poet'. This description, and subsequent ones by Dibdin and others, have coalesced into a standard way of speaking about the First Folio. The book is Shakespeare's 'Editio Princeps', his authoritative first appearance in print, which reproduced the plays precisely as he intended them. A recent description by Ian Wilson exemplifies this way of speaking: 'The monumental First Folio, the authorised complete canon of thirty-six of his *Comedies, Histories and Tragedies*, put together by Shakespeare's leading fellow-actors...With due allowance for inevitable minor infelicities of transcription, each play preserved in the First Folio is recognised as being very much as Shakespeare intended it.' First, complete, authoritative. The First Folio is none of these things.

When the First Folio appeared, half its contents had appeared in print already—some as early as twenty-five years before. For the eighteen plays already published, the quartos are the true first editions. The First Folio is not even the 'first collected edition'. Some quartos, including the 'False Folio' Jaggard–Pavier ones, had been sold as multi-play volumes. Irish scholar Edward Gwynn owned an extensive library that included eight Jaggard–Pavier quartos together in one volume (now in the Folger). Collectors also bound quartos together to create their own collected editions. Sir John Harington arranged for many of his plays, including Shakespeare quartos, to be grouped into composite volumes.

Part of the appeal of the 'first edition' concept is the idea of the satisfied author proudly handling the first copies of the edition as they come off the press. Shakespeare, though, never handled the First Folio; as already noted, he was seven years in the ground when it arrived. The quartos are the real thing, though the missing Shakespeare playscripts have an even stronger claim to 'firstness'.

The statement that the First Folio is complete and canonical has obvious shortcomings. Shakespeare made his debut appearance in print with the publication of the long poems *Venus and Adonis* (1593) and *The Rape of Lucrece* (1594). His first literary reputation was as a poet. Decades before the First Folio, Shakespeare's sonnets were circulating in manuscript. They first appeared in print in the small 1609 edition. The long poems and the sonnets, though, were excluded from the First Folio, as were a variety of poetical fragments that had been published under his name.

In another important respect, the First Folio does not include all of Shakespeare's writings. Through a minor oversight, *Troilus and Cressida* was left off the contents page but included in the body of the Folio. In a much graver omission, at least four 'Shakespeare' plays, and as many as sixteen, were not included in the Folio at all.

Pericles, Prince of Tyre is one of the excluded plays. Registered in May 1608, the play was published in a 1609 quarto version under the name 'William Shakespeare'. Advertising puff in the first quarto suggests the play was popular and extensively performed: 'The late, And much admired Play...diuers and sundry times acted by his Maiesties seruants, at the Globe on the Banck-side.' Contemporary sources corroborate this picture. Apart from attracting large crowds, the play was watched by the Venetian and French ambassadors. It was also performed by touring players, and was one of the most frequently reprinted of Shakespeare's plays, appearing in at least six quarto editions up to 1635. Despite that strong start, however, this obscure play is not well known today, and is seldom performed. The text is notoriously uneven, slow to warm up, and not very 'Shakespearean' until the third act. In creating *Pericles*, Shakespeare probably made extensive use of a prior play by another author. To the extent that he revised the play, he seems to have done so with a collaborator, most likely George Wilkins.

The Two Noble Kinsmen is also not in the First Folio. Probably a collaboration between Shakespeare and John Fletcher, the play was created in 1613 or 1614 but not registered until April 1634. Jonson's *Bartholomew Fair*, first performed on 31 October 1614, referred to the character 'Palemon' from *The Two Noble Kinsmen*. The play was based on three principal sources: Chaucer's 'The Knight's Tale' and Lydgate's 'Siege of Thebes', both of which appeared in the 1561 edition of *The Workes of Geffrey Chaucer*; and Boccaccio's *Teseide*, possibly the French prose version *La Theseyde*

(1597). Another First Folio exclusion, and another Shakespeare–Fletcher collaboration, is the lost play *Cardenio*. The Folio also excluded another lost play, *Love's Labour's Won*, along with the Shakespeare–Kyd collaboration *The Reign of King Edward III* (1596) and all the plays in the Shakespeare Apocrypha.

Apart from suffering from contentious exclusions, the First Folio also features some doubtful inclusions. Prior to 1623, nineteen of the thirty-eight plays in the canon (and eighteen of the thirty-six First Folio plays) had appeared in quarto format. Eighteen of the First Folio plays seem never before to have appeared in print. How they came to be included in the Folio is an enigma that goes to the heart of Shakespeare authorship and the scale of his achievements. The preliminary matter of the First Folio appears to convey a great deal of information, but in truth it holds a great deal back. It provides no details of how the playtexts were acquired, or the order in which they were written. It contains no biographical notes or authorial remarks. (Just as Shakespeare's manuscripts are missing, so, too, none of the First Folio working papers, such as marked-up quartos, has ever been found. Only one fragment from the First Folio's production is known to exist: a single page of the proofs for *Antony and Cleopatra*, now in the Folger.)

The list of plays published for the first time in the First Folio includes some of the greatest and most 'Shakespearean' texts—plays like *Macbeth*, *The Taming of the Shrew* and *The Tempest*. The list also includes runts and outliers. The 'misfit' status of *Timon of Athens* has already been pointed out. *The Comedy of Errors* was registered just before the First Folio appeared; it was a late inclusion in Shakespeare's œuvre. Some mainstream scholars attribute authorship of that play, along with another late First Folio addition, *Julius Caesar*, to Christopher Marlowe. If

Shakespeare had a role in these two plays, it seems to have been a modest and incremental one. Alexander Pope was one of the first to express such a view. In 1728 he argued Shakespeare had only a minimal role in creating *The Comedy of Errors*. Pope cast doubt on other First Folio plays, too.

An equally plausible theory, however, is that Shakespeare had *no* role in several of the eighteen non-quarto First Folio plays. That theory has attracted many followers. In the years since Pope expressed his doubts, mainstream and heretical scholars alike have argued First Folio plays must have been misattributed to Shakespeare; that the First Folio editors and publishers simply selected, from a cache of available plays, texts that would fit in to the First Folio and could plausibly be passed off as Shakespeare's.

In light of the 'inbetweener' view of Shakespearean author-ship, and the Jonsonian–Floriovian view of First Folio editorship, that theory is entirely plausible. Jonson and Florio would have known the scale of Shakespeare's authorship of the quarto plays. For these editors, therefore, it would not be much of a stretch to re-run the production process without Shakespeare's vitalis-ing stage—especially as the First Folio texts were intended for reading rather than performance. Jonson could have trawled the large body of available plays, found suitable works, knocked them into editorial shape, applied a degree of coherence with the other canonical plays, then sent them all to the printer. Common editing and presentation of the plays would have increased their 'family resemblance'.

This picture is congruent with Philip Henslowe's diary, which records him buying and staging plays with Shakespearean titles—such as *Henry VI* and *The Taming of the Shrew*—but with non-Shakespearean attribution and payment. It is also congruent with the evidence that Jonson had a stake in Shakespeare's œuvre.

And we know for sure that editors and publishers added plays to later editions of the Folio. By the Third and Fourth Folios, the number of 'Shakespeare' plays had risen from thirty-six to forty-three.

Jonson clearly had a motive to enhance the saleability of the First Folio. This commercial enterprise was undertaken when he was impoverished and indebted. The 'make-weight' of adding more plays would help justify the retail price and increase the perception of value, just as previous publishers had done by adding content to *Hamlet*; and just as the First Folio editors did by adding extensive preliminary matter—the portrait, the preface, the commendatory verses—running to eighteen supernumerary pages.

The bulky preliminary matter includes a dedication to Jonson's patron William Herbert, Earl of Pembroke (a contender for 'W. H.' in the *Sonnets* dedication). The First Folio dedication paraphrased an impeccable precedent: Pliny's dedication to Vespasian in his *Natural History*. Jonson's 1616 *Workes* received a vigorous critical response and a satisfactory commercial one. Most importantly, the volume helped make the dramatic arts more respectable. For Jonson in that year, Shakespeare's death may have planted a seed. The Bard was an ideal authorial vehicle for 'volume two', a way to repeat the venture and feed the public appetite with more plays, which Jonson would edit then see through the press. When it appeared, the Shakespeare First Folio reprised the model set down by the Jonson First Folio. It was a model others would re-use, including for Beaumont and Fletcher's 1647 folio.

Apart from plays being left out of the Shakespeare First Folio, some jointly authored plays were solely attributed to his author-ship. Thomas Middleton collaborated on *Timon of Athens* and possibly *All's Well that Ends Well*, but he is not mentioned in the Folio. Marlowe, Greene, Peele and Nashe are also not identified as co-authors. Jonson knew all about collaboration, and he knew it disrupted the neat authorial story he wanted to tell in his own *Workes*. The prelims for that 1616 edition state, probably misleadingly, that the contents were all his; that in readying his plays for printing, he had purged from them the work of other men. In the preface to the quarto edition of *Sejanus* (1605) he similarly stated,

> Lastly, I would inform you, that this book, in all numbers, is not the same with that which was acted on the public stage; wherein a second Pen had good share: in place of which, I have rather chosen to put weaker, and no doubt, less pleasing, of mine own, than to defraud so happy a genius of his right by my loathed usurpation.

If Jonson was behind the Shakespeare First Folio, he repeated this pattern there by gifting all the plays to Shakespeare alone.

Another objection to the picture painted by Beloe, Wilson and their ilk: calling the First Folio 'authorised' is baloney. The book was certainly not authorised by Shakespeare. The Folio editors created play titles he never used, and made textual changes he never reviewed. The preface denounced prior editions as fraudulent, and prior publishers as impostors, but we know from the Barrington books and the Wise case to take such protestations of integrity with salt. There were certainly pirates involved in the production of the First Folio, Jaggard principal among them (as noted, he had already been implicated in two Shakespearean misdemeanours: *The Passionate Pilgrim* and the 'False Folio') and there was certainly some fast and loose dealing with playtexts of dubious ownership. Let us be wary when pirates accuse others of buccaneering. Fundamentally, though, the 'authorisation' point is moot. In 1623, the likelihood of a competing bookseller or printer-publisher embarking on a rival edition of such a large and risky project was extremely low. Jaggard, Jonson and Florio had the field to themselves.

Faced with the opportunity to produce a monopoly edition of the plays, Jaggard and his collaborators fluffed it. As a piece of printing, the Shakespeare First Folio is a shoddy production. Executed 'on the cheap', the typography is certainly as 'disagreeable' as Dibdin labelled it, and as 'botched' as Shaw saw it. The end result was inferior to Jonson's *Workes*, and vastly below the best Continental printing of that period. There were also editorial problems. The First Folio texts are full of mistakes. (A few examples from *Antony and Cleopatra*: 'Anthony' for 'autumn'; 'foretell' for 'fertile'; and 'Thideus' for 'Thyreus'.) Shaw penned damning notes about the men who steered the Folio through the press. Apart from bungling the pagination, the editors left obvious misreadings.

> Macbeth's 'If trembling I in habit then'…is misprinted 'If trembling I inhabit then' which is nonsense, and has been changed by later editors to 'If trembling I inhibit thee' which is little better, and not authentic Shakespear. Mrs Quickly's vivid 'His nose was as sharp as a pen on a table of green frieze' appears as 'His nose was as sharp as a pen and a table of green fields,' which Malone, apparently ignorant of the fact that frieze is a very rough and tough woollen cloth with a rainrebuffing nap on it, much worn in Ireland before manual workers began to dress like gentlemen when off duty, corrupted into 'and a babbled o' green fields,' which is neither good Quickly, good Falstaff, nor good Shakespear.

Malone, it seems, was fallible. He did excellent work, though, on the relationship between the folios and the quartos. He was one of a bevy of leading Shakespeare scholars who compared meticulously the texts of the First Folio and the even firster quartos.

Some quarto editions are demonstrably superior. In many respects, for example, the 1608 *King Lear* surpasses the First Folio version, which lacks about three hundred lines present in the quarto, and which contains many misprints, some of them carried over from the 1619 'False' Jaggard–Pavier quarto. Some colourful parts of Shakespeare's plays were left out of the First Folio. As Colin Franklin noted, 'Thomas Bowdler, aware that here and there in *Othello* the 1623 folio was slightly less coarse of phrase than the quarto of the previous year, decided that the first folio could really be reckoned "the first *Family Shakespeare*".'

Readers searching for the 'best' edition of Shakespeare's plays should sidestep the First Folio. The very best editions—the most scholarly, thoughtful and complete ones—had to be carefully made up from the best quartos and folios. Editions of that editorial calibre were not available in the seventeenth century, nor for that matter in the eighteenth or the nineteenth.

When it comes to the search for information about Shakespeare's life and authorship, the First Folio is an unreliable source. Posthumous, incomplete, error-ridden; produced by piratical publishers and hidden editors. The volume is prefaced with ambiguous prefatory matter that is deliberately misleading and patently commercial. The story of the Folio is useful, however, in shedding light on Shakespeare's authorial achievement, and in helping in a practical way to scale his library. To the extent that some of the canonical plays are not his, for example, he probably didn't have manuscripts or proofs of them. More importantly, the production of the First Folio helps us picture the work of a nearby bookman, and that bookman's library.

The man who achieved a perfect score against Diana Price's ten criteria was sure to have had a library. We know with certainty that he did so; in fact, Jonson assembled at least *two* libraries in his lifetime. John Aubrey's *Brief Lives* included gossip about Jonson as well as Shakespeare. Aubrey portrayed him at his study at night, surrounded by documents, sitting on a 'chaire...of strawe' and affected by 'drinke'. William Drummond verified Jonson's love of liquor, recalling it as 'one of the elements in which [he] liveth'. (According to a well-known tradition, probably apocryphal, a stupendous Jonson-Shakespeare-Drayton drinking session was the immediate cause of Shakespeare's death. This is how Reverend John Ward recorded that piece of local gossip: 'Shakespear, Drayton and Ben Jonson had a merry meeting, and itt seems drankd too hard, for Shakspear died of a feavour there contracted.')

Alcohol. Piles of books and papers. A straw chair. Candles. This is all painting a dangerous picture. No surprise, then, that Jonson lost much of his library to fire. The conflagration occurred in the First Folio year, 1623. Suggesting that Shakespearean books and manuscripts are especially unlucky when it comes to documentary survival (a phenomenon that would, of course, help explain much of what the present book is about), none of Jonson's Shakespeareana survived the fire. The full extent of the damage is unknown, but some of Jonson's books did endure; today they bear singe-marks and other traces of inflammation. His *The Works of Claudian* (1585) is in the fire-anxious Bodleian; it features the telltale signs of scorching. Apart from marks of that kind, Jonson left behind underlinings, flower-doodles, his signature and extensive marginalia in his books.

Jonson provides the best model of what a Shakespearean 'writer's library' might have been like. He is also the best candidate for the role of 'master editor' who lifted and magnified the Shakespearean canon and Shakespeare's authorial legacy. If the First Folio is responsible for Shakespeare, and if Jonson was responsible for the First Folio, then in a real sense Jonson was responsible for the legend, and Jonson's library is intertwined with Shakespeare's.

CHAPTER 17

Closet Games

First published in the 1880s in a private, eleven-volume edition that extended to more than a million words, *My Secret Life*, by 'Walter', purports to be the memoir of a Victorian gentleman's sexual adventures. 'Walter' presents a small puzzle of authorial attribution. William Potter, author of *The Romance of Lust* (1873–76), has been put forward as the likely author of *My Secret Life*. But the most popular candidate, a known associate of Potter's, is Henry Spencer Ashbee, a book collector, author and bibliographer of early erotica. Biographer Ian Gibson referred to him as a subtype of the bibliomaniac: the 'erotomaniac'. It is likely that Ashbee either wrote the whole book, partly from imagination, or compiled and edited the text, adding the most remarkable index ever produced and seeing the book through the press.

Unlike Tolstoy and, more appositely, Henry Miller, Ashbee found in Shakespeare a kindred soul. He confessed to having read *Hamlet* 'hundreds of times', and to delighting in act 3, scene 2:

> *Hamlet*: Lady, shall I lie in your lap?
> *Lying down at Ophelia's feet*
> *Ophelia*: No, my lord.
> *Hamlet*: I mean, my head upon your lap?
> *Ophelia*: Ay, my lord.
> *Hamlet*: Do you think I meant country matters?
> *Ophelia*: I think nothing, my lord.
> *Hamlet*: That's a fair thought to lie between maids' legs.
> *Ophelia*: What is, my lord?
> *Hamlet*: Nothing.

(The title of *Much Ado About Nothing* has been read as a similar play on words, 'no-thing' or 'o-thing' meaning vagina.)

Ashbee found *Romeo and Juliet* 'full of incongruities and obscenities'. He expressed a practical view of the playwright's strategy: 'It would appear that Shakespeare, fearing that his play would not please the better class, endeavoured by means of obscene jokes to gain favour with the pit.'

Whoever 'Walter' was, he claimed to 'have had women of twenty-seven different Empires, Kingdoms or Countries, and eighty or more different nationalities, including every one in Europe except a Laplander'. Most of the action in *My Secret Life* takes place near the Lyceum, Drury Lane and other theatres. Like Ashbee, the secret author admired Shakespeare and made frequent references to his work. In a brothel, 'Walter' meets a girl who has seen *Hamlet*; he quotes Macbeth ('in my sear and yellow leaf'); and he presents a 'phallic parody' of Portia's court speech from *The Merchant of Venice*.

Apart from *Hamlet* and *Romeo and Juliet*, Ashbee relished Biron's long speech in *Love's Labour's Lost*. The speech includes the evocative line, 'Love's feeling is more soft and sensible / Than are the tender hooks of cockled snails', and it places women's sparkling eyes, which are 'the books, the arts, the academes, / That show, contain and nourish all the world', above religion.

The title of John Fry's *Pieces of Ancient Poetry* echoed those of respectable compilations of moralising verse, like *Elegant Extracts: or, Useful and Entertaining Pieces of Poetry, Selected for the Improvement of Young Persons* (1791) and *Fragments, in Prose and Verse* (1809) by the late friend of Henrietta Bowdler, Miss Elizabeth Smith, whose work was 'very popular in religious circles'. Fry's editions were popular in different circles. Parts of *Pieces* had to be expurgated to avoid problems with the authorities. His Carew book, too, ran risks. In life, Carew was accused of 'irregularities of his conduct'. Fry appreciated how Carew wrote, 'especially in the amorous way', mostly to a beauty called Celia. Carew was fascinated by every aspect of his lover. When he noticed a mole on her bosom, he wrote a poem. When a fly flew into her eye, he wrote a poem…

John Fry's bibliographical works are not just manifestos for bibliographical rigour; they are also polemics against prurience and prudery, celebrating the naughty side of Shakespeare. Fry was a teenager when he published Elizabethan poetry. Despite his illness, he had a healthy young man's interest in bawdry and innuendo. *Pieces* includes the wicked Scottish ballad 'Johnny Cock'; a much loved 1597 poem by Robert Devereux, Second Earl of Essex; and an ebullient song about Devereux's son, the Third Earl of Essex, to be sung to the tune of 'Whoppe! doe me now harme, good man':

There was a good Earle
Had gott a young girle
     His wimble did pierce her flanke;
His nagge was made able
By chaunge of his stable;
     O there was a brave quoad hanc!
This maide inspected;
But fraud interjected
     A Maid of more perfeçon:
The Midwives did her handle,
While ye Knt held ye candle
     O there was a clear inspeçon!

These lines refer to a pitiable episode in English history. At the age of thirteen, the Third Earl of Essex married fourteen-year-old Frances Howard. Before the marriage was consummated, Frances allegedly began an affair with Robert Carr, Viscount Rochester, later First Earl of Somerset. The young bride sought an annulment on the grounds of Essex's impotence. He for his part claimed he was perfectly capable with other women, and that his wife 'reviled him, and miscalled him, terming him a cow and coward, and beast'. Dual inspections were arranged, one in which Essex showed off his erection, and one in which his wife's virginity was examined—her face was covered, ostensibly for modesty but probably, as the song suggests, to conceal a substitute. After these spectacles the annulment was granted. Three years later a panel of Lords, led by Bacon, put the Somersets on trial for their roles in the murder of Sir Thomas Overbury. A juror in the trial, Essex pressed the King to send Frances to the scaffold. She and her new husband were condemned to death, but were pardoned before that sentence could be carried out.

~

Venus and Adonis was first published in 1593. According to the Bodleian Library, at least fifteen further editions were published over the next forty-three years, around ten of them in Shakespeare's lifetime. Very few copies survive from all these editions: most were read and shared so avidly they simply fell apart. One of the more enthusiastic readers was William Reynolds, who interpreted the poem as a coded personal love message from Queen Elizabeth. Among saner readers, *Venus and Adonis* rapidly earned a salacious reputation as an aid to 'solitary pleasure'. In the 1598 Cambridge play *The Return from Parnassus*, the character Gullio promises to 'worship sweet Mr Shakespeare, and to honour him will lay his Venus and Adonis under my pillow', just as an ancient king 'slept with Homer under his bed's head'. Samuel Johnson included *Venus and Adonis* in his list of the most scandalous and corrupting verse of the late sixteenth century. In support of that inclusion, Johnson cited a 1625 quarto, *A Scourge for Paper Persecutors*, by J. D., which included this revelation:

> Making lewd Venus with eternall lines
> To tye Adonis to her loves designes:
> Fine wit is shown therein, but finer 't were
> If not attired in such bawdy geer:–
> But be it as it will, the coyest dames
> In private reade it for their closet-games.

William Covell graduated MA from Cambridge in 1588. Alongside notes about other authors, Covell's 1595 *Polimanteia* included comments on *Venus and Adonis* and Shakespeare's other long poem, *The Rape of Lucrece*. The following year, Covell was accused of adultery with Brigett Edmunds, the wife of John Edmunds, another Cambridge MA. Yet another Cambridge MA, George Mountain, appeared as a witness in Covell's defence.

Mountain's evidence, though, was undermined by Brigett's testimony, which put Covell in a world of trouble, and pointed to a debauched culture among the university men: 'Mountain toulde me that Covell confessed that the sweeteste sporte that ever he had with me was in the chayre.' She claimed Mountain had heard Covell 'boaste that he laye with Licea, and by what meanes he gott to hir bedd'. ('Licea' is Giles Fletcher's *Licia, or Poemes of Loue*, Cambridge, 1593.)

Brigett's account also included an accusation against Mountain: he had read 'bawdrye' to her. Mountain contended that he 'never redd vnto hir anie of bawdrye, excepte she meanes it by this':

> that vpon a tyme when as she the said Brigett with diverse others wente to Elye or came from Elye by boate he (the saide Mr George Mowntayne) goeinge or commeinge with them alsoe: Mr Iohn Edmunds Iunior did instantlie requeste him the said George Mowntayne to take his booke or some storie booke to reade [on] the waye to passe the tyme awaie withall, and herevppon he tooke Bocchas [Boccaccio] in ffrence and reade of it in the boate to the companie there, and englished the same to them; wherein he saith there was no bawdrye at all.

Brigett's reply was damning for the man who aspired to ecclesiastical advancement, and who would in fact become Bishop of London. Her accusation, she said, was not about Mountain's reading of Boccaccio but 'an other tyme when as he red vnto hir an englishe book'. That volume was *The Palace of Pleasure* by William Painter. First printed in 1566, it went into multiple editions and earned a second volume. A saucy compilation of Italian and Italianate tales, Painter's book was a source for at least four Shakespeare plays.

Also in Johnson's scandalous grouping were Marlowe's edition of Ovid's *Elegies*, Thomas Cutwode's *Caltha Poetarum, or The Bumble-Bee* and 'some of the dissolute sallies of Green and Nashe'. The *Bumble-Bee* includes picturesque, orgasmic lines like this:

> She bends her branch, and bows it up and down
>   and to the heavens she doth exalt her eyes:
> And with a very fervent prayer doth frown,
>   looking aloofe unto the loftie skies:
> Somewhile to kneele, and otherwhiles to rise.
> Moving her body with a modest motion,
> As holy dames do use in deepe devotion.

Francis Freeling owned one of the only three known copies of the *Bumble-Bee*. Though the poem was much more salacious than the *Garden Plot*, Richard Heber presented an edition of it to the Roxburghe Club as his Member book. Shakespeare probably knew of the poem, and he may have owned it and used it as a source. Freeling drew a link between the poem, the mandrake and *II Henry IV*:

> Steevens quotes it in a note on the word mandrake in Shakespeare's *Henry IV Part II*, Act iii, Scene 2, and says he would give further extracts from it 'but on some subjects silence is less reprehensible than information.'

In his footnote, Steevens does expand somewhat on this point: 'In the age of Shakespeare…it was customary "to make counterfeit Mandrag, which is sold by deceyuers for much money." Out of the great double root of Briony (by means of a process not worth transcribing) they produced the kind of priapic idol to which Shallow has been compared.' The comparison appears in

Falstaff's speech:

> I do remember [Justice Shallow] at Clement's Inn like a man
> made after supper of a cheese-paring: when a' was naked,
> he was, for all the world, like a forked radish, with a head
> fantastically carved upon it with a knife: a' was so forlorn,
> that his dimensions to any thick sight were invincible: a' was
> the very genius of famine; yet lecherous as a monkey, and the
> whores called him mandrake: a' came ever in the rearward
> of the fashion, and sung those tunes to the overscutched
> huswives that he heard the carmen whistle, and swear they
> were his fancies or his good-nights.

Such salty content is consistent with what we know about how
Shakespeare operated. The authors of playscripts sometimes
shared in supernormal profits (the 'overplus') from the performance of plays. This created an incentive to add bawdy and
sensational content; what Dekker called, in 1612, 'filth'. When it
came to spicing up and 'vulgarising' plays, Shakespeare's talent
was obvious. *The Comedy of Errors* contains several examples of
this calibre:

> *Antipholus*: Then she bears some breadth?
> *Dromio*: No longer from head to foot than from hip to hip:
> she is spherical, like a globe; I could find out countries in her.
> *Antipholus*: In what part of her body stands Ireland?
> *Dromio*: Marry, in her buttocks: I found it out by the bogs.
> *Antipholus*: Where Scotland?
> *Dromio*: I found it by the barrenness; hard in the palm of the
> hand...
> *Antipholus*: Where stood Belgia, the Netherlands?
> *Dromio*: Oh, sir, I did not look so low.

This is the type of passage that eighteenth- and nineteenth-century editors preferred to remove. The best-known excisers were the siblings Henrietta and Thomas Bowdler. In 1807, Henrietta produced the first edition of the *Family Shakespeare*. Four little duodecimos printed in Bath, the edition contained twenty of the plays—more than half the canon. Henrietta's preface explained the project: 'For those who object to such alterations, there are many editions of Shakespeare, "with all his imperfections on his head"; but it is hoped that the present publications will be approved by those who wish to make the young reader acquainted with the various beauties of this writer, unmixed with any thing that can raise a blush on the cheek of modesty.'

Some darker and more difficult plays were among the twenty, including *Hamlet* and *King Lear*. Some spicier plays, too, such as *Measure for Measure* and *Othello*; Eric Partridge called these Shakespeare's 'most sexual, most bawdy plays'. Commercially, this first edition was a failure. Later editions, though, would succeed spectacularly, making the Bowdlers a household name and their *Family Shakespeare* a household favourite.

From *Othello*, the Bowdlers removed Iago's shout to Roderigo in the opening scene of the first act: 'I am one Sir, that come to tell you, your Daughter, and the Moore, are now making the Beast with two backs'. They removed, too, rude jokes like this one:

Clown: Are these I pray, call'd wind Instruments?
Boy: Ay, marry are they, sir.
Clown: O, thereby hangs a tail.
Boy: Whereby hangs a tail, sir?
Clown: Marry, sir, by many a wind instrument that I know.

From *Measure for Measure*, the Bowdlers excised most of the sexual innuendo, and especially the lines involving Lucio and

Pompey. In *Hamlet*, Ophelia's apparent suicide becomes an unfortunate riparian accident. The Bowdlers also removed Biron's speech in *Love's Labour's Lost*. In Noel Perrin's words, 'here was Shakespeare mutilated'.

Sir William Boothby directed much of his seventeenth-century book-buying towards lurid medical and social tracts such as *Confessions of a Maried Couple* and *The Tenne Pleasures of Marrage*. The founder of the Mitchell Library had similar tastes. Unmarried throughout his life, David Scott Mitchell retained a racy, bachelor's sense of humour. He devoured as a young man scientific and pseudo-scientific books on the nocturnal behaviour of debutantes, presbyophiles and nymphomaniacs; books on 'sexual relations, sexual organs and marriage' by such authors as Alexander Walker and Dr Edward B. Foote, the 'postbellum physiologist, health crusader and mail-order magnate'. Plain speaking, independent and broad-minded, Mitchell also collected heterodox religious texts and conventional erotica.

Knowing his character and interests, it is no surprise that he preferred to take his Elizabethan literature raw, and he disdained the Bowdlers' *Family Shakespeare*. His interest in Shakespeare was a radical act, just as it was for Fry and Wrangham. While the Bowdlers were making a PG-rated Shakespeare, John Fry and his collaborators were busy preserving and celebrating the adults-only version. The Bowdlers, Mitchell and Fry supply polar visions of Shakespeare's library: the wholesome family library against the surreptitious collection of an erotomaniac.

The idea of a Shakespearean porn library is as fascinating as Orville Ward Owen's obsessive vision of a mechanised, rotating one. The word 'pornography' did not exist in Shakespeare's time, and the field of erotica was ill-defined and fungible. If Shakespeare owned 'erotica', we would expect to see a wide variety of texts falling more or less into that category. Apart from the Boccaccio and Painter volumes that Mountain read, there would likely be a selection of other early Italian works such as Pietro Aretino's *Sonetti lussuriosi* (1534) and its accompanying erotic illustrations by Giulio Romano. English publishers reprinted with enthusiasm Aretino's works, including his 1534 *Ragionamenti* ('Dialogues'). John Wolfe's 1584 London edition of that work includes the anonymous *Ragionamenti di Zoppino*, a catalogue of Roman prostitutes.

Shakespeare may have travelled to Italy in his 'lost years' and encountered Italian erotica there. He certainly knew people who had been to Italy, including the Anglo-Italian John Florio, and some of the books certainly made their way to England at an early date. Julie Peakman, author of *Mighty Lewd Books* (2003), traced some of the titles that moved between Italy and England in the sixteenth century. She also found that the *Ragionamenti* 'retained its popularity' in Italy well into the twentieth century: 'My Italian friend recalls her father kept a copy in his library in Rome in the 1950s.'

Some sixteenth-century erotica circulated only in manuscript. Nashe's poem 'The Choice of Valentine's' is an example. Some material circulated only between lovers. A poem recently discovered inside a 1561 edition of Chaucer in the West Virginia University library was written by Lady Elizabeth Dacre to Sir Anthony Cooke. The poem ends unambiguously with an epigram by Martial: 'Long enough am I now; but if your shape should swell under its grateful burden, then shall I become to you a narrow girdle.'

Apart from manuscripts and imported Italian and French erotica, a Shakespearean porn library would have contained bawdy songs, ballads and lyrics, and English translations of Juvenalian satire and gory Senecan tragedy—all of which were guaranteed to get the blood flowing. In 1596, Valentine Symmes published an English version of Lucius Apuleius' *Golden Ass*. Other saucy translations included Marlowe's of Ovid's *Amores* (copies of which were sequestered and burned); and George Chapman's of Ovid's *Banquet of Sense* (1595). A self-respecting sixteenth- and early seventeenth-century erotic library would also include William Barksted's *Mirrha the Mother of Adonis: or, Lustes Prodegies* (1607, influenced by *Venus and Adonis* and *Measure for Measure*), Thomas Lodge's version of Scylla's *Metamorphosis* (1589), Thomas Heywood's *Oenone and Paris* (1594), Michael Drayton's *Endymion and Phoebe* (1595), Thomas Edward's *Cephalus and Procris* (1595), John Weever's *Faunus and Melliflora* (1600), Francis Beaumont's *Salmacis and Hermaphroditis* (1602) and Marlowe's *Hero and Leander* (1598).

These are the books we would expect to see in the library of the man who wrote these lines for Venus in *Venus and Adonis*:

I'll be a park, and thou shalt be my deer;
Feed where thou wilt, on mountain or in dale:
Graze on my lips; and if those hills be dry,
Stray lower, where the pleasant fountains lie.

Within this limit is relief enough,
Sweet bottom-grass and high delightful plain,
Round rising hillocks, brakes obscure and rough,
To shelter thee from tempest and from rain.

CHAPTER 18

All Perfect Things

It seems that nearly every second-hand bookshop in the English-speaking world has a dedicated Shakespeare section. And almost all the Shakespeare sections are the pits—the low points of their respective shops, to be jumped over when scanning the shelves. Odd volumes, silverfished, of *Shakespeare Quarterly*, *Shakespeare Survey*, *Shakespeare Studies*. Over-thumbed, marked-up school editions and cheat notes, covered in adhesive plastic. Cheap editions of the complete works, their microscopic printing completely unreadable. Study guides with pseudo-insights about Desdemona's motivations and their implications for the people of today and everyday life. The average Shakespeare section is enough to make those people of today take their own everyday life.

Every now and then, though, there is treasure to be found on the Shakespeare shelves. And few treasures are better than the 'private press' Shakespeares, the best of which, typographically, put the First Folio to shame.

Dating from the seventeenth century, the term 'private press' is notoriously hard to define. John Carter, the man who jointly exposed the forgeries of Thomas Wise, left behind these useful words on 'The fundamental principle of private press printing':

> the principle that, whether or not the press has to pay its way, the printer is more interested in making a good book than a fat profit. He prints what he likes, how he likes, not what someone else has paid him to print. If now and then he produces something more apt for looking at and handling than for the mundane purpose of reading, remember he is concerned as much with his own pleasure and education as with yours.

Started by Sir Egerton Brydges at Lee Priory near Canterbury in 1813, the Lee Priory Press was an early model for the modern private presses. According to private-press historian Roderick Cave, Brydges was 'a strange figure with his Gothic-romantic melancholy, his fondness for picturesque solitude, and his interest in the books and literature of the past'. Archdeacon Francis Wrangham's *A Few Sonnets Attempted from Petrarch in Early Life* (1817) was one of the press's few unarguably successful books. Nevertheless, Brydges helped mark out a path toward private-press excellence. Another bibliophile who helped delineate that path was Sir Thomas Phillipps, the ogre who had the colossal run-in with Halliwell. He forayed into the private-press field with his 'ill organised' Middle Hill Press, which produced what

Cambridge librarian Tim Munby called 'mediocre' books in very small print runs that still strained his printers. 'Distress'd and disappointed' (in the words of Phillipps's agent), they worked in premises without running water, except for the flooding rain that poured though the broken windows.

In the late 1880s William Morris turned these and other antecedents into a veritable artistic movement. By that time, Morris had already established himself as an author, a designer, an entrepreneur, and the foremost advocate for authenticity in the arts and crafts. On 15 November 1888, his friend and neighbour Emery Walker delivered a lecture on printing at the first exhibition of the Arts and Crafts Society. Using lantern slides that magnified type-specimens in a way that was as striking as it was useful, Walker took the audience through four centuries of good and bad typography. Oscar Wilde was in the audience; he afterwards praised the lecture effusively in the *Pall Mall Gazette*. Morris was also there, filled with inspiration. As he and Walker left the venue, Morris said, 'Let's make a new fount of type.'

Experiments with printing followed, one of which Morris called 'the best-looking book issued since the seventeenth century...I am so pleased with my book...that I am any day seen huggling it up'. After further practice runs, Morris established his own printery, the Kelmscott Press, with Walker as a close adviser. Displaying a fastidious regard for all aspects of book making, Morris described his aim thus: 'I began printing books with the hope of producing some which would have a definite claim to beauty, while at the same time they should be easy to read and should not dazzle the eye, or trouble the intellect of the reader by eccentricity of form in the letters.' He designed his own typefaces and bindings and decorative borders, and commissioned other work from leading artists and designers and illustrators, most notably Edward Burne-Jones. Burne-Jones was instrumental in the production of the greatest achievement of the Kelmscott Press: the 1896 *Chaucer*. The 'specials' of that book, which were printed on vellum, cost 120 guineas and became some of the most sought-after books of all time.

Morris established for the private-press movement a sound ethic of good craftsmanship in progressive reaction to industrial printing and ersatz typography. He and his successors would strive to match the best printing with the best of literature; to translate the most sublime poetry and prose into the most sublime book designs. The men and women who joined the movement were kindred spirits to those who built Britain's great private libraries: independent yet collaborative, eccentric yet rigorous, radical yet antiquarian in their interests. Roderick Cave described the Kelmscott books in terms that recall Francis Wrangham's creeping, all-consuming erysipelas: 'The books are heady, romantic, emotional typography; one almost feels that the type and ornament have grown together and could continue growing like some monstrous hothouse plant.'

The eleventh Kelmscott book was a beautiful edition of *The Poems of William Shakespeare*, printed from the original versions of *Venus and Adonis*, *The Rape of Lucrece* and the *Sonnets*. The elaborate border decoration of circling vines was carried over into beautiful, oversized initial letters, the whole printed in red and black, and bound in limp vellum. Five hundred copies were sold, at twenty-five shillings, plus ten vellum 'specials', price ten guineas. Today, the *Poems* volume is one of the rarest Kelmscott titles, very seldom seen on the market. The combination of Shakespeare and Kelmscott proved irresistible—people held on to the book. Shaw, though, sold his copy at the Sotheby's auction of books with his additional notes. A highly desirable association copy—Morris had inscribed it to Shaw—the book realised only twenty pounds. Today, it would command a price well north of ten thousand dollars.

Shaw also sold his copy of *The Tragedie of Hamlet Prince of Denmark*, edited by J. Dover Wilson from the second quarto text (1604–05), illustrated by Edward Gordon Craig and published in Weimar by the Cranach Press (1930). Shaw was sorry to see it go: 'Of all my Hamlets this is the most treasured. It is…a masterpiece of modern book design and printing, ranking my old friend Count Kessler and his Cranach Press with Morris and his Kelmscott Press and Acland with his Ashendene Press, as successors to Jenson and Caxton.'

A strong socialist strain runs through the private-press movement. The nature of fine printing, though, imposes an obvious paradox. Deluxe and fastidious printing necessitates small print runs and high prices. Morris was accused of 'preaching socialism and going away to prepare books that none but the rich could buy'.

Born in Geneva in 1866, Charles de Sousy Ricketts was orphaned at the age of sixteen. In 1882, while studying wood engraving at the South London School of Technical Art, he met a fellow student, Charles Haslewood Shannon. The two Charleses formed a lifelong partnership in their work and in their private life. Both men became mainstays of the London art world. Shannon achieved success as a portraitist, an etcher and a lithographer. Ricketts excelled as a painter, designer, sculptor, critic and historian.

At their Chelsea home, the Vale, Ricketts and Shannon formed a superb art collection. In 1889 they launched *The Dial*, a journal of art and literature. When the first issue appeared, Oscar Wilde called at the Vale to beg its publishers not to produce another volume, because 'all perfect things should be unique'. Thereafter, Ricketts designed and illustrated several Wilde books, including the superb first edition of *The Sphinx* (1894, small quarto, two hundred copies, printed in coloured inks, bound in gilt pictorial vellum, published by John Lane). Ricketts also produced, for the *Magazine of Art*, illustrations of two songs from *The Tempest*: 'Where the Bee Sucks' and 'Ariel's Song to Ferdinand'.

In 1896 the partners founded their own private press, which they called the Vale Press. This venture has been linked to the Arts and Crafts Movement, the Aesthetic Movement and Art Nouveau—but as much as anything it was inspired by book designs from the Italian Renaissance. Ricketts personally supervised the printing of Vale Press titles at a commercial printery, the Ballantyne Press. Like Morris, he designed his own typefaces, and paid close attention to every aspect of book making: paper, watermarks, binding designs, binding materials, texts, illustrations, typography. According to Thomas Sturge Moore, William Morris on his deathbed wept when he saw the first Vale Press productions.

The Vale Press produced some eighty-four titles, many of them with 'specials' printed on vellum, a deluxe material notoriously difficult to work with. The book that displayed the most ambition, and that most strained the partners, was the Vale Press edition of Shakespeare's works. For this edition, the partners assembled a small but experienced team. Thomas Sturge Moore was appointed editor. He had already edited two Shakespearean texts published by Ricketts and Shannon: the piratical *The Passionate Pilgrim* (1896) and the *Sonnets* (1899). (The press also produced an edition of Elizabeth Barrett Browning's *Sonnets from the Portuguese* in 1897.) Moore's assistant, Holmes, would read all the proofs.

The books were to be printed in the 'Avon' font, which Ricketts designed specifically for the Shakespeare edition. Thirty-seven volumes were planned (all the First Folio plays, plus *Pericles*). After pressure from subscribers, the publishers extended the edition to include two additional volumes: Shakespeare's *Poems* and his *Sonnets*. The volumes were published at the cracking rate of one per month, from April 1900 to June 1903. Production was difficult. Not only was there the special font, but also a new scheme of Kelmscott-esque decorative floral borders engraved by C. E. Keates from Ricketts' designs. Keates had produced similar borders for Morris. (Whereas the floral Kelmscott borders were vines 'full of wine', the Vale borders were 'full of light'.) Each volume was individually designed and painstakingly checked. The plays had to be character perfect; the brass blocks and wood engravings had to integrate seamlessly with the text. The pace and the level of difficulty tested the Vale and Ballantyne teams to the limit. Eighteen months into the project, Moore described his work on the Vale Shakespeare as 'rather a big order in the way of time'.

He recorded that work in his diary; his entries for *Cymbeline* provide an example of the steps taken for a single play. First, Moore prepared the text then sent it in manuscript to Ricketts, who read and approved it. A typewritten copy was then made, which Moore read, then sent to the printer, who used it to prepare the first set of proofs ('proofs in slips'), which were taken from unpaged galley matter. These were then sent to Moore to read and correct. The text was then set in pages and the printer prepared another round of proofs ('proofs in sheets'). Moore examined these and posted them to Holmes for final corrections. Ricketts, sometimes with assistance from Holmes, then supervised the final printing. In order to produce a play a month, these processes were run in parallel; at any given moment, each team member was working on multiple plays at different stages of production.

Hamlet was to be the first volume in the series. Its printed sheets were ready to be bound when, on 9 December 1899, a fire broke out at the Ballantyne Press. All the *Hamlet* sheets were destroyed, along with most of the Vale Press stock and decorative materials. This was a disaster for the edition and for the Vale Press as a whole. The reprinted *Hamlet* bore an additional press-mark—a burning Phoenix—and the motto '*Valeo sed non vale dico*' ('But I cannot say goodbye'). For the last volume of the series (*Henry VIII*) the motto was altered to '*Valeo sed Vale dico*' ('But I can say goodbye').

Further troubles would follow. Printing difficulties with *The Taming of the Shrew*. Binding problems, too: the binders went on strike 'over difficulties with the vellum copies'. The solution was to drop the idea of printing vellum specials for the Vale Shakespeare. The missing vellum copies are now an enduring fantasy for bibliophiles.

When the edition went on sale, it was greeted as an exquisite realisation of the playtexts and poems: a beautiful bookshelf of Shakespeare, in which, thanks to Ricketts' deep involvement in the books' every aspect, the contents harmonised seamlessly with the typeface, the decoration, the paper and the bindings. A total of 310 sets of the thirty-nine volumes were published. Despite the edition's success, however, the loss of the Vale Press stock and materials in the fire was an unrecoverable setback. Ricketts and Shannon closed their press in 1904.

Ricketts turned to writing, painting and sculpture, and to designing for the theatre. His costumes for *Lear* and *Macbeth* won wide acclaim, as did his books *Titian* (1910) and *Pages on Art* (1913). Fervently opposed to modernism, Ricketts 'had a great reputation as a connoisseur and in 1915 turned down the offer of the directorship of the National Gallery'.

In 1929 Shannon fell from a ladder while hanging a picture. Brain damage and amnesia were the result; Shannon required intensive nursing, and his career came to a tragic end. Devastated and exhausted, Ricketts suffered a fatal heart attack just two years after the accident. Shannon died in 1937, bequeathing most of the Ricketts–Shannon art collection to the Fitzwilliam Museum, Cambridge.

The paper and bindings of the Vale Shakespeare volumes are remarkably robust (the cloth used for the bindings was heavily infused with book glue) and they have stayed, for the most part, in very good condition. Though a 'rare' private-press edition, the Vale Shakespeare serves as a curious demonstration of the mathematics of rarity. An edition of 310 copies of thirty-nine volumes equates to a total print run of more than twelve thousand books! While complete sets of the Vale Shakespeare may be rare, individual volumes are common, and are frequently misfiled in bookshops. In my student days, Vale Shakespeare volumes were easy to come by at twenty to thirty dollars, despite being worth ten times that; the same thousand-per-cent margin that Wise forgeries attracted.

Other desirable Shakespearean private-press books that can be found without much difficulty include the Golden Cockerel Press edition of *Twelfth Night,* and the Nonesuch Press edition of *Shakespeare versus Shallow*—Leslie Hotson's remarkable book about William Gardiner, the corrupt Justice of the Peace who feuded with Francis Langley, owner of the Swan theatre, and who was behind the writ issued against Shakespeare. To solve the private-press paradox, Francis Meynell's Nonesuch produced both deluxe limited editions and 'trade' or 'unlimited' editions that adopted the same or similar typography but used industrial production methods such as offset printing. A socialist like Morris, Meynell planned to print an unlimited edition of Shakespeare—to bring a well-designed edition of the plays and poems to a mass audience—but the Great Depression made the project impossible.

Nonesuch published Charles Ricketts' final book, a poignant remembrance of Oscar Wilde. Late in his life, Ricketts had worried that his Vale Press typefaces could be used by others in a 'stale' and 'unthinking' manner. His solution was to do with his type equipment—all his letter punches and matrices—what Allen Lane had done with his autograph book: consign it to the Thames.

Allen Lane had moved from Bristol to London in 1919. Through a random act of serendipitous nepotism, his distant uncle, the great publisher John Lane, brought him into The Bodley Head as an apprentice. John Lane died in 1925, but Allen continued on at the firm. With the support of Lane's widow, Annie, Allen was made a director. His brothers, Richard Lane (who had worked as a Shakespearean actor in Egypt) and John Lane junior, would later join him at the firm. But in 1926 they had not yet arrived and there was no one at The Bodley Head to curb Allen's reckless approach to publishing. Without a minder, Allen was an accident waiting to happen.

The accident did indeed arrive, in the form of actor and author Hesketh Pearson, who presented The Bodley Head with a remarkable manuscript: *The Whispering Gallery: Being Leaves from a Diplomat's Diary*. Purportedly an anonymous tell-all memoir by a leading British diplomat, the manuscript consisted of jaunty and implausible anecdotes about world leaders—such as Kaiser Wilhelm, Cecil Rhodes and Mussolini—and literary lions—such as Kipling, Shaw and Twain. An example is the following story of a private audience with the Kaiser at Potsdam:

> [Wilhelm] was in one of his light-hearted humorous moods and tried to prove that Shakespeare was a German, the chief evidence that he could bring being that no German is introduced into any of the plays! When I informed him that the same sort of evidence proved conclusively that Homer was an Englishman, he laughed and said: 'You can have him! It doesn't matter much.'

Allen was eager to add the book to The Bodley Head's list. The firm's board agreed to go ahead on one condition: Pearson would have to tell one of their number the identity of the author. The board chose Allen, and Pearson named the diplomat and classicist, Sir Rennell Rodd. Allen quickly checked *Who's Who*; some of the details lined up, and he gave an assurance to his fellow directors, who authorised a large print-run. When the book appeared, Rodd furiously disowned it. Forced to withdraw it from sale, The Bodley Head sued Pearson for fraud.

Publicly, Allen Lane pretended to be Pearson's dupe, but privately he probably knew from the beginning that the book was a hoax. Pearson had already produced other fanciful writings, including *Modern Men and Mummers*, 'replete with exaggerated and often libellous tales of theatrical folk', and, in *Adelphi Magazine*, 'a collection of entirely imaginary conversations between Bernard Shaw and G. K. Chesterton which were (and still are) widely regarded as authentic'. (*The Whispering Gallery*, too, is sometimes taken seriously.)

After the fraud's exposure, Pearson was temporarily untouchable as an author, but Allen Lane (uncharacteristically) refused to bear a grudge. He even aided Pearson's resurrection as a legitimate author and Shakespeare biographer. Many years later, Lane told a retired army officer, 'there is no question that Hesketh Pearson did write the book himself, and I must say that despite the fact that the book got us into a great deal of hot water, I always had a high regard for him'.

Beset by such calamitous failures, The Bodley Head was soon in terminal financial trouble. Allen, Richard and John set up Penguin Books as part of their Bodley exit strategy. The goals were ambitious: the Lane brothers would bring the typographical care of fine printing to low-cost, mass-market paperbacks.

Inadvertently, the Vale Press had taken a stylish Shakespeare to a mass-ish market. Penguin would do it on purpose, and on an enormous scale. The Penguin Shakespeare—a Shakespeare library in pocket-sized volumes—was one of the firm's first series. Just two years after Penguin began, the Lane brothers launched their debut tranche of six plays. Edward Young, who designed the first Penguin logo, produced the Penguin Shakespeare cover design. It featured a wood engraving by the private-press publisher, author and designer Robert Gibbings. The books were well received, both critically and commercially. The *Sunday Times* reviewer wrote: 'Shakespeare for sixpence is well enough but this is Shakespeare well edited and well produced; books as bright as new pins, planned with care.'

The Vale Shakespeares were produced in just over four years; Penguin's took longer. The series editor, George Harrison from the University of London, was Allen's second choice for the role, but he went on to edit the Penguin Shakespeare for another twenty-two years. Over that period, one and a half million volumes were sold. Penguin took Shakespeare to an audience never imagined by the First Folio editors. (Like the Folio, though, the Penguins were not without glitches. Two examples: 'prostate' for 'prostrate'; and 'Queer Elizabeth I'.)

Apart from all the canonical plays and poems, Penguin published *Life in Shakespeare's England* (1944), *Principles of Shakespearean Production* (1949), *The Age of Shakespeare* (1955), *Shakespeare's Problem Comedies* (1960), *The Life of Shakespeare* (1963), *Shakespeare: A Celebration* (1964), *Shakespeare's Plutarch* (1964), *Shakespeare's Plays in Performance* (1969) and scores of other orthodox and unorthodox titles. *Penguin New Writing*, number twenty-five, criticised John Gielgud's *Hamlet* and put a powerful case for preserving the bawdiness and ribaldry in Shakespeare's plays, which dancer, theatre director and distant Shakespeare relative Rupert Doone saw as crucial to their coherence. Penguin's *Dr Johnson on Shakespeare* included helpful Johnsonian notes on Shakespeare's art. Johnson was not far away from Pope, or even the Bowdlers, in his views on the raw parts of Shakespeare: 'There are many passages mean, childish, and vulgar; and some which ought not to have been exhibited, as we are told they were, to a maiden Queen.'

In 1942, when Richard and John were serving in the Navy, Allen Lane issued a Penguin edition of Hesketh Pearson's *Life of Shakespeare*. Containing a staunch defence of Shakespeare's heterosexuality, the book marked Pearson's revival in the Penguin pantheon, nearly two decades after the *Whispering Gallery* affair. Looking back over Penguin's accomplishments since 1935, it is clear that no publisher did more to disseminate Shakespeare's work. No publisher did more to create a modern Shakespeare library.

CHAPTER 19

A Writer's Library

Writer and historian Ivan Southall won a string of literary awards in the 1960s and 1970s, including the coveted Carnegie Medal. As an author he shunned literary fashion, writing instead from untutored inspiration and experience (or, as a Shakespeare biographer might say, from Nature). Southall built his work on an insight that is fundamental to Shakespeare, as it is to Freud, Heidegger, Dickens and every significant modern novelist: that only through human beings and human interaction does reality occur and have meaning.

In the early 2000s I assembled a large collection of Ivan Southall books, many from his own library, including first printings of his first break-through successes, the 'Simon Black' series of adventure stories. The initial series of ten books had titles like *Simon Black in the Antarctic* (1956), *Simon Black in Coastal Command* (1953) and *Simon Black in Space* (1952). Ivan had inscribed these volumes proudly to his mother, who raised him and his brother Gordon after their father died when Ivan was fourteen.

Southall's personal copies reveal much about his methods as a writer. Like Shakespeare, he was a frequent reviser and recycler of his own work. To produce the children's book *Fly West* (1974), Southall scrawled all over his copy of *They Shall Not Pass Unseen* (1956), making dramatising additions and clarifying excisions to almost every paragraph. He did something similar when he abridged his book about bomb-disposal officers, *Softly Tread the Brave* (1960), into a version for young people, *Seventeen Seconds* (1973). Southall helped me picture what Shakespeare's working library might have been like: a dynamic resource of marked-up plays and manuscripts, subject to a continual process of revision and adaptation.

At Monash I would encounter other revelations about writing. In the 1950s, Australian readers had a voracious appetite for dramatic stories of crime and adventure. The stories appeared in squarish booklets, bound cheaply in thin paper but with lurid cover illustrations, usually of private dicks and discount damsels, under suggestive titles like *The Roots of His Evil* and *Deadly Reaper*. These 'pulps' (Allen Lane called them 'breastsellers') were sold at train stations, newsagents and other places where 'low literature' could be found. Publishers such as Horwitz and Transport Publishing Co. planned each series and engaged studios of hard-living, hard-drinking writers. The most popular pulps appeared under the names of authors such as Carter Brown, Tod Conrad, Marc Brody and K. T. McCall. Under intense pressure from publishers and editors, a typical pulp author would churn out books at the staggering rate of more than twenty a year. How did they do it?

First of all, the series names were a bit of a cheat. Different authors shared the same allonymous pen-names. 'Carter Brown' was mostly Alan Yates, but C. J. McKenzie and other authors also wrote under that name. 'Larry Kent' was mostly Des Dunn and Don Haring. 'Marc Brody' was mostly, but not exclusively, W. H. 'Bill' Williams. The second trick was to use crutches and shortcuts. The authors wrote to a formula: one slangy sidekick, one love triangle, two sex scenes, one chase, two murders. And they borrowed liberally from each other and especially from American authors of crime pulps and wild-west adventures and romantic potboilers.

In 2010, my wife, Fiona, and I found a revealing document inside a paperback we bought at auction. The book was Bill Williams' copy of US author Brett Halliday's *Murder Is My Business* (1957). Williams had scrawled notes throughout the book. On a separate manuscript he had mapped out his plan for another book that used Halliday's slang, plot points and characterisation. The manuscript shows Williams extracting the sharpest dialogue, the most evocative jargon and the sexiest plot elements. In the University of Melbourne library there is a similar document that shows Williams pinching from John Ross Macdonald's 1958 *Experience with Evil*. Williams' fellow authors did the same, ruthlessly plagiarising, appropriating and cannibalising other works. Fiona and I sold our Williams–Halliday manuscript to the rare-books library at Monash. That was the beginning of a long collaboration in which we helped the library build a rich collection of pulps that tell an important cultural story, and reveal much about allonymous authorship and sharp publishers.

When first published, the sixpence Penguin Shakespeares

sat on railway bookstalls alongside pulps by Dashiell Hammett, Dorothy L. Sayers and Edgar Wallace. In the Monash library the growing collection of pulps rubbed up against foundational volumes of Shakespeare heresy: Hugh Junor Browne's *The Grand Reality* (1888), Ignatius Donnelly's *The Great Cryptogram* (1888) and William Thomson's *On Renascence Drama* (1880). Shakespeare's quartos are the Elizabethan equivalent of Carter Brown and Marc Brody pulps. Early playwrights borrowed and stole from each other with the same voraciousness and ruthlessness. In Shakespeare's library, apart from marked-up copies of earlier versions of his own plays, there would no doubt have been scrawled-on copies of Thomas Kyd's *Hamlet*, Robert Greene's *Pandosto* and other prior plays and novels—an evidentiary trail of Shakespeare filching plot points, vocabulary, characters, settings.

Though it is almost blasphemy to say so, Shakespeare and his editors also relied on another pulp crutch: writing to a formula. Shakespeare's plays were built blockwise from standard characters and plot points. Young marriageable women and their dowries; adulterous monarchs; randy foreigners; unhappy bastards; madness; inheritance; betrayal; plays within plays; disguises and false identities. They were formulaic, too, in their structure, and in their blending of high and low humour, and tragic and comedic elements. Blockwise production made preparing and revising the plays easier. Among his peers, Shakespeare may have been the master of formulaic writing; this would help further explain why his peers showed such little respect for him and his work, and were so ready to call out his lack of 'art'. Perversely, though, the formula underpinned much of Shakespeare's appeal. Blending high thought and low melodrama, the formula had something for everyone—ideal for diverse Elizabethan audiences, and diverse modern ones.

Supposedly a Templar and the author of Rosicrucian manifestoes, Sir Francis Bacon spurred the hunt for anagrams, cryptograms, isopsephs and ciphers with his book *De Augmentis Scientiarum* (1623). After studying Bacon's writings, Umberto Eco wrote *Foucault's Pendulum*—a fictional attempt to link all the richness of the Baconian Shakespeare heresy to an epic conspiracy embracing the deepest mysteries from history: Gnostics, Psychics and Pneumatics. The Holy Grail, the Hollow Earth, the Freemasons. For Eco, *Foucault's Pendulum* was part of a lifelong exploration of textual, cartographical and bibliographical mysteries.

Some time between 1603 and 1611, John Donne produced *The Courtier's Library of Rare Books Not for Sale*. It lists thirty-four imaginary books—such as *Edward Hoby's Afternoon Belchings*, and Luther's *On Shortening the Lord's Prayer*—that would impart pseudo-wisdom on an aspiring courtier. Also in this tradition of imaginary booklists is François Rabelais' catalogue, in *Pantagruel*, that includes *The Codpiece of the Law*, *The Testes of Theology* and *Martingale Breeches with Back-flaps for Turd-droppers*.

The items from these lists are 'non-books' or 'promises of books'. Such volumes have a logical extension: the 'Library of the Mind'. After 'dreaming of the books which the famous have marked and annotated, and of being able to summon them from the ghostly shelves for his delight and reverent handling', the bibliophile F. W. Macdonald wrote of 'A Library that Never Was or Will Be'. Umberto Eco articulated this concept as the 'anti-library', made up of non-existent, unread and unending books. Given the history of the search for Shakespeare's library, and its meagre results, there is a strong temptation to see Shakespeare's library as a phantom; to group it among the imaginary libraries and anti-libraries.

George Barrington and James Wilmot supplied daunting images of empty Shakespearean libraries. Others, like Ireland, Collier, Owen, Browne and Gallup, railed against the documentary gaps, then resorted to all manner of fraud to fill them. Uncertainty permeates Shakespeare's writings and the search for his library. Though this uncertainty is a problem for most scholars, Eco elevated it to a central concept. His images of postmodern texts and postmodern libraries are useful counterpoints to Shakespeare's early modern ones. In a very real way, Shakespeare's texts are open; his plays are dynamic not static, flows not stocks. In Shakespeare's lifetime they existed in multiple versions, a living apparatus of the stage. There is no straightforwardly authoritative edition of any of his plays. In editing as in performance, the plays continue to be re-cast and re-imagined. Shakespeare's library, too, is dynamic. Hotly contested, it is subject to continual reinvention. Four hundred years of searching produced a rich portfolio of conceptions of the library, and commensurately of Shakespeare himself.

But Shakespeare certainly did have books, and he certainly read them. Why, then, have we found none of his manuscripts, and why are there no books with an authentic Shakespeare signature, bookplate, book label or inscription? Gaps such as these are what led many people to doubt his authorship. The gaps, though, are explicable in light of today's clearer picture of Shakespeare. Worldly, workmanlike, unsentimental. Pilloried and spurned. Occasionally dangerous. Accidentally talented. These attributes help explain why he was not an avid inscriber of books, nor much of a letter-writer. Practically minded and commercial, he does not seem to have been driven by abstract ideas of fame and posterity. Let us stop there. The further we take such talk, the further we stray into speculation, anachronism and the biographical fallacy in yet another guise. The nub is this: Shakespeare was not what we think of today as a 'literary' man. The value-laden distinctions we make between Shakespeare's literary and non-literary work are modern ones. So, too, are our expectations of what 'an author like Shakespeare' would leave behind.

In Elizabethan times, Shakespeare was not a celebrity. When John Manningham recorded the 'William the Conqueror' episode in 1602, he had to explain the punchline—otherwise it would not be clear that Shakespeare's first name was William. Nor, it seems, was Shakespeare a Jacobean household name. Through its scale and presentation, the First Folio created the retrospective impression of Shakespearean fame. It also brought a new polish and a new coherence to an œuvre that may in fact have been somewhat smaller and scrappier in Shakespeare's lifetime. Apart from the job done by the First Folio, the modern fame of 'literary Shakespeare' is indebted most of all to the eighteenth-century enthusiasm that had its richest manifestation in Garrick's Shakespeare Jubilee.

Some of the documentary silences that led to Shakespeare Authorship scepticism are not so silent after all. Though Edward Alleyn left Shakespeare out of his diary, he did acknowledge the Bard's existence by buying a copy of the 1609 *Sonnets*, in the year of their publication, and by making a note of the purchase. As we have seen, there are dozens of other contemporary references to Shakespeare. To the extent that documentary silences remain, some are not surprising. There is no evidence of Shakespeare attending Stratford Grammar School, for example, but there is little evidence about other students either, as the school's records for that period were destroyed. The school records of Robert Greene were lost, too, as were many other early documents. Shakespeare's contemporaries did not value historical records as we do today. Nor, often, did people have the resources with which to protect them.

Shakespeare's will famously makes no mention of books. (It does contain the notorious bequest, to Anne Shakespeare, of her husband's 'second best bed'.) The wills of many of his contemporaries, though, are similarly silent. Thomas Russell's, for example, does not mention books. Examination of a range of Stratford wills from Shakespeare's period shows very few bequests of books. Even some aristocratic bibliophiles did not mention books in their wills. There seem to be several reasons for this. First, books and other papers may have been regarded as ephemeral, or as miscellaneous chattels undeserving of a specific mention. Secondly, the market for books was highly liquid. There were many channels through which a dying bookman or his estate could convert books into cash. Thirdly, in Shakespeare's case, possessions such as books may have been listed in a separate codicil, initially appended to the will but now lost. These reasons should be enough to stop us worrying about the 'gaps' in Shakespeare's will.

Richard Field was born in the same town as Shakespeare and at around the same time. Like John Shakespeare, Richard's father Henry was in the leather trade (he was a tanner). In 1579, just before his eighteenth birthday, Field was apprenticed to George Bishop, a prominent London stationer. By agreement with Bishop, Field spent the first six years of his apprenticeship working under the printer-publisher Thomas Vautrollier. In 1587, Field 'was made free of the Stationers Company'. Five months later, Vautrollier died. The following year, at the age of twenty-seven, Field hit the jackpot. He took over his former master's business, and married his former master's widow, Jacqueline. With this head start, Field became one of London's leading printer-publishers. From his Blackfriars printery he issued *Venus and Adonis*, *The Rape of Lucrece* and hundreds of other titles, including dozens of major and minor Shakespeare sources.

Shakespeare's 'genius' was in appropriation, revision and synthesis. The search for his library has elucidated his extensive use of sources—and has helped preserve his reputation by showing the 'secret author' theories to be ill-founded. There are many theories, too, of how Shakespeare accessed his sources: reading at bookstalls in St Paul's Churchyard; borrowing volumes from wealthy booklovers; picking up content indirectly from source texts; and reading books in Richard Field's printery. Shakespeare may have visited Field's workshop and working library; he may have read sources there; and he may even have resided with Field to complete specific works, just as other bookmen did with other printer-publishers. Apart from all these reading pathways, though, Shakespeare also had a library.

Shakespeare's library. The biggest enigma in literature; the book-world equivalent of the Templar Treasure; less well preserved than the Dead Sea Scrolls; less well documented than the Great Library of Alexandria; more sought-after than any other bookish prize. In the course of our search we have glimpsed amazing but elusive riches. Playscripts of *Hamlet* and *King Lear*. Volumes decorated with Shakespeare's crest, or bound in fabric from his costumes. The *Sonnets* manuscript that circulated among his 'private friends'. Lost printed editions of *Othello* and *Love's Labour's Won*. Manuscripts of the missing play *Cardenio*, containing Shakespeare's Don Quixote and Sancho Panza. The ancestor-text of *Hamlet*, known as 'Ur-Hamlet'. Shakespeare's own copies of Ovid, Plutarch, Chaucer and Spenser. His books from the dawn of English printing, from the workshops of William Caxton and Wynkyn de Worde. Association copies, such as gifts to Shakespeare from Marlowe and Jonson. (Despite Shakespeare's many arguments with Jonson, the register of the Bard's death is satisfyingly unambiguous about his social status: 'Will. Shakspere gent'.)

At the turn of the millennium, the search for Shakespeare's library took a decidedly strange turn. Authors such as Brenda James, Diana Price, Bill Rubinstein, Graham Phillips and Martin Keatman brought the study of Shakespeare's life and works firmly into the realm of conspiracy theories. The 'anti-Stratfordians' have more than a superficial furtiveness in common with ufologists, crop circlers and great pyramid secretists. In their beliefs and writings about Shakespeare they are mostly wrong. Many errors, though, have also been made among the orthodox. Ultimately, the heretics serve a useful purpose by keeping the mainstream honest. I'm glad to say the Monash Nevillians and I have remained friends.

The quatercentenary of Shakespeare's death coincided with a golden age of print scholarship. New insights are regularly appearing; historical frauds and missteps can be seen more clearly; there are new lenses through which to view Shakespeare authorship, editorship and ownership. Despite all the Strat-Anti-Strat bile, the combatants' online conversation is vibrant and productive. They may even be inching towards consensus. For Shakespeare studies, ours is the best of times and the worst of times; an inflection point by any other name.

Epilogue

I sold the Ivan Southall Collection to John Thawley, a fellow bookseller who specialises in Australian literature. Courageously, John named his bookshop after Rodney Hall's novel *The Grisly Wife*. I hired a small truck and delivered the Southall books to the residence John shared with his decidedly ungrisly wife, Kay.

The Thawleys' house was built around a library designed by Sean Godsell, the acclaimed architect and former A-grade footballer. Godsell pioneered an open form of architecture that is normally terrible for private libraries. His signature Kew house, in which he lives with his wife, has windows and transparent metal grilles all round. Mrs Godsell complains she must get changed in the wardrobes or the bathroom, or put on a show for the neighbours. But the Thawley library was purpose-built to control the penetrating Australian light.

The library is a confusing multi-storey complex of staircases, bridges, ledges, mezzanines and twenty-foot-tall bookcases; a three-dimensional puzzle whose answer is a striking kilometre of shelf-space. Sean added a Shakespearean touch, a Juliet balcony upon which, at a Thawley party, Rodney Hall himself recited poetry to the guests below. John told me, and Sean later confirmed, that Umberto Eco had inspired the library's design. The inspiration came, not from Eco's concept of the anti-library, but from the mediaeval library-labyrinth in his novel *The Name of the Rose*.

Three years later, John and Kay decided to downsize and regionalise. They put their house on the market. After bidding against a family from New Zealand and a banker for Abu Dhabi, Fiona and I bought the house and its amazing library. (Fiona quipped that, when it came to me deciding whether I wanted to buy the house, John 'had me at Eco'.) Sean did a quick redesign to make the house child-safe. Our daughter, Thea, was twelve months old when we moved in to a space that looked, in its modified form, like a display home for toddler fences and baby gates. But it felt safe, and bookish in the extreme.

Fiona and I filled the reachable shelves with Shakespearean poetry, plays, journals and monographs. Few experiences are more pleasurable than assembling and organising a library. Workspace, research tool, biblio-retreat and biblio-temple, the library enabled and enriched our book-life, and became its anchor. Naturally, our John Fry collection, which had travelled with us since our first, tiny, hotel-room flat, was the library's heart.

What happened to Shakespeare's library? At the time of his death, some of the library was probably scattered. The will of actor

Nicholas Tooley hints at how that might have happened. Tooley required his executor to 'have a care to put off and sell my books to the most profit that he can'. And what of Shakespeare's books and manuscripts not sold upon his death? They were burned by Jonson, dispersed by Bagley, pulped by the Puritans, lost by Malone, filleted by Wise, defaced by Collier, dismembered by Halliwell, washed by Spencer and, innocently, unsuspectingly, kissed by Dibdin. Through such trials and vicissitudes a few of the books survived. They are sitting quietly, in cabinets and on shelves, in public and private collections around the world. We can say this confidently thanks to a newly discovered document, the Littlewood Letter.

After Samuel Ireland's disastrous search of Stratford-upon-Avon, he offered to trade half his library for a single Shakespeare signature. The biggest find from Edmond Malone's career-long search for Shakespearean books and documents was a short, unliterary and undelivered letter. On 25 October 1598 Richard Quiney drafted that letter to his 'Loving good friend and countryman, Mr Wm. Shackespere'. With his father and their friend, Quiney had hatched the idea of tapping Shakespeare for cash. The letter asks for a loan of thirty pounds. For some unknown reason, however, the men did not go through with their plan. The letter was never sent. The document is nevertheless an extremely important one. There are scores of letters in Shakespeare's plays, but the Quiney letter is the only authenticated Shakespearean letter in existence. The letter's importance speaks volumes about the scarcity of Shakespearean documents.

In early 2015, Fiona and I were preparing to exhibit at the Melbourne Rare Book Fair. A young woman, Caitlin Littlewood, had managed our stand in previous years. To plan our presence at the 2015 fair, I met with Caitlin and her father, Robert, at a cafe. From premises in Melbourne and Stoke-on-Trent, Robert deals in books and rare documents such as bookplates, prints and letters. Over his career he has made amazing finds. He brought to our meeting a stunning selection: early documents about trade and exploration; and early prints, including the famous image of Sir Joseph Banks as 'The Great South Sea Caterpillar transform'd into a Bath Butterfly'.

As I relished these examples I made an offhand remark about Shakespeare's library. 'I have a Shakespeare letter at home,' Robert said, in a tone that made his revelation sound unremarkable. Knowing the rarity of any kind of Shakespeare document, and especially a *letter*, I was immediately and obviously excited—as much as when, twenty years earlier, I first spotted Fry's *Pieces* at a college book sale. Robert and I arranged to meet at his home, where I would relish the chance to study the letter.

Robert is one of a long series of booksellers to figure in the Shakespeare story. Though the Littlewood Letter contains very little text, it is arguably the most important Shakespeare letter in the world today—provided, of course, it is genuine. Subject to that caveat, the document is the only surviving Shakespeare letter that was actually sent. Robert has traced the letter's English provenance, and we've been in touch with the Folger about testing and documenting its significance. If genuine, the letter provides spectacular confirmation that primary Shakespearean material—perhaps wrapped in Swedish lottery tickets—remains to be found. Where will the next Shakespearean discovery be made? In the words of John Baxter, the illustrious book-dealer who grew up in a tiny town near Wagga Wagga, 'anything can be anywhere'.

Further reading

CHAPTER 1

Schoenbaum, S. *Shakespeare's Lives*. (New York: Barnes & Noble, 2006).

Bate, Jonathan. *The Genius of Shakespeare*. (London: Picador, 1998).

Manningham, John. *Diary of John Manningham, of the Middle Temple, and of Bradbourne, Kent, Barrister-at-law, 1602-1603, edited from the original manuscript by John Bruce, Esq*. (Westminster: Printed by J. B. Nichols & Sons, 1868).

CHAPTER 2

Manningham, John. *Diary of John Manningham, of the Middle Temple, and of Bradbourne, Kent, Barrister-at-law, 1602-1603, edited from the original manuscript by John Bruce, Esq*. (Westminster: Printed by J. B. Nichols & Sons, 1868).

http://www.shakespearedocumented.org/

Wotton, Sir Henry. *Reliquice Wotioniaiue*. (London: 1651).

Henslowe, Philip. *Henslowe's Diary*. Edited by R. A. Foakes. (Cambridge: Cambridge University Press, 2002).

CHAPTER 3

Shakespeare, William. *Shakespeare's Sonnets: Revised*. Edited by Katherine Duncan-Jones. (London: Bloomsbury Academic, 2010).

Miller, Henry. 'Reading in the Toilet', in his *The Books in My Life*. (Norfolk, Connecticut: James Laughlin, 1952), pp. 264–286.

Jonson, Ben. *The Complete Plays of Ben Jonson*. Vol. II. Edited by G. A. Wilkes. (Oxford: Clarendon Press, 1981).

Jonson, Ben. *Ben Jonson's Every Man in His Humor*. Edited by Gabriele Bernhard Jackson. (New Haven: Yale University Press, 1971).

http://www.shakespearedocumented.org/

Bearman, Frederick A., Nati H. Krivatsy & J. Franklin Mowery. *Fine and Historic Bookbindings: From the Folger Shakespeare Library.* (Washington, D.C./New York: Folger Shakespeare Library/Abrams, 1992).
Catalogue of a remarkable collection of books in magnificent modern bindings, formed by an amateur (recently deceased), which will be sold by auction, by Messrs. Sotheby, Wilkinson & Hodge, ... at their house, no. 13, Wellington Street, Strand, W.C. on Thursday, the 11th day of November, 1897, at one o'clock precisely. (London: Dryden Press, J. Davy and Sons, [1897]).

CHAPTER 4

Rowe, Nicholas. 'Some Account of the Life, &c. of William Shakespear', in his *The Works of Mr. William Shakespear; in Six Volumes. Adorn'd with Cuts. Revis'd and Corrected, with an Account of the Life and Writings of the Author By N. Rowe, Esq.* (London: Printed for Jacob Tonson, 1709), pp. ii–xl.
Schoenbaum, S. *Shakespeare's Lives.* (New York: Barnes & Noble, 2006).

CHAPTER 5

Malone, Edmond. *An inquiry into the authenticity of certain miscellaneous papers and legal instruments, published Dec. 24, MDCCXCV. and attributed to Shakspeare, Queen Elizabeth, and Henry, Earl of Southampton: illustrated by fac-similes of the genuine hand-writing of that nobleman, and of Her Majesty; a new fac-simile of the hand-writing of Shakspeare, never before exhibited; and other authentic documents: in a letter addressed to the Right Hon. James, Earl of Charlemont.* (London: Printed by H. Baldwin, for T. Cadell, Jun. et al., 1796).
Shapiro, James. *Contested Will: Who Wrote Shakespeare?.* (New York: Simon & Schuster, 2010).
Keen, Alan & Roger Lubbock. *The Annotator: the pursuit of an Elizabethan reader of Halle's Chronicle, involving some surmises about the early life of William Shakespeare.* (London: Putnam, 1954).
The Bible and Holy Scriptures conteyned in the Olde and Newe Testament. Translated according to the Ebrue and Greke, and conferred vvith the best translations in diuers langages. With moste profitable annotations vpon all the hard places, and other things of great importance as may appeare in the epistle

to the reader. (Geneva: Printed by John Crispin, 1570). Folger Library
STC 2106 copy 1.

CHAPTER 6

Dibdin, Thomas Frognall. *The Bibliomania: or, Book-madness; Containing
some account of the history, symptoms and cure of this fatal disease, in an
epistle addressed to Richard Heber, Esq.* (London: Printed for Longman,
Hurst, Rees, and Orme, by W. Savage, 1809).
*A catalogue of the library of the late John, Duke of Roxburghe, arranged by G.
and W. Nicol, booksellers to His Majesty, Pall-Mall; which will be sold by
auction at His Grace's late residence in St. James's Square, on Monday, 18th
May, 1812, and the forty-one following days, Sundays excepted, at twelve
o'clock, by Robert H. Evans, bookseller, Pall-Mall.* (London: Printed by W.
Bulmer & Co., 1812).

CHAPTER 7

Bell, Alan. 'Archdeacon Francis Wrangham, 1769-1842', in *The Pleasures
of Bibliophily. Fifty Years of the Book Collector. An Anthology.* (London &
New Castle: British Library/Oak Knoll Press, 2003), pp. 118–126.
Blainey, Ann. *Immortal Boy: A Portrait of Leigh Hunt.* (London: Croom
Helm, 1985).
[Fry, John.] *Pieces of Ancient Poetry: From Unpublished Manuscripts and
Scarce Books.* (Bristol: Printed by John Evans & Co., 1814).
[Fry, John.] *Bibliographical Memoranda: in illustration of early English
literature.* (Bristol: Printed by R. Rosser, 1816).
[Fry, John.] *The Legend of Mary, Queen of Scots, and Other Ancient Poems;
now first published from ms.s. of the sixteenth century. With an introduction,
notes, and an appendix.* (London: Printed for Longman, Hurst, Rees, and
Orme, 1810).

CHAPTER 8

*Catalogue of the Curious, Choice and Valuable Library of the Late Sir Francis
Freeling, Bart. F.S.A. …which will be sold by auction by Mr. Evans, at his
house, No. 93, Pall-Mall, on Friday, November 25, and nine following days
(Sundays excepted).* (London: Printed by W. Nicol, 1836).

Greene, Robert. *Greene's Groats-Worth of witte, bought with a million of Repentance. Describing the follie of youth, the falshood of make-shifte flatterers, the miserie of the negligent, and mischiefes of deceiuing Courtezans. Written before his death and published at his dyeing request.* (London: Printed by William Wright, 1592).

Catalogue of the Library of the Late Rev. John Morgan Rice, containing many articles of distinguished rarity and curiosity in early English poetry, … which will be sold by auction, by Mr. Evans, at his house, No. 93, Pall-Mall, on Wednesday, May 14, and three following days. (London: Printed by W. Nicol, 1834).

CHAPTER 9

Anderson, Mark. *'Shakespeare' by Another Name. The life of Edward de Vere, Earl of Oxford, the man who was Shakespeare.* (New York: Gotham Books, 2005).

James, Brenda & William D. Rubinstein. *The Truth Will Out. Unmasking the Real Shakespeare.* (Harlow: Pearson Longman, 2006).

http://www.shakespearedocumented.org/

Casson, John & Mark Bradbeer. *Sir Henry Neville, Alias William Shakespeare: Authorship Evidence in the History Plays.* (Jefferson: McFarland & Co., 2015).

Bryson, Bill. *Shakespeare. The World as a Stage.* (London: HarperPress, 2007).

O'Donnell, John. 'Alias William Shakespeare'. Lecture delivered at Duneira, Mt Macedon, on Sunday, 6 April 2014. http://www.duneira. com.au/wp-content/uploads/2014/09/Alias-William-Shakespeare-Duneira.pdf

CHAPTER 10

Caldwell, George S. *Is Sir Walter Raleigh the Author of Shakespere's Plays and Sonnets?* (Melbourne: Printed by Stillwell & Knight, 1877).

Thomson, William. *On Renascence Drama, or, History Made Visible.* (Melbourne: Sands & McDougall, 1880).

Browne, H. Junor. *The Grand Reality: Being Experiences in Spirit Life of a Celebrated Dramatist Received Through a Trance Medium.* (Melbourne:

George Robertson & Co., 1888).

Browne, H. Junor. *The Baconian Authorship of Shakespeare's Plays Refuted.* (Melbourne: George Robertson, 1898).

Wantrup, Jonathan. *Australian Rare Books, 1788-1900.* (Potts Point: Hordern House, 1987).

Lambert, Richard S. *The Prince of Pickpockets. A Study of George Barrington Who Left His Country for His Country's Good.* (London: Faber, 1930).

Garvey, Nathan. *The Celebrated George Barrington: A Spurious Author, the Book Trade and Botany Bay.* (Potts Point: Hordern House, 2008).

Barrrington, George. *A Voyage to New South Wales; with a description of the country; the manners, customs, religion, &c. of the natives, in the vicinity of Botany Bay.* (London: Printed for the Proprietor, sold by H. D. Symonds, 1795).

Ferguson, John. *Bibliography of Australia.* (Canberra: National Library of Australia, 1975-1977).

CHAPTER 11

Gosse, Edmund. *Critical Kit-Kats.* (New York: Dodd, Mead & Co., 1903).

Wise, Thomas J. *A Bibliography of the Writings in Prose and Verse of Elizabeth Barrett Browning.* (London: Printed for private circulation only by R. Clay & Sons, 1918).

Pollard, Graham & John Carter. *An Enquiry into the Nature of Certain Nineteenth Century Pamphlets: with an epilogue.* Edited by Nicolas Barker & John Collins. (Aldershot & New Castle: Scolar Press/Oak Knoll Press, 1992).

Drake, Nathan. *Shakespeare and His Times: including the biography of the poet; criticism on his genius and writings; a new chronology of his plays; a disquisition on the object of his sonnets; and a history of the manners, customs, amusement, superstitions, poetry, and elegant literature of his age.* (London: Printed for T. Cadell & W. Davies, 1817).

Collier, J. Payne. *The History of English Dramatic Poetry to the Time of Shakespeare; and Annals of the stage to the Restoration.* (London, John Murray, 1831).

Collier, J. Payne. *New Facts Regarding the Life of Shakespeare: in a letter to Thomas Amyot, esq., F.R.S., Treasurer of the Society of Antiquaries, from J.*

Payne Collier, F.S.A. (London: Thomas Rodd, 1835).

Hamilton, N. E. S. A. *An Inquiry into the Genuineness of the Manuscript Corrections in Mr. J. Payne Collier's Annotated Shakspere, Folio, 1632: and of certain Shaksperian documents likewise published by Mr. Collier.* (London: Richard Bentley, 1860).

The Ashley Library: a catalogue of printed books, manuscripts and autograph letters collected by Thomas James Wise. (London: Printed for private circulation only, at the Dunedin Press, Edinburgh, 1922–1936).

Foxon, D. F. *Thomas J. Wise and the Pre-Restoration Drama. A study in theft and sophistication.* (London: Bibliographical Society, 1959). Supplement to Bibliographical Society's Publications No. 19.

CHAPTER 12

James, Brenda & William D. Rubinstein. *The Truth Will Out. Unmasking the Real Shakespeare.* (Harlow: Pearson Longman, 2006).

CHAPTER 13

Allott, Robert (Compiler). *England's Parnassus: or the choysest flowers of our modern poets, with their poeticall comparisons.* (London: Printed for N.L. C.B. and T.H., 1600).

Greene, Robert. *Greene's Groats-Worth of witte, bought with a million of Repentance. Describing the follie of youth, the falshood of make-shifte flatterers, the miserie of the negligent, and mischiefes of deceiuing Courtezans. Written before his death and published at his dyeing request.* (London: Printed by William Wright, 1592).

CHAPTER 14

Shaw, Bernard. *Flyleaves.* Edited with an introduction by Dan H. Laurence and Daniel J. Leary. (Austin: W. Thomas Taylor, 1977).

Owen, Orville W. *A Celebrated Case. Bacon vs. Shakespeare. In the court of 'The Arena.' Request to reopen. Brief for plaintiff.* (Detroit: Howard Publishing Co., 1893).

Owen, Orville W. *Sir Francis Bacon's Cipher Story. Discovered and deciphered by Orville W. Owen.* (Detroit: Howard Publishing Co., 1893-95).

Gallup, Elizabeth Wells. *The Bi-literal Cypher of Sir Francis Bacon:*

discovered in his works and deciphered by Mrs. Elizabeth Wells Gallup. (Detroit: Howard Publishing Co., c.1899).

Strong, Archibald. *Peradventure. A book of essays in literary criticism.* (Melbourne: Thomas C. Lothian, 1911).

Crosse, Henry. *Vertues common-wealth: or the high-way to honour wherin is discouered, that although by the disguised craft of this age, vice and hypocrisie may be concealed: yet by tyme (the triall of truth) it is most plainly reuealed.* (London: John Newbery, 1603).

Pollard, Alfred W. *Shakespeare Folios and Quartos: A study in the bibliography of Shakespeare's plays, 1594-1685.* (London: Methuen & Co., 1909).

Pollard, Alfred W. *Shakespeare's Fight with the Pirates and the Problems of the Transmission of his Text.* (London: Alexander Moring, 1917).

Price, Diana. *Shakespeare's Unorthodox Biography: New evidence of an authorship problem.* (Westport: Greenwood Press, 2001).

Mendenhall, Thomas C. 'A Mechanical Solution of a Literary Problem,' *Popular Science Monthly*, Vol. 60, No. 7, 1901, pp. 97–105.

CHAPTER 15

Tangye, Richard. *Reminiscences of Travel in Australia, America and Egypt.* (Birmingham: Printed at the Herald Press, 1883).

Chanin, Eileen. *Book Life: The Life and Times of David Scott Mitchell.* (North Melbourne: Australian Scholarly Publishing, 2011).

Charles Stitz (Ed.). *Australian Book Collectors: Some Noted Australian Book Collectors & Collections of the Nineteenth & Twentieth centuries.* (Bendigo et al.: Bread Street Press/Books of Kells in association with the Australian Book Auction Records et al., 2010–16).

Souter, Gavin. *Lion and Kangaroo: The Initiation of Australia.* (Melbourne: Text Publishing, 2000).

CHAPTER 16

Sidgwick, Frank. *Frank Sidgwick's Diary and other material relating to A. H. Bullen, & the Shakespeare Head Press at Stratford-upon-Avon.* (Oxford: Blackwell for the Shakespeare Head Press, 1975).

Shakespeare, William. *Mr. William Shakespeares Comedies, histories & tragedies, published according to the true originall copies.* (London: Printed by Isaac Jaggard & Edward Blount, 1623).

Jonson, Benjamin. *The Workes of Beniamin Jonson*. (London: Printed by Will Stansby, 1616).

Franklin, Colin. *Obsessions and Confessions of a Book Life*. (New Castle et al.: Oak Knoll Press/Books of Kells/Bernard Quaritch, 2012).

CHAPTER 17

Anonymous [Henry Spencer Ashbee]. *My Secret Life*. Vols I–III. (Amsterdam: Privately printed for subscribers, 1888).

Ian Gibson. *The Erotomaniac: The Secret Life of Henry Spencer Ashbee*. (London: Faber, 2001).

Bowdler, Thomas (Ed.). *The Family Shakespeare, in Four Volumes*. (London: Printed by Richard Cruttwell for J. Hatchard, 1807).

CHAPTER 18

Watry, Maureen M. *The Vale Press: Charles Ricketts, a publisher in earnest*. (New Castle & London: Oak Knoll Press & The British Library, 2004).

Cave, Roderick. *The Private Press*. (London: Faber, 1971).

Peterson, William S. *The Kelmscott Press. A History of William Morris's Typographical Adventure*. (Berkeley: University of California Press, 1991).

[Pearson, Hesketh.] *The Whispering Gallery: Being Leaves from a Diplomat's Diary*. (London: John Lane, The Bodley Head, 1926).

CHAPTER 19

Eco, Umberto. *Foucault's Pendulum*. (London: Secker & Warburg, 1989).

Index

Drake, Francis 230
Drake, Nathan 68, 107, 110, 154
Drayton, Michael 21, 23, 25, 140,
    189, 220, 256, 269
Droeshout, Martin 243
Drummond, William (Laird of
    Hawthornden) 199, 247, 256
Dudley, Robert (Earl of Leicester)
    31, 116
Dunn, Des 285
Dyer, Edward 24, 97
Dyson, Humphrey 30, 244

Eco, Umberto 287, 288, 294
Edmondes, Sir Thomas 22
Edmunds, Brigett 262, 263
Edmunds, John 262, 263
Edwards, Richard 72
Edwards, Thomas 269
Eliot, John 29, 100, 209
Eliot, George 149
Elizabeth I 9, 13, 24, 25, 42, 48,
    54, 83, 89, 93, 100, 101, 104, 116,
    119, 120, 175, 194, 197, 200, 220,
    237, 262, 282
Elizabethan Club, Yale University
    185
Ellis & Elvey 240
Emerson, Ralph Waldo 13
Eton College 22
Euphorbus 188
Evans, Robert Harding 71, 104, 110
E. W. & A. Skipwith 150

Fastolf, Sir John 201

Fellows, Virginia M. 59
Ferguson, Sir John Alexander
    136, 137, 143
Field, Henry 290
Field, Richard 27, 29, 61, 63, 184,
    230, 290, 291
Fitzwilliam Museum, Cambridge
    278
Fletcher, Giles 263
Fletcher, John 25, 26, 143, 180,
    189, 210, 249, 250, 252
Florio, John 7, 27, 60, 61, 103, 107,
    197, 209, 214, 243, 244, 251, 254,
    268
Folger, Henry Clay 35, 229
Folger Shakespeare Library 35,
    37, 58, 64, 104, 158, 229, 248,
    250, 296
Foote, Dr Edward B. 267
Forman, Harry Buxton 150–54,
    163
Forman, Maurice Buxton 152
Fox, Charles James 134
Foxe (Fox), John 76, 220
Foxon, David F. 159
Francis II, Dauphin of France 93
François I 37
Franklin, Benjamin 234
Franklin, Colin 70, 255
Fraser, Michael 48
Frederick, Sir John 234
Freeling, Sir Francis 88, 89, 94,
    96, 99, 100–03, 110, 187, 264
Freeman, Mrs (Anna Maria de
    Burgh Coppinger) 46, 48

Freeman, Thomas 190, 207, 212
Free Public Library, Sydney (see
  Public Library of New South
  Wales)
Freud, Sigmund 13, 283
Fry, John 4, 88–103, 105–08, 110,
  111, 187, 260, 267, 294

Gallup, Elizabeth Wells 8, 9, 206,
  207, 288
Gardiner, William 278
Garnett, Richard 99
Garrick Club 155
Garrick, David 126, 131, 132, 196,
  239, 289
Garrick, Eva Marie (née Veigel)
  131
Garvey, Nathan 137, 139, 143
Gascoigne, George 98
Gates, Sir Thomas 176
Gayley, Charles Mills 176, 177
George III 70, 83, 88, 132, 138
George, Prince of Wales (George
  IV) 51, 52, 84, 110
Gerard, John 63
Gesner, Conrad 37
Getty Jr, Sir John Paul 241
Gibbings, Robert 281
Gibson, Harry Norman 59
Gibson, Ian 258
Gibson, John 84
Gielgud, John 282
Godsell, Sean 293, 294
Golden Cockerel Press 278
Golding, Arthur 24

Goldingham, Henry 86
Goodge, William Thomas 129
Gosse, Sir Edmund W. 146–49,
  153
Gosson, Stephen 103
Gower, John 24, 100, 213
Grammaticus, Saxo 210
Great Library of Alexandria 291
Greene, Robert 26, 57, 101–03,
  110, 140, 142, 190–96, 199, 205,
  207, 212, 247, 253, 264, 286, 289
Greene, Thomas 109
Greer, Germaine 130, 207
Grenville, Thomas 75
Grey, Lady Catherine 119
Grey, Sir George 240, 241
Griffiths, Mark 63
Griffiths (reviewer, *Monthly
  Review*) 92
Grolier de Servières, Jean
  (Viscount d'Aguisy) 36
Gullett, Henry 238
Gwynn, Edward 248

H., Miss 131
Hagué, Louis 37, 38
Hake, Edward 103
Hakluyt, Richard 230
Hall, Arthur 104
Hall, Edward 166
Hall, Dr John 21, 23, 25, 40
Hall, Rodney 293, 294
Hall, Susanna (née Shakespeare)
  21, 40
Hall, William 174

Halle (Hall), Edward 60

Halliday, Brett 285

Halliday, Frank Ernest 59

Halliwell, James 156, 161–64, 215, 271

Halliwell Phillipps, Henrietta Elizabeth Molyneux 161, 162

Hamilton, Nicholas 157

Hammett, Dashiell 286

Hammond, John 166

Hanger, Major George 132

Harding, John 24

Hardyknute 77

Haring, Don 285

Harington, Sir John 42, 49, 248

Harrison, George 281

Hart, Joan (née Shakespeare) 40, 104, 105, 109

Hart, John 40

Hart, Thomas 105

Harvey, Gabriel 101, 185, 186

Harvey, Sir William 174

Hatcliffe, William 174

Hathaway, Anne 46, 47, 142, 290

Hathaway, William 174

Hawkins, Sir John 77

Hazlitt, William 107, 110

H. D. Symonds 134, 135

Heard, Sir Isaac 51

Heber, Richard 68, 70, 264

Heidegger, Martin 283

Hemmings, John 18, 19, 41, 42, 48, 217, 242

Hemmings, William 41

Henri II 37

Henri III 37

Henri IV 119

Henry II 119

Henry VII 31

Henry Frederick, Prince of Wales 22

Henslowe, Philip 23, 24, 251

Herbert, Mary (Countess of Pembroke; née Sidney) 125

Herbert, William (Earl of Pembroke) 174, 252

Herbert, William 70, 104

Heywood, Thomas 23, 24, 26, 91, 97, 141, 269

Hoby, Sir Thomas 166

Hogarth, William 46

Holinshed, Raphael 50, 57, 101, 166, 180, 241

Holland, Hugh 177, 243

Holme, William 174

Holmes, Charles J. 275, 276

Homer 92, 104, 262, 280

Hone, William 84

Hooker, Richard 220

Horace 66, 169

Horne, Richard Hengist 150

Horwitz Publications 284

Hotson, Leslie 278

Howard, Frances (later Frances Carr, Countess of Somerset) 261

Howard, Henry (Earl of Surrey) 24

Howell, James 106

Huband, Ralph 41

Hughes, William ('Willie') 174

Acknowledgments

Modern Shakespeare scholarship owes a huge debt to generations of researchers and archivists who assembled what little we know about the Bard and his life. Those researchers and archivists include Charles and Hulda Wallace, who painstakingly scoured thousands of uncatalogued documents at London's Public Record Office, searching for references to Shakespeare and his circle. True masters of archival research, the Wallaces found priceless Shakespearean court documents and other invaluable records.

Apart from Charles and Hulda and their peers, I acknowledge the more recent scholars and librarians who made *Shakespeare's Library* possible. Major documentary and textual sources are identified in the 'Further reading' section. Full source notes are available at my author site (stuartkells.com). For practical help and guidance I am also indebted to the custodians of the Bodleian Library, the British Library, the Folger Shakespeare Library, the State Library of New South Wales, the State Library of Victoria, the New York Public Library, and the libraries of Meisei University, Monash University and the University of Melbourne.

I also gratefully acknowledge the support and advice of Fiona, Thea and Charlotte Kells, Don and Sheila Drummond, Elizabeth and Louise Lane, Bill Leslie, Wallace and Joan Kirsop, Jacky Ogeil, John O'Donnell, Lorna Lawford, Maurice Hanratty, Lisa Ehrenfried, Ed Schofield, Charles and Mary Stitz, Richard Overell, and the teams at Text Publishing and Counterpoint

Press, particularly Michael Heyward, Penny Hueston, Alaina Gougoulis, Khadija Caffoor, W. H. Chong, Lucy Ballantyne, Jane Watkins, Anne Beilby, Jack Shoemaker, Alisha Gorder, Wah-Ming Chang, Jennifer Alton and Yukiko Tominaga.

© Sarah Walker

STUART KELLS is an author and historian. His history of Penguin Books, *Penguin and the Lane Brothers*, won the prestigious Ashurst Business Literature Prize. *The Library: A Catalogue of Wonders* was short-listed for the Australian Prime Minister's Literary Award and the New South Wales Premier's General History Prize, and has been published around the world in multiple languages. Find out more at stuartkells.com.